PERSONAL RESPONSIBILITY AND CHRISTIAN MORALITY

Josef Fuchs, S.J.

Translated by William Cleves and others

Georgetown University Press, Washington, D.C.
Gill and Macmillan, Dublin

First published 1983

Georgetown University Press
Washington, D.C. 20057

ISBN: 0-87840-405-8

Gill and Macmillan Ltd
Goldenbridge, Dublin 8

ISBN: 0-7171-1104-0

Library of Congress Cataloging in Publication Data

Fuchs, Josef, 1912-
    Personal responsibility and Christian morality.

    1. Christian ethics--Catholic authors--Addresses,
essays, lectures.   I. Title.
BJ1249.F76 1983   241'.042   83-1548
ISBN 0-87840-405-8

TABLE OF CONTENTS

Preface

Preface

The question of the characteristic features of Christian morality has different aspects. It is especially important with respect to normative morality. Here both the "specific" and the "distinctive" — which is an element of the "specific" — have to be taken into consideration.

In Christian morality, as in every morality, the problem arises as to how both behavioral-material norms and concrete solutions are to be found. This problem is especially urgent when the normative aspects of Christian ethics must be determined in their material content as a morality of human beings and therefore as a "human" morality.

Insofar as it is a question of moral *norms* of action, it becomes important to know what its true, though still not fully formulated, expression is and then what its exact value is. This question can be posed theoretically, but it becomes most pressing when it is a matter of finding imperatives for concrete decisions. In this case, a "question of conscience" is raised.

Whether in formulating behavioral-material norms or in finding imperatives of conscience, it is the personal responsibility of the individual Christian which in different ways is put in question. Even the behavioral-material norms already formulated are not fully adequate to determine a concrete imperative for the voice of conscience.

As a continuation of the earlier publication, *Human Values and Christian Morality* (1970), this author's contributions to the above-mentioned problematic have already appeared in various languages. Some of the more representative ones have been collected in this English version, *Personal Responsibility and Christian Morality*. These essays were written at different times and independently of one another, a factor which should be kept in mind while reading them. They are published here without essential changes, and therefore occasional repetitions are to be found, for which the author apologizes.

Rome, September 1981   JOSEF FUCHS

1. Moral Theology as Sacra Doctrina

Sacra doctrina is a technical term in medieval theology.[1] Aquinas employs it as a fundamental concept at the beginning of the first part of his *Summa Theologiae*. According to him, sacred doctrine exists only in virtue of the revelation which has been given to us. Sacred doctrine "believes" what is revealed. Nevertheless, it is at the same time a "science" which theologians "pursue" (*tractant*). Such a theology even enters into details, which "introducuntur in exemplum vitae, sicut in scientiis moralibus," yet it is primarily concerned with divine existence (*res divinae*) and not with human action. The fact that sacred doctrine presupposes a revelation which is believed has two consequences: (1) since it takes for granted faith in the God who reveals himself to us, it is fundamentally "wisdom"; whatever it treats is seen in reference to God, whether because it has to do with God himself or because it deals with a matter related to God as its beginning and end; and (2) due to the authority of sacred doctrine we can discuss matters with heretics in a way different from that possible with unbelievers. This is the thought of St. Thomas.

Doctrine can be understood as teaching or as content. In what follows this term is used in its original lexicographic meaning, that is, as instruction, lesson, or teaching. In this sense, theology (and therefore moral theology) is doctrine. It is interesting that one of the Vatican Congregations deals primarily with sacred doctrine as teachings = content of teaching: the Congregation for the Doctrine of the Faith (formerly the Holy Office). Another is primarily responsible for sacred doctrine as teachings = instruction in the faith: the Congregation for Catholic Education (formerly the Congregation for Sacred Studies). The word "sacred" should not be colored by any de-mythologizing-Platonic or metaphysical-Aristotelian understanding of divine knowledge. Rather, sacred doctrine means the attempt, within the believing Church, both to deepen continually, in an ever new and extensive manner, our understanding of faith in the historical self-revelation of God to us in Jesus Christ and to teach this enriched understanding of faith.

Thus it follows that theology as sacred doctrine differs essentially from the study of religion. In the United States several Catholic universities have altered the traditional obligation that students of all departments attend theology lectures. Instead, for the sake of a well-rounded education, all must hear lectures in religious studies which, although compulsory, entail free choice as well; among these is theology. The reason is that students who do not believe do not really study "theology" with a professor who teaches sacred doctrine, for theology presupposes faith. For this reason, obligatory attendance at theology lectures could be seen as an unjust requirement.

Thus, in what follows we will speak of the discipline of theology exclusively as sacred doctrine. We should not be dissuaded from choosing this term by the fact that medieval theology was not as conscious as is contemporary theology of the historicity which characterizes one's understanding of faith.

I. THEOLOGY AS UNDERSTANDING OF FAITH

A few years ago the editors of *Concilium* organized a theological congress in Brussels on the occasion of the tenth anniversary of the magazine. In the course of the proceedings there emerged a tendency, coming for the most part from France, not to reserve the title "theologian" for specialists in theology, or for professors and students of theology. The reason was that anyone who believes is also a theologian; for the believer has at least an initial understanding of faith. This is certainly true; an understanding of faith can be called theology. One who believes will put into words his understanding of what he believes, even if at first only in the presence of those who enabled him to discover faith: for faith comes from hearing (Rom. 10:17). The more the believed word of revelation is understood as a message concerning the ultimate meaning of individual and social existence (with their different possibilities, interest, and requirements), the more will this word be extended in an ever-widening dialogue of faith. Faith, which is proclaimed in dialogue and gradually more clearly grasped as the hopeful power of love, becomes in turn capable of an ever more profound understanding of itself. Thus, according to the tendency which emerged at Brussels, all faith involves theology.

In this sense theology is always practiced by the entire Church. The emphasis belongs on the words "the entire Church". The Church in its totality is the mediator of the Word by whose power we can arrive at a hopeful and loving faith and at its true understanding. It follows that the believing community which is the Church, composed as it is of many mediators of the Word and at the same time hierarchically structured, is not simply the "place" where the above-mentioned theological dialogue always takes place. As a universal structure, the Church is officially interested in and committed to the faithful conservation of the message of revelation, as well as in the transmission and ever deeper understanding of that message. This nascent theology present everywhere in the Church, is not enough, although it is indeed important and fruitful. The Church must also regard theology — that is, the knowledge and understanding of faith — as a science. Although this is not the place to explore at length the penetrating question of analogy which arises as soon as one speaks of theology as a science based on faith, something should be said about it. Therefore, in the rest of this chapter we shall follow the common usage and speak of theology as a science. Above all, we shall concentrate on that theology which is taught as a science by the specialists who are entrusted with this task by the Church, the community of believers. We shall, in short, consider theology as sacred doctrine.

II. THEOLOGY AS A SCIENTIFIC DISCIPLINE

Even as a science, theology is essentially directed toward proclamation — toward the clarification which faith brings to the existence of human meaning and hope, and toward the encounter with the mystery of God who is the ground and revealer of this meaning. In the same way, theology is also characterized as an academic subject. It is proclamation which takes place as a science and not as meditation or as "theology on its knees", to use the words of H.U. von Balthasar. In calling for such a theology he, not without reason, opposes a theology marked by much too sober concepts, which has nothing to do with life. Certainly a lucid and genuine theology must be able to lead one to meditate and to "put one on one's knees". In doing this, however, theology remains the science of faith and makes use of all the scientific means which can aid an exact presentation of its objective contents. This holds for theology in general, and therefore albeit in different ways, for the areas of specialization in theology, e.g., canon law and Church history, which basically concern themselves with the mystery of the believing Church. Naturally, this also holds true for moral theology.

The proclamatory character of theology is not contradicted by its painstaking scientific research into minute details which do not reveal — at least not immediately — its function as proclamation: careful research of the sources (Scripture, tradition, magisterium), study of the history of theology itself (by which contemporary theology is necessarily influenced), and finally, philosophical endeavors within theology. No matter what his level of study, the student of theology should not be afraid of being introduced to this painstaking work, but should welcome it. Only with the help of scientific effort of this kind can the discipline of theology contribute to some extent to the type of proclamation which the present situation demands.

Due to the necessary affinity of proclamation to the present experience of believing Christians and theology students, one should not be astonished at the fact that sacred doctrine, and thus the "teaching" of theology, which one could have experienced forty years ago in the very same lecture halls of the same Roman universities, was very different from the teaching and "doing" of theology today.

Revelation itself, and even more so tradition and the magisterium, already adhere to some theological assertions which are formulated as propositions. We should not forget, however, that these assertions are always necessarily formulated in the language of a particular horizon of thought, with its own way of posing questions. We have need not only of interpretation but also of a hermeneutic, in order correctly to translate into contemporary ways of questioning and understanding those things put differently in the sources of our faith and in the theology (theologies) of times past. Only in this way can we guarantee a genuine transmission of the content of our faith, and not just a verbal correctness which could produce a falsification or an inexact rendering of the tradition. It is only through this process that new facts, new problems and new forms of human self-understanding can raise questions for faith and theology; in turn, theology must lay bare and make intelligible the answers to such questions which are hidden in faith and revelation. Only in this way is it possible for theology critically to view the understanding of faith which the Church has at any given moment and, if necessary, free it from one-sidedness. Only in this way, too, can theology shed light on the questions and concerns which weigh down upon man today as he lives with his contemporaries both within and outside of the Church. Theology can remind modern man of important values, ideals and dimensions of human existence which he has inadvertently dismissed. This is true not only with regard to what is specifically Christian, but also with regard to a fuller humanization of man himself and of society.

This means that theology has the difficult task of getting to know both the spirit of the present age and the men who embody it (all of whom are not the same); theology must also grasp what modern man's capacity for understanding and what his tendencies are, both within and outside of the Church. Such knowledge, even if it were only partial, would have significant consequences: e.g., what theological questions, given the students' particular intellectual development, should even be dealt with today? How should these questions be approached in the light of the present state of the believing Church community and of the believing student of theology, or how should they not be approached? What are the aspects of God's saving action which can best be formulated for students in clear concepts and which aspects are more suitable to a richer expression through the use of picture and symbols, the method that corresponds to the narrative theology, as it is called, of the last few years?

What are the central questions that must be brought to the attention of students who might still be untouched by them? These may be those that are directly concerned with the mystery of salvation, or those that make possible an encounter, enlightened by faith, with current ideologies (e.g., Marxism, humanism) or with the findings of other disciplines (e.g., the human sciences). What stimulus contained in the Christian doctrine of salvation would be attractive to man's present situation? I am thinking, for example, of J.B. Metz's attempt to construct a political theology,[2] especially if this attempt could be carried even further, with the help of theological reflection, in the direction of a political ethics.[3] What affirmations can theology make or not make which will affect the future, and more specifically, the future of man's temporal world and its meaningfulness?

Certainly many fear that, in the face of such questions, theology may possibly foster more doubts than it can give answers. But if theology is aware of its nature as proclamation, it must in fact seek to say what is a dogma, what is a solid theological opinion, what are thoroughly possible ways of asserting the truth, and what ways are open to debate – and all this in spite of a healthy theological pluralism and taking account of the opportunities that may or may not be available. Above all, however, faith, which alone makes possible the most radical critique of ideologies, ought not itself to be misused as an ideology reinforced by theological assertions. In face of all the dangers which have been pointed out here, theology finds help in the entire believing Church which expresses itself authoritatively through the magisterium. On the other hand, theology, through its task of research and teaching by which it too proclaims the Gospel, is answerable to those who bear an office in the Church. The contribution of Bishop Christopher Butler, auxiliary of Westminster, published in the *Clergy Review* of 1975, should also be considered.[4] Butler cautions against opposition between the teaching of theologians and the authority of bishops. Both have their own proper authority, both learn and teach according to the different degree of authority which each group possesses and which must in all honesty be recognized. It is not usually the case that he who holds an office is also an authority on sacred doctrine, but it does occur at times. What has been said here leads us to another problem.

III. SACRED DOCTRINE: TEACHER AND STUDENT

The last few years have witnessed a new phenomenon: groups of bishops or entire bishops' conferences gathering, for instance, for a month for an intensive study of contemporary theology. At these study sessions an invited professor of theology is recognized as having his own proper authority as a scientifically trained proclaimer of the Christian message. This, however, is not the normal relationship between teacher and student when theology is taught. We should rather concentrate on the normal teacher-student relationship in theology because of the special character of this discipline.

Teaching theology is the same, objectively speaking, as teaching any other subject. There is however, an awareness, seldom mentioned but nonetheless real, that both teachers and students come together expressly as believers, that they are one in their faith in God's word and work; such faith reveals to them the mystery of hope in their lives and in that hope the mystery of God himself. It is precisely for the purpose of a deeper understanding of their common faith that they commonly engage in studying theology. Paraphrasing what St. Paul wrote to the Philippians, we may say: having been taken hold of by faith, they are trying through theology to grasp faith even more firmly (Phil. 3:12). Nor should we think that it is always the teacher who stimulates; the opposite can also happen in the classroom itself through a common attempt of understanding, and it can happen, too, outside a formal teaching situation through personal questions, dialogue, and research seminars.

If theology is essentially oriented toward proclamation, we should not overlook the fact that the great majority of theology students purposely choose this field of study for the sake of further proclaiming faith. This is the case whether as priests or laymen they intend to serve the Church in directly announcing the Gospel, or whether they intend, as a result of a more profound understanding of faith, to live a Christian life which clearly gives better witness to faith, even if often only implicitly.

The role of a teacher of theology is clearly and explicitly one of witnessing to faith and proclaiming it. Consequently, in theology the person of the teacher, his life and his faith, are involved more than in teaching any other subject, even more than in philosophy. Students will note or sense something different in a theology professor.

This does not alter the indispensable requirement that the teacher's pursuit of "sacred doctrine" has to be a scientific labor. The following are necessary elements of this task: providing an introduction to the general problematic of theology, discussing individual problems and theological method, disclosing the various forms of thought and expression which theology itself historically opted for and which thus characterize this discipline. Since theology has developed historically, it cannot be pursued without translating past forms of thought and expression into a language accessible to the students of today, without necessarily adopting the language of catechetical instruction.

At present, it is often said that many study theology because of a personal search not only for a more profound but also for a more certain faith: in other words, these students are seeking more certainty regarding the meaning of the existence which is given to them in Christ. The teacher of theology must know this, and indeed he will sometimes also be made aware of it in the classroom. But even he can never give anyone faith or the ability to believe. Still, many students may not be experiencing a genuine uncertainty or doubt about faith, but may be undergoing a crisis due to a misunderstanding or ignorance of their faith, or they may be perplexed at experiencing the darkness of faith. Much misunderstanding and ignorance can be eliminated through theology, even that resulting from faith's confrontation with the different horizons of thought and the pressing problems of a new age. Theology in its totality as well as its individual assertions can also bring about a less threatened, more genuine and fruitful certainty of faith, in spite of the inherent obscurity which always remains.

Thus it often happens that in the process of treating questions the teacher of theology has the responsibility of purifying his students' understanding of faith. In turn, the students, as a result of being purified in their faith, will have the task of proclaiming it wisely, without running the risk of being considered destroyers of the faith they have inherited. This, by the way, is a danger to which even the teacher of theology is exposed when he is evaluated by those who, because of their office, are authoritative witnesses to the Church's faith and defenders of it. Those who hold such responsibility should not forget, however, that theology as sacred doctrine is not given once and for all, but for various reasons has had to undergo and must continue to undergo a history, in order to ensure an untainted and enriched knowledge of faith.

For his part, the teacher of theology must be aware that in some way a difference of perspective, with regard to how one should understand and question faith, can exist between him and his students. It is necessary to take this into account, since in the broader society as well as in the Church these perspectives change either with the passage of time or with the evolution of culture. The same holds true when the teacher makes a serious attempt to understand contemporary patterns of thought. It can happen, for example, that between the older teacher and the younger student there exist intellectual attitudes and kinds of questions which are not exactly identical or which render the words spoken by the teacher irrelevant to the student's understanding of faith, so that it is difficult for the student to accept them or necessary for him to understand them in a different way. Moreover, it should be noted that it is not always chronological age which decides who is older and "the man of yesterday", and who is younger and "the man of today" or even "the man of tomorrow". Nonetheless, the difficulty of arriving at a common understanding of a common faith invariably exists in one way or another between teachers and students.

IV. THE PLACE OF SACRED DOCTRINE AMONG OTHER ACADEMIC DISCIPLINES

In addition to the special nature of the teacher-student relationship in theology, its unique place among other academic subjects in Catholic or public universities ought briefly to be pointed out. In earlier centuries, because society was basically Christian, theology was ranked highest among university studies. Theology enabled citizens, presumed to be believers, to reach the highest level of human knowledge, precisely through study of the divine revelation contained in faith. Theology mediated both ultimate knowledge and certainty regarding not only the true meaning of human existence, but of the *humanum* as such, and of the divine and Christian foundation of human existence. In this process the analogous nature of the concept of science caused no decisive difficulty. It is important to note that the primary purpose of these universities was not the formation of priests, but the promotion of an ever deeper knowledge of faith through scientific elaboration.

It seems that there is basically no reason why such a vision and organization of academic subjects could not exist today, above all in Catholic universities. To be sure, difficulties could arise from such a vision since not all representatives of other academic disciplines would be inclined to give theology a privileged place, especially because the concepts of other sciences are very different from those of theology. They can be compared only by analogy. The fact that some scientists are opposed to a science which by its very nature presupposes and builds on the knowledge derived from faith does not mean that they thereby deny theology as such its right to exist. One might well ask if individuals engaged in other academic disciplines do not, either secretly or openly, bring to their research some other system of thought, perhaps even an extremely influential one, which is in some way a "faith." Furthermore, we should note that teachers in other fields not infrequently encounter many questions in their own academic fields (e.g., in the natural or human sciences) which touch on the meaning of the totality of existence; it is in this totality that individual questions seem to be deeply embedded, even that question which philosophy, and especially theology, treat in a systematic manner. Should not theology show itself ready in this respect to be a partner in dialogue with other academic disciplines? Would not theology's dialogue with them be enriching, and indeed would not a mutual enrichment be possible and desirable for both sides? In the light of these reflections, it is understandable why what happened in the city of Milan, for example, puzzled many theologians. There a regional Catholic faculty of theology was founded, without incorporating it organically into the already existing Catholic (!) university.

In a basically secularized society there exists the danger that at lay universities the presence of a theological faculty might be regarded by many either as only an institute for the formation of priests (this ought not to be the case and, in German-speaking countries, is not) or as serving a purely confessional purpose. That other systems of thought or ideologies are sometimes in fact the basis of more or less openly and systematically determined departments is, when it comes to theology, easily overlooked. In some German universities, nevertheless, theology has its place, sometimes even in fact the traditional place of honor. Theology's presence there is not without extreme importance in a society which was originally built on Christian values but is now, according to some, post-Christian. The dialogue between representatives of different academic fields and their colleagues in theology, who deal thematically with questions of meaning which are basically common to all fields, has great significance, as does the dialogue between students of different disciplines. Such dialogue even touches at times upon particular concrete questions of our society; this happens in spite of, or even because of, the unique and inimitable character of sacred doctrine, which is proper to the discipline of theology.

V. MORAL THEOLOGY AS SACRED DOCTRINE

What has been said thus far makes it easier to arrive at insights into the problematic which is of particular interest to this author, namely, moral theology as *sacra doctrina*. It should first of all be made clear that moral theology is basically and formally sacred doctrine in the same sense that, for example, dogmatic theology or exegesis is. This truth has not always been kept in mind throughout the history of theology, and there are historically conditioned reasons why this insight was neglected. As a result a thoroughly Christian understanding of moral theology was lost to a great extent. Thus moral theology was deprived of its character as a form of knowing and proclaiming faith; this fact also had negative consequences for Christian spirituality and pastoral theology. New theological perspectives, which were created during part of the last century and then again in this century from the 1930s onward, met with much resistance at first. These, however, finally found authoritative recognition at Vatican II, chiefly in a short remark found in *Optatum totius* (n. 16), and they have had more and more influence on moral theology since then. In this conciliar recognition, moral theology is seen, along the lines presented earlier, as sacred doctrine: as a scientific discipline which has as its subject-matter the sublime vocation of the believer in Christ.

Accordingly, in moral theology, understood as a branch of *sacra doctrina* which only for practical reasons was separated from the other theological disciplines, the search is undertaken to help Christians reach a more profound understanding of their faith in the more practical aspects of the mystery of Christian life, including even its very concrete details. It is not really important that one cannot draw a theoretically exact line of demarcation between moral theology on the one hand and dogmatic theology, spirituality, etc., on the other. What is important is that the Council wanted to restrict the mystery of man's sublime vocation in Christ neither to the discipline of dogmatic theology nor to that of spirituality. Were this to happen, it would mean that the most profound and mysterious aspect of Christian behavior would be eliminated from moral theology.

Nevertheless, one would not be interpreting the admonition of the Council correctly if one were to understand "vocation" or "calling" exclusively or even primarily in terms of demand or command. For the Christian vocation is above all grace, and indeed the grace which is accepted precisely through the power of grace; for the refusal to accept grace would otherwise not form the basis of a theology dealing with the real status of the believer. The conciliar affirmation therefore corresponds to Johannine and Pauline theology as well as to Augustine's teaching in *De spiritu et littera*[5] and to Aquinas' doctrine on the grace of the Holy Spirit as the principal element within the new law of Christ.[6] Also in line with these theologies is the conciliar teaching which regards the gift of vocation as a gratuitous self-actualization of the Christian precisely as a person; though it expresses itself in the concrete, this self-actualization is still not of the world but a true gift. Furthermore, this self-actualization takes place (since it is a real result) and must take place (since it is a demand and command) only in particular decisions, actions, deeds and works in accord with the way in which man's world is also formed in other respects. This self-actualization is thus present in all these particular personal actions; it should animate them and bestow on them their most profound theological and Christian meaning and value.

If, as has been said, theology has and carries on its own history, this obviously holds true, and indeed in every respect, for moral theology as well. As history itself shows, moral theology is not simply a "once for all" matter. The horizon against which human and Christian existence has been understood is, in the history of moral theology, ever changing. Thus certain aspects of Christian morality which have been, at times, in part parallel to the concerns of philosophical ethics, have been highlighted. New, or at least partially new, aspects have been discovered and aspects which were one-sided or known to be misleading have been eliminated. A prime example of this phenomenon would be the problematic question of the "Christian-ness" and the "human-ness" of Christian morality, an issue which has always been and is still being discussed today and which has been solved differently at different times.

As a further example, we may consider the fact that neither before nor after St. Thomas have theologians totally agreed on a clear understanding of the new law of Christ. In fact, some had not even taken note that for St. Thomas only the interior grace of the Holy Spirit is to be considered as the primary element of this law, while the Gospel, since it is something exterior, becomes almost a secondary element. This does not mean that for St. Thomas the Gospel, the proclamation of what is new, has no importance for moral theology. This is surely not the case! Without the Gospel we would have no way of understanding or of proclaiming the Christian vocation in Christ. We should be aware, however, that revelation and vocation have to do with man in his totality as a human person. It would also be misleading to categorize Christian revelation and vocation as "partial elements" or as Christian "trimmings" instead of relating them to man and to humanity as such, and therefore to his totality. The human person and all mankind are fundamentally freed from the situation of "being fallen." As a "new" reality, mankind thus stands before a fresh horizon which gives everything in his existence (not only its partial elements) a new meaning and thus a new potential. The man "of the Spirit" is no longer the man "of the flesh", but in his total person a new creature; he remains, however, always a "man." The Gospel as the proclamation of what is new and the Spirit as the one who dwells and works in us do not primarily give us this or that new "trimming", new demand, expectation, or command (not even for a particular man as such), but they call the man, who is now freed, to be sure, from the situation of "being fallen" (however one wishes to interpret this) to a "life in the Spirit." Hence we are not to search in a positivistic way for specifically Christian demands and commands in the Gospel.

We should rather say that man as such (even though he never exists only as such) can understand objectively correct behavior, as well as the demands of justice, of love and of renunciation; he is conditioned, however, by his life in the world, where he is limited by being a creature and where he thus experiences himself as a weak and fallen being. But man, as a concrete "existential", does not easily succeed in understanding correct behavior without at least the fundamental freedom from being fallen which comes from the Spirit and the Gospel. On the other hand, the vocation in the Spirit (grace and Gospel) alone is the new existential which allows him to understand himself and his society and the demands of human morality much more easily and correctly. This happens through the existential vistas opened up by his being freed and being called in the Lord, despite the fact that a not inconsiderable residue of his being fallen remains. Moreover, he understands that his human morality is specified interiorly by this new freedom, in spite of the material sameness of human and Christian morality.[7] Thus, the reality of God the Father, proclaimed in the Gospel as the one who affirms, redeems and loves man by calling him in Jesus Christ and in the Spirit to his true worth, makes possible not only an understanding of who God is but also of what man's life as man is like if he lives within the framework of the Christian existential. The Gospel creates more than the full self-understanding of man; it moves beyond this so as to facilitate and indeed to make possible the full self-realization of man as he experiences the Christian existential.

On the basis of this new and more profound understanding of self and of God, which N. Rigali in particular has pointed out,[8] the man who is called in Christ will often, in spite of the material identity between the human and Christian moral order, find himself faced with individual callings and decisions which cannot be prudently judged or made by his humanity alone. This experience is grounded in the fact that man in his totality is laid hold of by the Spirit and by the Gospel; this necessarily means that his personal Christian individuality is empowered and enabled here and now to make concrete inferences under certain conditions.

Furthermore, in the course of human history new types of problems continually arise not only for individuals, but for interpersonal relations, for special groups or for human society. As human problems they find human solutions. However, since it is not specific elements of human existence but man in his totality who is given this Christian call, what becomes clear in human solutions to new human problems is the meaning which the message of the Gospel and which being-called-in-the-Spirit (e.g., Christian love or Christian justice) lend to these new problems. In other words, what the Gospel and the Spirit have always implicitly contained is made explicit. In this sense an increase in concrete moral knowledge also means an increase in knowledge of the Gospel and of the Spirit who is given to us. Moral knowledge is, for this reason, an understanding of faith; always new, always excellent, it is in turn transformed by the academic subject of theology into an enriched means of proclaiming the faith. The material identity of the "human" and the "Christian" moral order does not contradict this phenomenon.

What has been said about new types of moral problems also holds true for new ways of understanding man and his world. That there have been and always will be new horizons of understanding is certainly beyond question. By way of example, we might note the at times more contemplative and at times more active view of man's responsibility with regard to his world and his history, or the at times more static and at times more dynamic definition of man. We could also point out the changing conception of the dignity of man, and indeed of each individual man and woman (and the legitimately different consequences of each view); there is also the evolving sensitivity regarding the value and above all the function of women in human society. These mutations could possibly give rise to a very different understanding of the kind of behavior which has always been expected or required of man in the past, but they can also lead to new expectations and to consequences not previously perceived. It might be that Christian revelation itself was responsible or co-responsible for such a changed understanding and therefore for such an evolving understanding of man along with its consequences, but this is not necessarily true. In any case such an understanding, together with its consequent expected or required modes of behavior, has a Christian meaning which is rooted in the Gospel and in the Spirit; thus it brings the essence of Christianity to light.

Furthermore, one who is engaged in moral theology today must be prepared to heed the more or less certain knowledge which is being discovered, for example, by the human sciences. He must also be ready to reflect seriously on the possible moral consequences which can arise from these sciences even if he senses the danger that these consequences do not fully correspond to the moral demands which theologians previously recognized on the basis of insufficient or mistaken knowledge. If the moral theologian does not listen and reflect in this way, he sets himself in opposition to God's creative Spirit who is shaping man's world. The search to understand faith and the willingness to proclaim it through moral theology demand open and serious research, with concomitant reflection, if this proclamation is to be true to itself in every detail. Only in this way can one arrive at correct moral knowledge which, of itself, possesses specifically Christian meaning in spite of its specifically human subject-matter. It should be said again here that theology, including moral theology, is a Christian endeavor of man; it is thus not unconditional and not a once for all matter in every respect. If Vatican II understands the Church as "semper reformanda" *(Unitatis redintegratio)*, we should realize that theology too, which takes part in the Church's existence, is "always in need of reform". The same, therefore, is true of moral theology. We must always consider what theological pronouncements we can honestly affirm; in no case ought we to misuse them as ideologies. We shall never completely exhaust either the theoretical or the practical implications which the term "new creature" affords the history of Christianity. Such insights guard moral theology both against opting for static rigidity and against advocating total discontinuity. A further result of these insights, as history itself proves, is that with new horizons of understanding regarding man and revelation and with new knowledge concerning both the latter, as well as with new problems of humanity, a number of key questions arise: in any given age, what are the most urgent topics to be taken up by moral theology? How are these topics to be developed? History itself shows that these questions recur continually.

Thus, we never have a comprehensive understanding of man, independent of history and as such always ready at hand. The same can be said of our understanding of morality, even that which emerges from our faith. For precisely this reason it is legitimate to debate the extent to which the hierarchy and theologians can and should intervene in moral problems, and the form which this intervention should take. Moreover, the problem of teacher and student having conceivably different horizons of understanding is one which still exists in moral theology today. The teacher must always examine himself critically to discover if his knowledge of facts and his horizon of understanding are able to meet the challenge posed by many of today's human questions. It may become evident to him that he has to rethink his position; yet it may also become clear to him that he must try to change those viewpoints of his students which depend on fallacious arguments. Finally, the moral theologian cannot enter into the fruitful dialogue which is so often desired by many and is indeed desirable, if he does not take seriously the scientific knowledge attained in other fields — of course in accord with the degree of certainty it contains — and if he does not apply himself to the task of understanding the intellectual perspectives of those in other fields — even their moral and theological perspectives. If the theologian makes this attempt, however, the ensuing interdisciplinary dialogue can have far-reaching results for moral theology; in fact, seen within the context of our understanding of faith, this dialogue can rightly be called a proclamation of the faith, even if the "moral" discussion takes place totally on the level of the "human."

NOTES

1. Thomas Aquinas, *S.T.* I, q. 1; cf. art. 1c and ad 2; art. 2c and ad 1; art. 3 ad 1; art. 6; art. 7c; art. 8c.
2. Cf. G. Bauer, "Christliche Hoffnung und menschlicher Fortschritt. Die politische Theologie von J.B. Metz als theologische Begründung gesellschaftlicher Verantwortung des Christen", Mainz 1976 (dissertation, Pontifical Gregorian University).
3. Cf. J. Jankowiak, "Critical Negativity and Political Ethics within the

Context of the Political Theology of J.B. Metz", Rome 1975 (dissertation, Pontifical Gregorian University).

4.   Cf. R. Coffy, "Lehramt und Theologie-die Situation heute", *Orientierung* 40 (1976), 63-9, 80-3; F.B.C. Butler, "Authority and the Christian Conscience", *The Clergy Review* 60 (1975), 3-17. Cf. also Avery Dulles' contribution, "What Is the Magisterium?", *Origins* 6 (July 1976), 81, 83-7 (giving an American bibliography).

5.   Migne, *Patrologia Latina*, 44, 199-246.

6.   Aquinas' doctrine on this point is systematically presented in *S.T.* I-II, qq. 106-8.

7.   This "formal" specification is naturally also a "material" one, insofar as every formal dimension contains a material element. It is called formal and is formal in reference to another type of materiality.

8.   Cf. N.J. Rigali, "New Epistemology and the Moralist", *Chicago Studies* 11 (1972), 237-44. The reference here is to 243ff.

2. Moral Theology and Christian Existence

If it is true that the spiritual formation of those who study theology should be related to their studies and should be considerably influenced by them, this holds in a special way for moral theology. Praxis itself confirms this; and the unique character of lectures on moral theology makes it necessary. For it is the task of moral theology not only to transmit the Christian doctrine of the relation between man and the God of his salvation, which is elaborated in exegesis and dogmatic theology, but also to translate it into a treatise on Christian life and action in this world. If this transmission and translation are not done well, then theology itself will fail to make clear how one's acceptance of the salvific work of God may be put into effect in the daily living of Christian existence. If it is truly done well, however, the moral life practiced each day will be understood to be the chief means by which the Christian actualizes his theological existence in faith, hope and love, and thus deepens his relationship to the God of his salvation.

The most proper and decisive aspect of the Christian's existence is not so much his morality — that is, his correct human behavior; it is much more his theological reality, his continual relationship to the God of salvation, which includes a total giving of himself through a hopeful and loving faith. What is essential in this regard is that such a total giving of self be comprehended and lived, actualized and expressed through moral action. If moral theology can achieve the goal of making theological existence understood, then it can contribute decisively to the formation of genuine Christian values in those who study theology.

In what follows, (1) the theological existence of the Christian will be described as a total giving of self by which he answers the call of the God of his salvation. Then, (2) the possibility of making this response of total self-giving through one's daily moral life will be discussed. Finally, (3) the possibility of living out Christian existence through right relations with one's neighbor will be set forth.

I. THEOLOGICAL OR CHRISTIAN EXISTENCE AS A GIVING OF SELF

The immediate relation of the Christian to the God of salvation, which is called theological, is not only treated in moral theology in the tract which deals explicitly with the theological virtues. Faith, hope, and love essentially form a single reality; Christian existence is faith which hopes and loves. Theological life, therefore, is the one total relation to the God of salvation, such that the Christian gives his entire self to God and thus answers his call in Christ. This relation and this giving of self do not, from a moral point of view, signify any particular and categorial mode of action through which the Christian expresses himself, but the transcendental "being-given-away" of the total person, which underlies every particular and categorical Christian action. This giving of self in faith, hope, and love can be presented in moral theology under various aspects. In what follows, these aspects are developed: (1) the acceptance of the Christian vocation, (2) the following of Christ, (3) the life of the new law, and (4) the complete openness of the Christian person.

1.   In the *Decree on Priestly Formation* of Vatican II, the vocation in Christ is regarded as the central reality which ought, above all else, to be studied and explained in moral theology: "[Moral theology] ought to show the loftiness of the vocation of the faithful in Christ and their obligation to bear fruit in love for the life of the world...."[1] This vocation is first and foremost neither a collection of Christian precepts nor a call to this or that way of living the Christian life (as a layman, husband or wife, priest or religious, etc.); nor is it a call to a specific profession (teacher, politician, craftsman, etc.); rather it is a call to salvation in Christ. Even the latter, however, is not a precept or mandate, but a gift. Furthermore, this gift is not only the offer of God, present in a general sense to the world of man in Christ, but also the offer made to each and every individual in a personal way. This gift is not only an offer, but God's activity in the individual. For the God of salvation not only holds out a personal relationship of friendship to man, but effectively removes him from his state of alienation, and produces that faith in him which makes trust possible as well as the total giving of self to the Father in love. In other words, faith brings about in man that life which is a continuation of the interpersonal relation between Christ and the Father. Faith is salvation and one day it is to pass into unending salvation.

Nonetheless, the call to salvation is a demanding one. Not that man's vocation primarily demands this or that particular thing; rather it requires the acceptance and active realization of that life which is salvation. For salvation is indeed a gift, but this gift is a personal life which is realized in liberty. It is not some object imposed upon us, but is simultaneously both demanded and given. The life which is the Christian vocation, or Christian salvation, consists in a mutual giving, that is, in God's giving of self to the Christian and in the Christian's giving of self to God. The initiative lies with him who alone can take the initiative and who in fact "loved us first" (1 John 4:10) and who accordingly expects and demands our reciprocal giving of self and seeks to bring this about in us.

The fulfillment of individual precepts and each particular attempt at acting rightly are to be understood as a specification and embodiment of one's acceptance of the call to salvation. The latter takes place through the various concrete ways in which one realizes the good in a double sense, namely, both as gift and demand, and through the act of accepting both senses freely. In each and every particular act the God of salvation gives himself, calls the whole man to salvation and brings about in him its acceptance; thus God facilitates the self-giving which occurs in the faith which hopes and loves. In other words, Christian existence, as the "toward-each-other" and "with-each-other" of the God of salvation and the man destined for it, is realized in each particular moral action, even if this happens in a noncategorial and for this reason in a nonvisible manner.

2. A readiness on the part of Christians to follow their call corresponds to the belief that such a call issues from the Father through Christ. Thus, following this call is really the following of Christ. We now know that even within the New Testament the concept of following Christ underwent some changes.[2] Exegetes tell us that for the pre-Easter disciple the call of Christ was not primarily a call to salvation, but to a profession, so to speak. The disciple was challenged to live his life in the service of the work of Christ himself; the disciple was to fulfill the mission of Christ and prepare others for salvation. Such a mission demanded of the disciple a strict communion with Christ and an acceptance of the corresponding consequences for his life.

The post-Easter disciples found themselves in a very different situation: now they looked to the glorious Lord. Thus the words of Christ concerning discipleship take on a new meaning. They no longer primarily mean the sending of individual disciples to carry out the work of the master, but the call of all people to salvation. This is especially evident in the Gospel of John. A call to discipleship and to following Christ is now to a great extent identical with being called to faith, hope and love – the vocation to exist and to remain in Christ. Thus, at Antioch, as is recorded in the Acts of the Apostles (11:26), the disciples – that is, those who follow Christ, are as such simply called Christians.

The familiar words of the Lord about taking up the cross and denying oneself (Luke 14:27 = Matt. 10:38; Mark 8:34 = Matt. 16:24 = Luke 9:23) illustrate quite well the changing meaning of the concept of Christian discipleship. It seems that carrying the cross was originally understood as a state of life for the disciple who follows Christ in fulfilling his mission in this world. The few who are called to this ought to be prepared to die with Christ – that is, to carry the cross together with the Lord himself. The post-Easter Christians, however, began to understand these words of the Lord as directed not only to the few disciples but to the "people" (Luke 14:25; Mark 8:34), and even to "all men" (Luke 9:23). And by the cross they understood not so much the cross of Christ himself which the disciples who accompanied the earthly suffering of Jesus had to be prepared to carry, but the cross which belonged to each and every one of them, and which had to be carried daily in communion with and imitation of the Lord (Luke 9:23) and in the spirit of self-denial (Mark 8:34 = Matt 16:24 = Luke 9:23) in order to gain salvation. In John (12:26 a) the concept of carrying the cross is totally lacking; it is only said that one should follow the Lord. To be a Christian means to follow Christ in the sense that a total communion, in suffering and in joy, is to be sought with the now glorified Lord.

Some have observed that in the writings of St. Paul the call to follow Christ is changed into the call to conversion through baptism.[3] This sacrament is truly a call to total self-giving, to dying and being buried with Christ, and all this precisely so as to live daily with Christ. This new way of existing in Christ implies accepting the moral imperative of transforming the sinful man according to the image of Christ. Consequently, to follow Christ means to believe, to allow oneself to be taken up in Christ, and to express through one's daily moral actions the self-giving love of Christ toward his heavenly Father and toward his brothers.

3.   Inspired by the New Testament writings and those of St. Augustine, Christian theology through the centuries developed a doctrine of the "new law" in contrast to the "old law" and the "natural law." Thomas Aquinas in his *Summa Theologiae* made a distinction between the primary and the secondary element of the new law, that is, between the grace of the Holy Spirit and the precepts of the new law.[4] Precepts, even those of the Gospel, are in themselves lifeless and bring death to man the sinner. The grace of the Holy Spirit, on the contrary, is a life-giving gift. Precepts demand various things of us, while the grace of the Holy Spirit creates a new man in us. Christian morality is not determined by new moral precepts but by the grace of the Spirit which transforms man. What the Sermon on the Mount sketches is not so much a superhuman Christian morality, but the new man of the kingdom whom Christ himself creates. The man who is selfless and who gives of himself to his neighbor in the presence of his heavenly Father will begin to be a genuine human person, that is, to live a truly human moral life. Through such a human existence a person makes visible his self-giving love, or the reign of God present in him. Similarly, the specific element of the "spiritual man" (*pneumatikos*) about whom St. Paul writes does not consist in a unique Christian moral code, but precisely in that new spirituality which the grace of the Holy Spirit produces within a person's essentially carnal (*sarkikos*) or self-centered nature. In fact, the "spiritual" man does those things which man as such ought to, but which, as a "carnal" man, he refuses to do. St. Paul does not contrast a "Christian" and a "human" morality, but the "spiritual" and the "carnal" man.

Therefore, the primary element of the new law is that Christian freedom by which man, as a son along with Christ, not only *can* give himself in a loving way to the loving Father, but also in fact *does* give himself. This freedom is the immeasurable, Spirit-worked openness of the fallen man who on his own opts for a carnal-egotistic way of life; the same man is now ready to receive the love and call of the Father. Thus a dialogue of love begins between the Father and the man transformed by the Spirit into a son of God.

This dialogue of love needs some medium in which to express itself. St. Paul calls good works the "fruits of the Spirit" (Gal. 5:22). Aquinas agrees when, by way of explanation, he says that precepts (as secondary elements of the new law) are in the service of grace,[5] which is the primary element of Christian existence. Therefore, the decisive element of the new law is the new man himself who, as a totality − that is, as a person − enters into a dialogue of love with the Father through the power of the Spirit. This relationship, which is the core of Christian existence, expresses itself, as far as morals are concerned, in the "observance of the commandments" (see John 14:15-24).

4. The interior freedom of the man who believes in and follows Christ makes him fully open and available to the Father. The new reality which Christ made possible for man is not this or that particular thing, but an immediate dialogic relationship with the Father in total communion and in generous self-giving. This does not deny that man by his very nature is fundamentally open to God. However, since he exists concretely in a fallen state, man tends to act egotistically and in fact receives this generous availability and openness from Christ, as a participation in his total openness to the Father.

Those who consider excessively rigorous the position that one is obliged always to do the better thing have perhaps not yet sufficiently reflected on the nature of the Christian who exists before the Father. For how could a man who loves God in full generosity and total openness restrict his moral activity to precepts which hold for all and correspond to common structures, if in a certain case the better mode of acting here and now is perfectly clear to him? The existence of such cases follows from the very nature of the Christian's new life; for, as the one who dedicates himself totally to the God who calls him, the Christian cannot in fact experience any advice simply as advice. How can the total reality of such a relationship to God be conceived without including an interior readiness to correspond to the expectations of the Father? What has been said here is made particularly clear by Karl Rahner who has worked out a form of Christian situation ethics called "existential ethics".[6] According to the latter, the gracious love of God the Father creates the innermost being and the individual-personal vocation of each man. This central truth far surpasses the generally formulated norm of the "Christian person," even though the personal call, as long as it is stated exactly, never contradicts the general norm. Thus, the individual-personal call can be recognized as such only through the experience of full Christian faith and love. This means that the individual-personal call depends on the Christian's relationship to God through concrete acts of faith and love. Only in this way is it possible to determine if an apparent personal call really is one or not. Christian existence is openness and availability which know no self-imposed or generally understood boundaries in the face of the God who calls the individual in love and grace and who has complete disposition over him.

II. CHRISTIAN EXISTENCE AND CONCRETE MORALITY

The Christian's life in faith, hope and love — that is, the acceptance of one's vocation, the following of Christ, abiding by the new law and total openness and availability to the heavenly Father, does not fundamentally mean some particular activity and behavior or this or that virtue, such as justice and friendliness. Faith, hope and love deal with the relation of the Christian in his totality, therefore as person, to God the Father. Explicit "acts" of faith, of love or of readiness to follow Christ are not in the last analysis faith, love, or readiness to follow Christ themselves, but their actual forms of expression. It is very important, however, to insist that Christian existence manifests itself not only in such religious acts but in every aspect of the believer's life. Moral theology should therefore shed light on: (1) the presence of theological life in concrete moral behavior, (2) its different modes of presence in moral activity which is either fully human or only peripheral, (3) its presence in activity which is called "secular", and (4) its special presence in "religious life."

1. The decisive question is this: how can daily life with its multiple aspects, marked as they are by creaturely contingency, truly be the life of faith, love, discipleship and self-giving? If concrete acts of justice and chastity or the daily fulfillment of personal obligations, etc., are only themselves and nothing more, then Christian life can hardly or seldom be called "theological." Moral theology, if it deals simply with moral virtues and norms of acting, even if it presents the latter only along with or in connection with the values of Christian existence and even if in doing so it attributes primacy to theological values, is a poor moral theology, and thus hardly Christian. The question posed here is therefore of great importance.

How will one find a solution? Moral tendencies and acts are in their execution always something more than that which they indicate; they are more than freely willed tendencies and acts corresponding to certain moral categories. The reason for this is that in every free act the person who is its subject actualizes himself. Morality ultimately consists in the entire person's self-actualization before the Absolute through the categorial moral acts. The categorial moral act is not truly moral unless in and through it the acting person realizes himself before the Absolute. In turn, the moral self-actualization of the person is only possible in and through an act of a particular moral category.

Faith and love, the following of Christ and the full disposition of one's self, do not belong to any definite moral category, but are the way of behavior made possible by Christ, who is totally related to the Absolute. Through his moral actions in accord with different moral categories the human person makes actual his Christian relation to

God the Father. Particular moral deeds allow him to realize himself as a believing person, as one following Christ, and as one offering himself in Christian freedom. Therefore, through categorial moral acts he actualizes his own Christian existence. He does this, however, at that deepest core of his being where he is consciously present to himself but where he is not able to make an adequate reflection on his own self-fulfillment. It is only the moral act in its categorial particularity which is the object of his conscious reflection.

There are certainly reflective and thematic acts of faith and love, of being close to Christ and of opening oneself to grace. These acts, however, are essentially categorial religious acts which, as we have said, express faith and love, the personal following of Christ and the availability of the self before God. Such expressions not only take place in religious acts but also in the various moral acts of the truly believing and loving Christian. As a result, all such acts concretely and *de facto* constitute Christian existence. Not only do acts of Christian religiousness deepen the relation of the sons of God to the Father of Jesus Christ, but so do the categorial acts of morality. This is true of the latter even if in them – in contrast to the acts of Christian religiousness – their Christian relation to God is hardly or even not at all brought to thematic reflection, but remains on a nonthematic and transcendental level of consciousness, which is in itself a deeper and richer level.

2. Some attention must now be given to an important distinction between two different ways of behaving morally. For not all moral acts are personal in that they proceed from the person as a totality and from the core of his ego. In other words, some acts are considered moral which are not such in the full, but only in the analogous sense. Through them one neither experiences oneself directly nor is one truly engaged, for one does not take a position with regard to the Absolute from the true core of one's person. In these acts a man exists in a somewhat superficial way for the very reason that they hardly cause him to actualize himself or to determine his true relation to the Absolute. Such acts are not those of Christian existence in the proper sense. Much like the venial sins of a believing and loving Christian, they are nothing other than superficial ways of acting which do not place the reality of Christian existence in question, that reality which belongs to the core of the person.

Nonetheless the moral life which is lived at surface level, so to speak – that is, one's "light" moral activity (so called because of the parallel to "light" or "venial" sins) is not simply outside the sphere of

Christian existence. Even the "light" acts of genuine virtue are consequences and expressions of the Christian relation to the Father through faith, hope and love. Yet they are not moral acts in the full sense of the word, because they are not personal in a strict but only in an analogous sense, and are thus only analogously "human".

3. The active presence of theological or Christian existence in daily moral activity is of special importance above all because such activity is thoroughly regulated only by a "horizontal" norm; that is, it is determined by the this-worldly framework of meaning, by the "secular" or "human". This statement must not be understood as a recent invention and as a concession to the secularized or secular worldview. Rather, it is derived from Christian tradition itself, in that Christianity brought not a new moral code,[7] but a new man, who embraces and fulfills the genuinely human moral code from the depths of his being. This does not prevent the Christian, because of the categorial nature of his faith, from understanding many values in terms of their ultimate meaning. Nor does his human ethics prevent him from opening himself in a special way to the promptings of the Spirit of Christ. It must be emphasized, however, that the moral manner of behaving has a basically horizontal this-worldly, human norm.

For centuries men have asked how such moral activity can have Christian value and "merit". Above all, the question has been asked whether such merely human morality ought not somehow to be based on motives of faith. But how seldom moral activity is de facto based on or motivated and occasioned by faith in the true sense! Yet it is true that Christian meaning and motivation — for example, in the exercise of temperance, chastity or truthfulness — are operative when a Christian fulfills the demands of human morality. But there is another factor of even greater importance, namely, that human morality, which is determined by horizontal, this-worldly norms, be penetrated by Christian existence, so that it becomes an expression of the Christian relation to God. For the Christian's life of faith, hope and love is realized neither simply in itself, nor only in purely religious acts, but also in and through daily moral behavior. Does not the Christian, even in his search for a human moral order and norms, also ultimately seek a way of expressing and translating into daily action his Christian existence, his faith and love?

Therefore, theological or Christian existence, and especially its vitality, is at work not only in acts of reflective consciousness but also in those nonthematically and nonreflectively conscious acts which animate and penetrate conscious moral behavior. For this reason, not only profound meditation and solemn worship, but also the moral practice of justice and mercy, as well as the fulfillment of daily obligations and the shaping of this world, can in a very true sense constitute Christian existence.

4. In a special way attention must be given to the active presence of Christian existence in religious life – that is, in piety and worship. Again, one should distinguish between religious life and "theological" life or Christian existence. Explicit acts of faith and love, of following Christ and being open to the Father, of meditation and prayer, of religious recollection and solemn liturgy, constitute religious life. They have their roots, as religious expressions, in Christian existence which is the total actualization of the person and likewise the foundation of both religious and moral life.

Religious life, however, must also be distinguished from moral life which is horizontally determined. The moral and religious aspects converge at an essential point, though, since both are categorial expressions of man's total dependence on and self-surrender before the Absolute; it is for this reason that they are also expressions of theological existence which is the decisively Christian relation between God and man.

In a certain respect, religious life is closer to theological existence than is moral life, even though each is a categorial expression of the life of faith, hope and love. This is why religious life enjoys a special place in the process by which theological existence animates moral life. To a certain extent religious life brings the reality of Christian existence into the sphere of reflective and thematic consciousness, as is the case in explicit acts of faith, hope and love, as well as in other acts of reflective religiousness. It seems evident that religiousness promotes Christian existence in a more forceful and immediate way than does moral life. Religious practices contribute to the steadiness, depth and vitality of Christian existence, and make moral life itself a dialogue between us and our heavenly Father.

III. CHRISTIAN EXISTENCE AND LOVE OF NEIGHBOR

It is clear that transcendental or theological existence chiefly actualizes and expresses itself in the field of morality through love of one's neighbor. The best humanists, even those who confine reality to the immanent, consider love of neighbor the preeminent moral act, and indeed the only truly absolute postulate of human morality. We spoke earlier (in section II) of the moral and religious life as that reality in and through which Christian existence realizes and expresses itself, and we must here dwell briefly on the specific implications of this affirmation for the moral sphere of love of neighbor. In doing so, we must consider the special relation of brotherly love both to the rest of morality and to the love of God. We must therefore treat the following topics in order: (1) love of neighbor as an expression of Christian or theological existence, and (2) the identity of love of neighbor and the life of faith, hope and love.

1. In this context Karl Rahner calls love of neighbor the "fundamental moral act of man".[8] He considers this statement to be founded on the following considerations: (a) seen from a personal and moral perspective, the world of things is not to be understood as closed on itself but as a part of man and of his personal environment; (b) this fact, however, taking account of the personal nature of man, is not to be interpreted in an egocentric manner but in terms of personal communication and openness; (c) man's first personal partner, as far as his "categorial" life is concerned, cannot be God himself, because a mediation is always needed, due to man's historicity and factitiousness; the mediator is the human person and his world.

Love of neighbor, like love of God, should be carefully distinguished from the actions by which it expresses itself. It is true that works of goodness, mercy, etc., are called works of love and are thus distinguished from, for example, works of justice. Nonetheless, this mode of categorizing is not fully justified, for love does not mean this or that good work, but the total openness of the person to another. Love of neighbor as such does not induce a person to give this or that but to give himself. Therefore he who gives much, perhaps even all he has, and indeed even his life, may thereby have truly given himself − that is, his love − but then again, he may not! In the same way, the sum of the virtues by which a man acts rightly toward his neighbor does not in itself constitute love. Love is more than this. One need only reflect on what St. Paul says in this respect in his hymn on the love of neighbor. (1 Cor. 13). In order to express itself, brotherly love needs the acts of other moral virtues. Love expresses itself both in works of goodness and in works of genuine justice, as long as the one who performs these works really loves his neighbor − that is, makes himself freely available as a total person in full openness to the other. Thus we can say that Christian existence − therefore faith and love, following Christ and being open to the Father − expresses itself in a special way through love of neighbor, which for its part finds expression in manifold forms of the right behavior toward one's neighbor. One who stands in relation to God through faith and love lives and actualizes his Christian existence through love of neighbor and through works which for this reason manifest a right relation to his brother, even though they do not necessarily spring from conscious reflection on the fact that "acts ordered by charity" are being carried out.

2. Here the question arises whether this formula of ours can stand as it is or should be made somewhat more specific. Theological tradition not only holds that love of God is present in love of neighbor, as in the rest of moral activity. The tradition goes further and even affirms a true identity between love of God and love of neighbor; this means that love of neighbor not only *expresses* Christian existence but *is* Christian existence; it is therefore Christian love of God, which manifests itself in many different ways of acting rightly toward one's neighbor.

Rahner distinguishes "explicit" from "nonexplicit" love of God.[9] The latter, according to him, not only is present in the love of neighbor as a supernatural and transcendental act, but also sustains the explicit love of God itself, because charity is the primordial way of loving God. In similar fashion, must one not distinguish between a "categorial-explicit"[10] love of neighbor and a prior, more profound relationship of love to one's brother which is primordial and in fact totally open and Christian? Must it not therefore be said that the latter is identical with the primordial, transcendental and total Christian love of God? In other words, the Christian experiences the other in his true reality — that is, as one with whom God identifies himself in Christ. The explicit categorial love of neighbor and the nonexplicit but transcendental love of God *and* neighbor mutually condition each other, in the way in which Rahner described the mutual conditioning of categorial-explicit love of neighbor and transcendental love of God. Love of neighbor is, in its deepest roots, not brotherly love "for God's sake," but truly Christian or theological existence; it is love of neighbor as love of God. Transcendental love for others sustains explicit and categorial acts of loving one's neighbor, penetrates and animates every right manner of behaving toward one's brother and in this way allows the latter to be an expression of theological love of neighbor and therefore a living expression of Christian love of God.

This brief exposition has intended to show how the teaching on Christian life as the life of faith, hope and love can be of great importance for the personal formation of students. This will be the case if: (1) the nature of Christian existence is clearly explained as total availability to the heavenly Father who lovingly calls man to salvation; (2) the possibility of the presence of this living relationship with God in daily moral life is made intelligible; (3) the special relation of brotherly love both to love of God and to the rest of morality is illuminated.

NOTES

1.   I wrote a commentary on this text: "Moral Theology According to Vatican II," *Human Values and Christian Morality*, Dublin 1970, 1-55. Cf. also B. Häring, "Theologia moralis speciali cura perficienda", *Seminarium* 18 (1966), 357-68.

2.   From a rather vast bibliography of recent years I cite the following: E. Neuhäusler, *Anspruch und Antwort Gottes*, Düsseldorf 1962, 186-214; E. Larsson, *Christus als Vorbild. Eine Untersuchung zu den paulischen Tauff- und Eikontexton*, Uppsala 1962; A. Schulz, *Nachfolgen und Nachahmen. Studien über das Verhältnis der neutestamentlichen Jüngerschaft zur urchristlichen Vorbildethik*, Munich 1962; H. Zimmerman, "Christus nachfolgen", *Theologie und Glaube* 53 (1963), 241-68; T. Aerts, "Suivre Jésus. Evolution d'un thème biblique dans les Evangiles synoptiques", *Eph. Theol. Lov.* 42 (1966), 476-512; R. Thysman, "L'Ethique de l'imitation du Christ dans le N.T.", *Eph. Theol. Lov.* 42 (1966), 138-75; H.D. Betz, *Nachfolge und Charisma. Eine exegetisch-religionsgeschichtliche Studie zu Mt. 8:21 f. und Jesu Ruf in die Nachfolge*, Berlin 1968; A. Klingl, "Nachfolge Christi — ein moraltheologischer Begriff?" in K. Demmer and B. Schüller (eds.), *Christlich glauben und handeln. Fragen einer Moraltheologie in der Diskussion*, Düsseldorf 1977, 78-85.

3.   E. Neuhäusler, op. cit. (see note 2 above), 282.

4.   Thomas Aquinas, *S.T.* I-II, q. 106, a. 1s.

5.   Ibid., a. 1.

6.   K. Rahner, "On the Question of a Formal Existential Ethics", *Theological Investigations II*, London 1963, 217-34; idem, *The Dynamic Element in the Church*, London 1964, 84-170.

7.   Cf., for example, Thomas Aquinas, *S.T.* I-II, q. 108, a. 2.

8.   K. Rahner, "Reflections on the Unity of the Love of Neighbor and the Love of God", *Theological Investigations VI*, London 1969, 241.

9.   Ibid., 237-8.

10.   Ibid., 247.

3. Vocation and Hope: Conciliar Orientations for a Christian Morality

Post-conciliar moral theology has taken seriously the Council's desire for the renewal of moral theology. Even before the Council, efforts were under way to place moral theology on a new level by making it more Christocentric. However, this pre-conciliar approach of "Christianizing" moral theology met with a certain amount of skepticism from most moral theologians. Nevertheless, the Council (as can readily be seen in the document *Optatum totius*)[1] adopted this Christocentric approach and made it its own. By so doing, the Council brought to maturity a theological concept that had already been some ten years in the making, thereby changing overnight the climate of moral theological opinion. Today, then, the principal concern of moral theology should be to focus on the nobility of the Christian vocation of the faithful in Christ. Everything else — worship, the works of charity, the transformation of the world — is really the fruit of this basic Christian vocation of the faithful.

Some years ago, I wrote about some of the conciliar guidelines for the renewal of theology set forth in *Optatum totius*.[2] But it would be a grave mistake to think that *Optatum totius* was the last or only word on the subject of the renewal of moral theology. The Council was not satisfied to adopt the Christocentric approach in moral theology and leave it at that. In the Constitution *Gaudium et spes*, it had already begun to advance toward a position vis-à-vis problems that were facing the Council then and in which we are engaged today. Thus, in *Gaudium et spes* — though in a preliminary and fragmentary fashion — the Council began to grapple with questions that have become most important for Christians living in the world, especially in recent years. In this perspective the world is seen as a place not merely to be lived in but to be transformed and humanized. From the moral viewpoint we can formulate this perspective as follows: what specific actions performed by Christians in this world and for its transformation can be said to be the fruit of the Christian vocation? What is being examined in this question is not simply the

Christian's duty, to be carried out in the world, but, above all, the very hope of the world.

It should therefore be clear that if moral theology is to renew itself, the conciliar documents *Gaudium et spes* and *Optatum totius* must be considered jointly. In this chapter I intend to reflect on the content of both documents in order to discuss more fully the idea of Christian (moral) behavior in this world both as the fruit of the Christian vocation and as the hope of the world — vocation and hope.

I. A NEW MAN OR A NEW MORALITY?

The intention behind the formulation of the conciliar decree *Optatum totius* is clear. The Council Fathers desired a moral theology whose dominant motif would be the sublime vocation of the faithful in Christ rather than a catalogue of laws and obligations. In other words, a separation of theological disciplines that would make the Christian vocation the focal point of dogmatic theology while failing to make it at the same time the focal point of moral theology cannot help but result in a misunderstanding of the very content of Christian moral theology and Christian ethics. If moral theology polarized itself so as to be preoccupied only with a codification of divine precepts rather than with an interpretation of the meaning of Christian life as being "vocation in Christ", it certainly would not be responding authentically to its essential task.

The Council repeatedly employs the concept of vocation (as divine and Christian) in a variety of its documents. The concept is certainly a familiar one in both the Old and New Testaments, and provides the basis for interpreting man and the world. Nonetheless, given the influence of our own cultural ambience, it is still a familiar concept for modern man. "Vocation" always indicates a loving initiative in which God makes himself the horizon of man's being; it is, moreover, an active "coming-to-be" by God in the heart of every individual in such a way that man in turn opens his own core of being to the divine vocation by freely accepting it. For fallen man such a vocation means redemption, salvation. Salvation, then, is simply the interior transformation of the egocentric human heart — a conversion, the fruit of grace, from a state of enclosed self-centeredness to a total openness to God that is the only means to communion with God founded in Christ.

Thus, that men let themselves be taken up radically into communion with the Father, that God calls us in Christ and begets in us the acceptance of vocation, that he continually calls us from the self-ishness of our own egocentrism to a communion of mutual giving, that he even succeeds in calling us out of ourselves despite our egotistical tendencies — all this can surely be called a miracle: a miracle which is indeed worthy of being the central theme of moral theology. Abstractly, the implications of this central theme will be sketched out in several disciplines — theological, anthropological, psychological, ethical and pedagogical. However, it should be stated clearly at the beginning that the divine vocation never comes to us in a global and abstract manner; it is always translated into concrete and categorial modes of our behavior in a very concrete and categorial human world. In this perspective one can surely distinguish be-tween those behavioral modes of being in the world and of human interpersonal action that are capable of expressing man's loving openness to the God of creation and redemption, and those be-havioral modes that do not express the openness of love. Such dif-ferentiated behavioral modes can be stated universally in the form of principles and norms. These modes can also be understood as the appropriate, concrete ethical demand of the concrete, individual re-ality, inasmuch as such a reality can never be totally expressed in principles and norms; at the same time, it does not contradict them either. This ethical demand (if one were to carry it to its ultimate term of realizing, externally and internally, the human task) will always ap-pear subject not only to the pressures of external reality but also and equally to the dynamism of human personal growth and the promptings of grace. Thus, we should never lose sight of the fact that ethical imperatives are categorial translations and, as such, are sup-ports for man's vocation — in his entire personhood — in Christ.

In this same line of thought it is easily seen that the primary ob-ject of the Christian moral message is not a new morality (or a new material content), but rather the proclamation of a new man. It was not a new moral code that humanity had hoped for from Christ, but rather redemption — the transformation of the old man into the new, of the egocentric man into the man wholly under the influence of the Son's love of the Father. Christ's mission was not primarily to teach men the difference between good and evil works: it was the redemption which would make them men "of the Kingdom". Christ's task was not to impart moral lessons, but to create a man who would produce good works as the "fruit" of his transformation and "newness" (John 15, Gal. 5:22). Thus the Sermon on the Mount is not presented as a new morality, if by "new" one means going beyond a genuinely human morality. The word "new" must be seen as contrasted with "old", and not with "genuinely human". When we speak here of the old and the new, it is with reference to man — that is, the old man who is selfish, egocentric, and closed, as distinct from the new man who opens himself in surrender to love. What is brought out in the Sermon on the Mount is what (whenever the situation demands it) the new man is capable of (as the fruit of his newness) in the Kingdom, and this is put in strict contrast with the old man who is imprisoned in his own ego and is never able to raise himself to the same level. Thus, in dealing with the concepts of the old and the new man, we are dealing with an actual morality of oldness and newness, but not in the sense of a new doctrine called Christian as opposed to an old doctrine that was merely human and simply taught the difference between good and evil. At the same time, a certain newness should not escape us; namely, that good works which arise out of a true ethic should not be simply treated as a praiseworthy human achievement: they already express the filial love that transcends fallen man's egotism and egocentrism.

We may be certain that the moral doctrine underlying the real distinction between good and evil behavior will not be banished from the discipline of moral theology. On the other hand, it should not be allowed to assume a place in moral theology which would result in allocating only a marginal significance to the central theme of Christian morality. Certainly, the work of defining what is concretely good and evil is important, even for the Christian, especially since man lives, for the time being, in the flesh and does not yet experience the fullness or definitiveness of redemptive grace; and thus, alongside his response to grace, he continues to be exposed also to the powerful influence of his own egocentric tendencies. In reading the Gospel, therefore, one does not get the impression that Christ's message can be summarized as a new ethic, but rather as a total and efficacious vocation to the newness of men of the Kingdom. Granted that the factors for the formation of ecclesial communal life and human society are extremely important, has not the preoccupation of moral theology (and also of a ministerial Church) with such factors alone, more often than not ended in a rather one-sided view which frantically searches for right norms to safeguard itself from errors? Was not Christ's true and proper intention — the liberation of the (ever present) "old" man from his egocentrism as he is called to faith in a trusting gift of self to the Father (by the great gift of grace) — more than once obscured by such a narrow vision, despite the fact that from the moral viewpoint the surrender of ourselves in faith, hope and love should be the universally decisive fact? And isn't this especially the case when the decision to surrender ourselves shows itself, as it must, in the effort to produce through good works the fruit of our personal self-giving?

The Council Fathers intended first of all to give the proper stress to the corpus of moral theology. They openly shared the concern of many that the Church, in its moral theology, was all too often presented as the instructor and defender of truths and norms and was not seen sufficiently as a community conscious of its vocation in Christ and faithful above all else to that vocation and to its indispensable accompaniment, "bringing forth fruit". However, given the necessary link between fidelity and "bringing forth fruit", and the logical impulse to determine objectively what is good and what is evil, still it is noteworthy that Christ only discussed the material determination of good and evil when someone else raised the question; the only exception to this was the case where the perverse heart of the "old man" attempted to justify its own evil (cf. the controversy on the indissolubility of marriage). What is important to Christ is the new man of the Kingdom and that he bring forth fruit: but the question of what works to produce this fruit, whether in its consideration or in its resolution, has no major prominence.

The genuine response to the vocation in Christ rises from the depths of the human heart, where man (in his freedom) makes his choices not for this or that particular good (or evil) but where he decides to commit his entire personal being for good or for evil − that is, where he makes a choice for faith, for love, and for following Christ, or where he chooses not to accept Christ's call. This fundamental choice in freedom is the basic and genuine decision, and is certainly more central than all the external and internal confessions of faith, love, and the following of Christ for, in the last analysis, such confessions are only expressions of the decisive commitment to faith, love, and the following of Christ. A fortiori, the fundamentally decisive commitment we have defined will be much more central and all-encompassing than one's free choices for individual tasks or right works because, in themselves, these latter are but the fruit and categorial expression of that same fundamental and profound decision of commitment. It is precisely for this reason that while a categorial work is truly a right work and not simply an apparent one, it will not be the determining factor in the communion of love with the Father (and hence of salvation) merely because it is right. Instead, the determining factor will be the sincere and morally possible effort to bring to reality in a truly right work the person's profound and fundamental decision.

If, therefore, in the documents *Optatum totius* and *Gaudium et spes* the pledge of Christians and of the Church in the world and for the world ("world" meaning humanity and its world) is identified as the fruit of the Christian's vocation and of the vocation of the Church in Christ, then what is being presented primarily is the true newness of the Christian in the Church (to the extent that the Christian is the "new man" of redemption and the Kingdom, and not the "old man" of egotism and sin). Indeed, the new man and the Church will not bring forth the fruit of their new reality unless they sincerely and readily attempt a true, authentic (as opposed to an erroneous, artificial) transformation of the world. The selflessness of the man prepared for such a task will cause him to steer away from the dead end of his own egocentric "I" and will more easily open him up to the avenues of his own authenticity and truth. His sincere availability will be turned to its best advantage when, in his search for the best solution to mankind's problems, he finds the knowledge of the reality of man and human society drawn from revelation and nurtured in the Church.

II. A HUMAN MORALITY OR A NEW MORALITY?

The old man and the new man reap the fruit of their own moral being in the diversity of their personal morality. The morality of the old man, unredeemed and enclosed in his own egocentric "I," will basically be an inhuman morality, i.e., one that is incapable of bringing out of itself man's interpersonal and social character. Seen in this light, the vocation of Christ is a message of liberation for human authenticity and for a morality worthy of man. Correlatively, ethics or moral doctrine essentially demands of man's behavior in the world of men that it should be "human", as is worthy of man, and not "inhuman." If the vocation of Christ had given rise to a moral doctrine that imposed on man in the world of men a behavior different from an (authentic) *humanitas*, Christianity would have become a sect and the Church a ghetto. Societal life and cooperation with men of good will in the building up of human society would never have been possible. However, this is not to say that those called in Christ do not nourish their authentically human morality from motives born out of the newness of a transformed heart or from the revelation of a living faith. Nor is the grace of the Christian heart and the content of the Word of God prevented from having their own special insight into genuinely human forms of behavior.

Likewise, one cannot simply deny the right of the ecclesial community, over time, to crystallize certain types of authentically human behavior in its own verbal formulations. Above all, one cannot deny to Christian existence its own special modes of being, accessible only to the reality of faith and the Church; these modes are presupposed by, and a living condition of, a Christian person who makes an existential decision to live an authentically human life but in a special way; for example, a life of virginity "for the sake of the kingdom", a docility with regard to the urgings of the Holy Spirit, the unselfish works of love inspired by the crucified Lord. For these reasons one can speak intelligibly of a "Christian" moral doctrine as also of a "Christian social teaching" (*Gaudium et spes*, n. 23). Yet, while it is indeed possible to speak of a certain distinctiveness of the "specifically Christian" in contrast to the "authentically human" elements in "Christian" morality, we should never lose sight of the fact that the newness of those called in Christ is postulated on a personal morality that is really distinct only from that of the old man, but not essentially from an ethic or moral doctrine which is an authentic expression of *humanitas*.

Gaudium et spes brings this out very clearly. It affirms that whatever is genuinely human is not alien to the Church (n. 1). In fact, the Church offers its sincere cooperation to humanity in man's quest for establishing the fraternity of men because they share in the same humanity (n. 3). The Church (and Christians themselves) is not participating in this task in a self-interested manner in order to establish its own exclusive society as an isolated ghetto adrift in a sea of non-Christians, nor is it fashioning a human society that is distinctively Christian; rather, it is seeking to help build a genuinely human society. We ought also to be able to see how modern man's rapid, tumultuous discoveries contribute to "humanizing" the world (n. 15). And, in this sense, it should also be understood that there is a "legitimate independence of earthly affairs" (n. 36) – that is, an autonomy that should not be restricted to the scientific field alone (cf. Galileo), but also includes every creative cultural endeavor which shapes human and social life.

The Council is quick to point out, however, that while the Church does not picture itself as forming its own isolated culture (n. 42), neither does it bind itself to or canonize any particular form of human culture, not even when it merges with a genuinely human culture. In view of this, the twofold Christian commandment of love of God and love of neighbor (the foundation and summary of all moral precepts) can be seen as profoundly connected with *humanitas*; namely, as the first commandment of Christianity, it is a demand to make man more genuinely human not only because we are brothers in our shared humanity but also because we are all, in the last analysis, created as images of God (n. 24). This great commandment again illustrates the concept of "newness" (n. 38): it is a newness to the "old man" in that Christ has challenged him to go beyond his own egotism once more; it is a newness to the "new man" in that it shows that the love of the new man de facto (in Christ) is elevated so as to become the love of the Son for the Father. In line with this, *Gaudium et spes* continually affirms the idea that not only does Christ's message not oppose mankind's pledge to shape the world in a genuinely human fashion, but it even requires this (nn. 34, 39, 43). Christ, in fact, "frees all of them so that putting aside the love of self and bringing all earthly resources into the service of human life", they may prepare the future of this world and with it also the future of the definitive *eschaton*. Such a human ethic of "putting aside the love of self and bringing all earthly resources into the service of human life" is a challenge to fallen man redeemed in Christ — a challenge that Christians call the cross, whose ultimate significance cannot be understood outside of faith.

However, affirming the essentially human character of Christian ethics in regard to human behavior in the world of men in no way prevents the Gospel of Christ from offering the light of its word. Here we are thinking not so much of the particular assertions that can be found in the Gospel about certain concrete manners of behavior, but rather of the fundamental affirmations of its anthropology and of its genuinely human-Christian task. To pass on to an outline of norms, precepts and imperatives, it is necessary to follow the method of *Gaudium et spes* in order to discover the guidelines to be observed in carrying out the works entrusted to humanity in today's world "in the light of the Gospel and of human experience" (n. 46). Similarly, in interpreting the phrase "the signs of the times...in the light of the Gospel", the Council asserts that Christian revelation greatly aids the work of deepening our understanding of the dignity of the human person and the laws that govern his social life (n. 23) and, for that reason, there flow from the Church's religious mission "the task and the energy" and also the "light" which can serve to form and consolidate the human community according to divine law (n. 42). Recognizing, then, that there is a rapport between man's genuinely human achievements and the revealed Word, and following in the footsteps of the Council, we can be confident that the Spirit will help us to discern what is truly God's design in historic events and what judgments we should express about the values that are historically conditioned in any age (n. 11).

In speaking of the judgment of earthly realities, we have already mentioned that the Council used a specific principle – i.e., these realities must be judged "in the light of the Gospel and of human experience". However, this principle, as the word is used in *Gaudium et spes*, has yet to be precisely explained. On the one hand, we will have to be patient because the many contingent realities of our human world cannot be given an adequate human-ethical evaluation before all the data are in. On the other hand, we must explain how this expressed judgment is reached "in the light of the Gospel".

Karl Rahner interprets the Council's idea as being the moral instinct of faith.[3] He admits, however, that in exceptional cases such an instinct does not guarantee us the correct answers to concrete problems. He immediately adds that the light of the Gospel cannot serve as a substitute for experience or professional expertise. Thus, Rahner is led to conclude that the attempts toward concrete solutions should be characterized as "imperatives".[4] Edward Schillebeeckx[5] finds himself approaching the problem along the same lines as certain philosophers (particularly W. Adorno)[6] and as the "political theology" of Johannes Metz.[7] He prefers to speak of judgments made in the light of the Gospel as the negative experience of contrast, by which he means that there are realities which are offensive to human dignity when they are contrasted to the light of the Gospel. Thus, according to Schillebeeckx, any positive attempts made to overcome those situations which trample man's dignity under foot are not founded on faith as such. He is right in his suspicions that while many political movements and parties claim that their programs are derived from the content of faith, they are, in reality, simply ideologies.[8] Z. Alszeghy and M. Flick come to a similar conclusion.[9] Yet they do not exclude the possibility of elaborating (on the basis of the data of revelation) "an objective *image* of revealed reality". However, it is also their opinion that the concrete problems of human life cannot have concrete prefabricated solutions posited a priori in faith or theology itself. We should conclude, therefore, that the Christian always judges in the light of the Gospel, but not without human experience and scientific knowledge. The real solutions to men's problems in the world are always going to be "human" solutions, and thus, they will be solutions of a "human" morality. In this way *Gaudium et spes* sought to bring out a fuller appreciation of the evaluative problems surrounding the human realities of the family, marriage, sexuality, cultural progress, socioeconomic life, politics, war and the brotherhood of mankind.

Given this understanding of the morality of human behavior in the world of men, some further observations by the Council, concerning the limits of moral knowledge, may be cited. According to the Council, from the Word of God deposited in the Church one can reach some (very generic) principles of a religious or moral bent. However, the Church "does not always have at hand an answer to every particular question", and therefore it desires "to add the light of revealed truth to mankind's store of experience so that the path that man has taken in recent times will not be a dark one" (n. 33). The Council is speaking of a path which all men can and ought to travel together, and hence a path that is not interiorly conditioned by reflections stemming exclusively from revelation: a path, which, in turn, would not be unacceptable to nonbelievers. In this context the Council inserts a wise admonition to the laity, not to imagine "that their pastors are such experts that they can readily give them a concrete solution to every problem which arises, however complicated" (n. 43). Within this same section, the Council adverts to the fact that Christians, with a sincere conscience, frequently and legitimately can and do make different evaluative judgments of the very same concrete questions (n. 43). Even the light of the Gospel does not prevent uncertainties and discrepancies from arising in human and ethical evaluative judgments, despite human experience and expertise. The Council also explicitly reckons with the possibility of continuing uncertainties and of a legitimate pluralism (even among sincere Christians) in moral questions of how to behave in the world of men. The intentions and imperatives of human behavior have to be ascertained — even when viewed in the light of the Gospel — through a human evaluation of the knowledge available to us and human experience (which is not always the same) in particular situations.

It should go without saying, then, that Christians are seeking, finding, and living the intentions and imperatives of a substantially human morality as modes of a day-to-day realization of their faith, hope and the following of Christ. In this respect, this substantially human morality of human behavior is thoroughly Christian and is conscientiously practiced as such. We should also explicitly add that, according to *Gaudium et spes*, non-Christians who, without benefit of the light of the Gospel, seek and live out the genuinely human intentions and imperatives of human behavior, may well "come into contact, in a manner known only to God, with the paschal mystery" (n. 22). In this sense, the human morality of behavior in the world of men should be considered "Christian" in its deepest significance, which would also include some form of "participation" for non-

Christians. The reason for this lies in the fact that, according to revelation, all men — in virtue of creation and redemption — have their existence in the one God-man Christ (Col. 1:15-18). And for this reason there exists — even though by analogy — for Christians and non-Christians alike, an intrinsic hope-filled relationship between the attempt to build an ever better world and the reality of the definitive *eschaton* (n. 4, etc.).

III. *A STATIC OR A DYNAMIC INTERPRETATION OF MAN?*

The difficulty of reaching definitive solutions to man's problems in our world, coupled with the admitted possibility of a legitimate pluralism in finding answers for a number of problems, could have a tremendous impact on our world. *Gaudium et spes* addresses itself to this contemporary situation, describing the situation thus: "Today, the human race is passing through a new stage of its history marked by profound and rapid changes which are spreading by degrees around the world" (n. 4). The Council Fathers further note that "the human race has passed from a rather static concept of reality to a more dynamic, evolutionary one" (n. 5). These dynamic and evolutionary changes are not simply happening to man, but man himself is responsible for them when, going beyond a magical and superstitious view of the world, he accepts it as his duty to transform the world. The fact of the (active) changing of man and his world, along with a more dynamic and evolutionary understanding of the order of earthly reality, can lead to new types of behavior and behavioral norms which, when confronted with a static conception of the order of reality, will inevitably provoke an upheaval (n. 7).

Hence the Council shows clearly enough to anyone inclined to understand it that the change in man and his world and the changed human understanding of man and his world (keeping in mind that the changed understanding plays a part in the change in man himself) can have the consequence of altering established attitudes and behavioral norms in various sectors of human life. Thus, what creates anxiety and upheaval for a static mentality becomes, in a dynamic and evolutionary understanding of human existence, the very process itself. It will become even more natural to man as he realizes, after some reflection, that it is his task to shape mankind and the world into an always more "human" world and a more "human" humanity. It will be man himself, therefore, who — in "the light of the Gospel" — is called to seek and discover the pattern of an authentic (i.e., a truly human) mode of behavior and active engagement within this world. Through this sincere search he will already be fulfilling the "natural moral law" as the expression of the will of Him who willed man as man (i.e., even before man had gotten around to observing conscientiously the modes of behavior he considered a genuinely human response). Such an understanding of human existence and behavior escapes the illusion that notable changes in the existence and conception of man and his world will have no consequences for a legitimate human order of behavior.

In this "new epoch" announced by the Council we may perhaps find ourselves menaced by the danger of not distinguishing precisely enough which changes give rise to alterations in man's behavior in the world and which do not. In any case, man, in the course of a history that has been evolving for millions of years, will always find himself confronted anew with the question of what constitutes genuinely human behavior in the world of men, and this is precisely because man's reality and that of his world will never fully realize all the multitude of possibilities whose source is the Creator. However, this does not mean that all ethical orders will change or could change, but only that necessary changes are not to be ruled out from the beginning. This holds for Christians and history verifies it. Is it not perhaps true that *Gaudium et spes* has specifically begun this work of appraising a world in the process of change, and indicated the main criteria: on the one hand, the light of the Gospel, and on the other hand, professional expertise and human experience?

In many respects, the Constitution remained within traditional behavioral modes in its understanding, while in other respects it affirmed new modes. It never denied the fact that changes occur, and according to the principle *agere sequitur esse*, changes can require that behavior also must change anew. The Council very carefully acknowledges, however, that "beneath all changes there are many realities which do not change and which have their ultimate foundation in Christ, who is the same yesterday, today, and tomorrow. Hence, in the light of Christ...the Council wishes to speak to all men in order to...cooperate in finding solutions to the outstanding problems of our time" (n. 10). (For those Christians who, in the perspective of *Gaudium et spes*, would see certain difficulties in regard to Church pronouncements on questions of human behavior in the world, one should keep in mind that such declarations will never be made outside a concrete context, and for a proper reading, they are in turn subject to an appropriate hermeneutic, just as we have hermeneutical principles for biblical studies.)

Using *Gaudium et spes*, we could produce several examples of human changes and the changed understanding of man and his world, along with the respective consequences for human behavior. In dealing with examples, the Council does not speak about them merely as facts. Limiting ourselves to a single example, let us consider the deepened understanding of the human person (e.g., nn. 9, 27-29, 41), where there is the growing "conviction not only that humanity can and should increasingly consolidate its control over creation, but even more, that it devolves on humanity to establish a political, social, and economic order which will to an ever better extent serve man and help individuals as well as groups to affirm and develop the dignity proper to them" (n. 9). *Gaudium et spes* was not content simply to list examples, but went further by giving support to the many just pleas of underdeveloped peoples, of women, of farmers and laborers — just pleas which have their roots in the changed understanding of man.

IV. CONSCIENCE OR OBJECTIVE NORMS?

If the man who believes in, loves and follows Christ, according to the light of the Gospel and with the help of professional expertise and human experience, must seek out a way of expressing the evolving human reality in today's world, we may ask where this seeking and finding takes place, i.e., where is man's referential core? In paragraph n. 16 *Gaudium et spes* points toward reason and above all conscience. It seems to me that this paragraph is of primary importance, even though it is a compromise text typical of commissions. The text is excellent in some parts and rather unclear in others, but it merits close examination because it is intended to be a conciliar directive to Christians (and hence moralists).

Using the words of Pius XII, the Council calls conscience "the most hidden center and sanctuary in man where he finds himself alone with God..."[10] It would therefore be at man's most profound level of interiority, where he experiences his totality as a person and where he pledges and binds himself to God (the Absolute). The text is quite clear in saying that it is in his conscience that man hears the voice of God and perceives a law that he does not give to himself but which he must obey and by which he will be judged. This law imposes on him the task of doing only good; moreover, it tells him what good and its opposite consist of. In conscience man perceives that law which "has its fulfillment in the love of God and neighbor" and which is, according to Paul, a law "written in the heart". It can be said further that in being faithful to their conscience men are seeking the truth and letting themselves be guided by objective norms of morality and not by some blind arbitrariness. However, it can also happen that conscience (in which God speaks to man) makes erroneous judgments through ignorance of the objective norms of morality.

In the texts we have been considering, the assertions which suggest that the proper source of moral knowledge is the conscience are not sufficiently harmonized with those assertions that make objective norms (found outside the conscience) the source. There is also a failure to distinguish between the experience of being bound absolutely in conscience and the possession of moral knowledge in conscience, and a failure as well to determine their proper reciprocal relationship. Thus, it will certainly be worth our while to come to a more accurate understanding of the intention of the Council's assertions.

It is first of all important to conceive of conscience as the most intimate experience-knowledge of man's total state of dependence and submissiveness in the face of the Absolute and thus, ultimately, in the face of God. For the believing Christian, this fundamental experience has the same character of absolute submissiveness as that formed in faith, in love, and in following Christ. In short, the experience is a summons — that is, man has (through moral knowledge in conscience) the conviction that there is a concretely correct mode of realizing his own proper contingent "I" (before God) every time he acts. It is for this reason that this conviction (of moral knowledge in conscience), even though it comes under the heading of knowledge, rarely rises above the rank of "moral certainty". It has, however, the character of absolute obligation corresponding to man's absolute submissiveness in the experience-knowledge of absolute certainty. Sincere conviction, to the extent that it is "knowing in conscience", is the criterion according to which man's actions will be definitively judged, independently of whether his conviction is previously or subsequently considered as right either by the subject or by another authority — i.e., when judged by reason (in the light of the Gospel). The judgment that man must himself realize as a concrete here-and-now reality, together with his sincere conviction (knowing in conscience) of the rightness of his actual behavior, is truly right and therefore an objective norm. In the strict sense, it is this judgment that is presented as the "voice of God" in the conscience, which is the "hidden center and sanctuary in man where he finds himself alone with God". This does not mean, however, that "knowing in conscience" in concrete acts as such is the voice of God, or that it will always stand up to the test of rightly judging reason.[11]

Consequently, knowledge of the total and absolute state of man's submissiveness in the face of God, together with knowledge of the absolute obligation to act upon the sincere conviction of "knowing in conscience", can be said to be legitimately "the voice of God" and "objective norm"; it can further be said that every man is conscious of this objective norm, at least in a pre-reflexive way, with absolute certainty. But on the other hand, sincere convictions known in conscience will not be objective norms of behavior when they are not confirmed by right reason; subjectively, for the most part, they will be nothing more than morally certain.

Quite frankly, the framers of *Gaudium et spes* had a difficult time resolving the debate concerning the problem of the "objective norm of morality" (n. 16). The distinctions we have employed do not appear clearly in the text. In other words, the text does not hold a firm line of argument: part of it seems to attribute simply to conscience the knowledge of what is morally right (thus, loyalty to conscience on the part of Christians and non-Christians alike is seen as the possibility of finding common and true solutions to the problems of man's social life), while another part of the text assigns to conscience the function of taking particular cases and applying to them objective norms of morality which are to be found outside conscience. It seems to us that the whole question is left unresolved except with regard to the knowledge of conscience about the rightness of categorial ways of behaving as these relate to the concept of "objective norms".

Little attention has been paid, however, to the very significant reliance on the Scholastic concept that the forming of a convinced conscience (as "knowing in conscience", i.e., moral consciousness of what is right in the concrete) is an inquiry of "right reason". This means that the objective ethical norm is nothing other than "right reason", not only in "knowing in conscience" at the moment of acting but also, to a certain degree, "outside of the situation", even in scientific reflection on morality that always presupposes the experience of conscience. Here "reason" does not so much mean discursive reasoning but rather, evaluative comprehension, since one is dealing with moral values. This does not mean that someone may not act by himself to solve a problem for the first time, a problem that requires a response here and now: the correct solution would be according to "right reason". It is in just this manner that the situation is always to be fully evaluated. In fact, even the person who, during the formation of his "knowing in conscience", accepts and applies previous ethical knowledge and norms from outside sources, must make an evaluation of the concrete reality (his personal knowledge of norms will help him here) before discovering what norms should be realized in regard to the concrete reality, which in itself can never be expressed exhaustively in universally valid norms. Raising the problem of objective norms in connection with the conciliar text will help prevent the arbitrary formation of the conviction of conscience — and for many, this is a purpose that has become even more urgent in the years since the Council.

It is our opinion that the real problem does not lie so much in the relationship between convictions of conscience and objective norms, but rather in the question of defining the nature of the "objective norm". It is not uncommon that many, in adopting the notion of objective norm, see it (perhaps unconsciously) as having objectivity exclusively because it has been derived from an exterior objectivization expressed in the discoveries either of the positive formulations of moralists, tradition, or the magisterium of the Church, or in the belief that there are divinely received precepts. (Here it is appropriate to ask whether God at any time or any place has really given us these kinds of precepts and, indeed, how we even know them.) If norms of correct behavior in man's world are substantially "human" norms (i.e., from the natural moral law), their objectivity consists only in the necessity of man's right reason rightly judging precisely what human behavior best corresponds to the given human reality. Therefore, whether the *recta ratio* of acting is expressed in previously stated or accepted norms, or is first known in "knowing in conscience", has nothing to do with the question of objectivity in itself.

The importance of formulated norms derives from their inevitable influence on the process of forming our own convictions of conscience (i.e., of moral knowledge in the conscience). In this formation the individual must not content himself with his own examination of the data (and the opinion thus formed) but must also weigh what can be found in other sources, especially those regarded as "authority" (scholars, generally accepted convictions, tradition, the magisterium, the Scriptures). It is only on the basis of a consideration of the proportional weight of the various instances (and this includes one's own personal examination of the data) that we reach a stage where we can responsibly make a judgment of conscience as to what is right in the concrete. (We prescind from discussing further the precise relationship between normative formulations and concrete reality as the moral norm, since that would entail another long essay.) In this way, then, one is able to discover whether "knowing in conscience" is objective "right reason". This is what *Gaudium et spes* wished to affirm by its two interpretations of conscience in paragraph n. 16.

This is not the most apt place to explore the question of what weight one should assign to the *locus theologicus* (especially, the magisterium and tradition) for the formulation of a conviction of conscience in a given case. Nor is it the best place to discuss which hermeneutical rules should be applied in answering such questions. However, it is an opportune place to conclude our reflections on the complex problem (underlined by the Council) of our "new epoch", especially as it is marked as a time of rapid changes. On the one hand, in such an age questions will continually arise which were not conceived in their concreteness and were therefore not formulated in corresponding norms. Often individuals or groups will have to find solutions to these questions or, driven by the need for action, they may have to make a decision. On the other hand, it could be (as noted above) that formulated norms presuppose a different context from that of the "new epoch", and that, therefore, we find it necessary to examine whether or not the new context requires a different type of behavior. This should not be presumed a priori, but at the same time it should not be excluded as a new opening.

In his conscience, therefore, the new man "of the Kingdom", being guided in "the light of the Gospel" and by expert knowledge and human experience, and evaluating clearly the considerations we have discussed and their application, will attempt the task of discovering what concrete behavior in man's world can here and now be genuinely human and, therefore, be the expression of faith, love and following Christ. In so doing, Christians are following their vocation in Christ and are really becoming, in fidelity to their vocation, a hope for the world of men.

NOTES

1. "Special care should be given to the perfecting of moral theology, which, nourished more fully by the teaching of Scripture, should, in a scientific presentation, shed light on the grandeur of the vocation of those who believe in Christ and on their obligation to bear fruit in love for the life of the world."

2. J. Fuchs, "Moral Theology according to Vatican II", *Human Values and Christian Morality*, Dublin 1970, 1-55.

3. K. Rahner, "The Problem of Genetic Manipulation", *Theological Investigations IX*, London 1972, 238ff.

4.   K. Rahner, *The Dynamic Element in the Church*, London 1964, 13-41.

5.   E. Schillebeeckx, *God the Future of Man*, New York 1960, 190-6; cf. idem, "The Magisterium and the World of Politics", *Concilium* vol. 6 no. 4 (1968), 12-21, especially 16ff.

6.   T. Adorno, *Negative Dialektik*, Frankfurt a.M. 1966. Cf. also Schillebeeckx, art. cit., 21, n. 8.

7.   Cf. inter alia J.B. Metz, "The Church's Social Function in the Light of 'Political Theology'", *Concilium* vol. 6 no. 4 (1968), 3-11. Cf. also Schillebeeckx, art. cit., 16ff.

8.   Schillebeeckx, art. cit., 14ff.

9.   Z. Alszeghy and M. Flick, *Metodologia per una teologia dello sviluppo*, Brescia 1970, 47-68; 91-9.

10.   Cf. J. Fuchs, "Moraltheologie und Dogmatik", *Gregorianum* 50 (1969), 689-716.

11.   Cf. D. Capone, "Antropologia, coscienza, e personalità" in *Studia Moralia* IV (1966), 73-113. Cf. also H. Vorgrimler, "Das zweite Vatikanische Konzil" in *Lex. f. Theol. u. K.*, Teil III, Freiburg-Basle-Vienna 1967, 328ff.

PART II

Christian Normative Morality

Is There a Distinctively Christian Morality?

Is There a Normative Non-Christian Morality?

Autonomous Morality and Morality of Faith

4. Is There a Distinctively Christian Morality?

Was it Paul VI's intention to offer a specifically Catholic or Christian solution to the problem of birth control in his encyclical *Humanae vitae?* A significant number of oral and written positions on this question — both before and after the encyclical's publication — seem to answer in the affirmative. Such a view implies that there is a Catholic or Christian morality which is valid only for Catholics or other Christians and which differs from another, a non-Christian, morality. Is such a view legitimate? If we read Paul VI's encyclical carefully it will become clear that the Pope in no way intended to provide a specifically Christian solution for a universal human problem. It was precisely this that enabled him to address himself also to non-Christians, in order to put before them a "human" solution to a universal human problem. In the same way his predecessor, John XXIII, had addressed himself in his encyclical *Pacem in terris* to all men and women of good will, thereby implying that his statements about human dignity and human rights were not specifically Christian, but universally human.

Many questions of Christian morality are not merely Christian, but universally human problems; consequently, Christians and non-Christians can discuss them together. Norms are not distinctively Christian simply because they are proclaimed officially within the Church. Rather, we might put it as follows: to the extent to which they proclaim truth they are universally human and therefore also Christian — hence, not distinctively Christian. When, however, a statement does not truly address genuine humaneness, the norms it sets forth are not authentically human, hence also not Christian, let alone specifically Christian ethical norms.

If, on the other hand, we take as our starting point not the aforementioned encyclical, but the Sermon on the Mount or Jesus' words about carrying the cross, we will presumably tend to think — at least at first — that we have here a morality which contradicts all human morality and which is therefore — insofar as it is a morality proclaimed by Jesus and Christianity — distinctively Christian.

Our subject, "Is there a distinctively Christian morality?" cannot have as its purpose a comparison between a lofty morality of good Christians and a less lofty one of bad non-Christians. Rather, our concern is to discover whether Christian morality is, in content, basically different from, or even in contradiction to, a morality concerned with the dignity of men and women everywhere.

I. THE "CHRISTIAN INTENTIONALITY" OF CHRISTIAN MORALITY

No doubt many Christians formulate this question for themselves as follows: human beings are capable of discovering moral values and norms; the Christian is sustained, in addition, by the revelation of higher ethical values and norms, which either surpass the values and norms of a genuinely human morality or, at least partially, challenge it. Is such a view correct?

Others may state the question differently: Christians consult Scripture, the tradition and the teaching authority of the Church about the norms and values of Christian morality. Insofar as they derive these from Christian sources they will consider such a morality as "specifically Christian". Such a solution, however, proves too simple. For the concrete directives of Scripture are relatively few and must each be carefully studied in their context and meaning. Neither Christian tradition nor the Church's teaching authority provide us with a closed and readily applicable morality, in themselves. We must keep in mind, moreover, that the Christians of the first centuries did not yet possess such directives from the Christian tradition and teaching authority; nonetheless they sought to live a "Christian" morality. Finally, much of what we find in Scripture, in Christian tradition and the Church's teaching authority is universally human morality. The question therefore remains: what is distinctively Christian in Christian morality?[1]

1. Perhaps we shall discover in the pages that follow a better approach to the solution of our question. Christian morality is the morality of men and women who believe in Christ. This does not simply mean believing that Christ is the one the Scriptures say him to be and whom the Christian community proclaims. To believe means to set our ultimate hopes for life and our expectation of salvation on Christ —more yet: to give him our entire love and capacity for dedication. Whoever thus loves and believes—that is, all those who follow Christ with their entire heart and soul—will ask what form a life of such an imitation of Christ, a life of such faith and love, should take.

They will ask how such faith and love, how such an imitation of the Lord, can manifest and express themselves in external deeds and in the secret depths of the heart.

It is already clear that we must distinguish two elements of Christian morality. They are basically different from each other, yet belong together, and constitute Christian morality in their unity and interpretation. On the one hand there is the particular categorial conduct, in which categorial values, virtues and norms are realized — values, virtues and norms of different categories, such as justice, faithfulness, and purity. On the other hand, there are transcendental attitudes and norms, which inform various ethical categories and go beyond them, virtues such as faith, love, allowing oneself to be redeemed, living as a sacramental person, following Christ, etc. Such transcendental attitudes and norms refer to and involve, obviously, not only one's conduct in a specifically human sphere — such as justice, faithfulness, purity — but the human person in his or her entirety. It is the whole human person, as person, who gives her or himself in faith and love, in imitation of Christ, in surrender to Christ who died and rose again.

Scripture speaks unambiguously and frequently about transcendental and Christian attitudes, making quite clear that they are distinctively *Christian* attitudes. Scripture speaks more rarely about the particular, categorial approaches to the various spheres of life (social attitudes, family and conjugal morality, etc.), and is less clear about their meaning for and application to various historical periods. The question now arises: are there distinctly Christian categorial ways of conduct, or are genuinely human attitudes and life styles in the various areas of life not also those of Christians?

2. However we answer this question, one thing should now be clear: the specific and decisively Christian aspect of Christian morality is not to be sought first of all in the particularity of categorial values, virtues and norms of various human activities. Rather, it resides in the believer's fundamental Christian decision to accept God's love in Christ and respond to it as one who believes and loves, as one who assumes the responsibility for life in this world in imitation of Christ — that is, as one who has died with Christ and is risen with him in faith and sacrament, thus becoming a new creation. If, in what follows, we refer to this Christian decision and fundamental attitude as "Christian intentionality", our reason for this will soon become evident.

This Christian intentionality should not of course be mistaken for a pious mood or peak religious experience. Let us keep two things in mind. First, Christian intentionality refers to a full, personal decision that is made — not, however, once and for all, or as an occasionally repeated past act, but as a full, personal, enduring decision in each particular situation; hence, the permanent, present, and not past act of decision. Secondly, Christian intentionality refers concretely to an actual presence in the particular attitude and conduct of various spheres of life, a living, conscious presence in the daily shaping of life and the world, so that this daily life in its manifold particularity — whether distinctively Christian or simply human — represents at the same time and in its depths the living, conscious and free actualization of the decisiveness of Christian intentionality.

How are we to understand this conscious presence and actuality of Christian intentionality in the categorial variety of daily life? Let us not forget that morality always has a twofold aspect: On the one hand, it makes concrete a particular moral value, such as justice, kindness, faithfulness; on the other, man actualizes or realizes himself as a person in the living of certain specific values, ultimately in the light of the Absolute. Whoever practices justice, does not turn away the poor, educates children, in so doing realizes not only this, but also himself. For in and precisely through his concrete deeds, he himself enters as person into a specific relationship with the Absolute — that is, with God. We must keep in mind, however, that there is a considerable difference in the various types of consciousness of both these aspects of moral conduct. For we tend to reflect more or less thematically and explicitly on the particular-categorial aspects of our lives. The self-realization of the person as person before the Absolute, on the contrary, tends to escape thematic reflection: indeed, it cannot properly be accessible in the center of the "I" to a full thematic reflection. Nonetheless, we are conscious of this self-realization as person before the Absolute, as flowing from the concept of self-realization as an act of freedom. Just as the realization of a particular attitude, insofar as it is particular, tends to take place in a thematic-reflexive consciousness, so too our self-realization before the Absolute takes place in the awareness, but largely without thematic reflection. This nonthematic, unreflexive consciousness must not be considered as a lower degree of awareness, but is at bottom deeper and richer than the thematic-reflexive consciousness. The aspect of self-realization of the person before the Absolute constitutes objectively the more essential and decisive element of the moral act, in contrast to the aspect of the particular-categorial doing of justice, of one's duty to the family, etc. The self-realization of the human person before the

Absolute God thus takes place through — and manifests itself in — the realization of particular individual acts.

We spoke of the realization of the self as person before the Absolute, and said that this Absolute is, in the last analysis, God. The Christian, however, does not simply know the Absolute or God, but knows him as Father, who is our life and salvation in Jesus Christ. And as believer in the full sense of the word, he not only knows God as Father of Jesus Christ, but lives — as person — in the decision for him. He makes this commitment at times, and as far as possible, part of the express reflection of his consciousness; but not ordinarily, not in the everyday shaping of life and the world. And yet the believer is aware, in unthematic, unreflexive consciousness, of his salvation, of his self-realization as Christian intentionality. This intentionality is, therefore, present, alive and conscious in the Christian's daily moral life, as Christian realization of the self, as the deepest and most challenging element of morality, which addresses the whole person, and not only the individual deed. "Christian intentionality", as actual decision for Christ and the Father of Jesus Christ, consciously active in daily moral conduct, is to be seen as the most important and decisive element of Christian morality.

3.   Christian intentionality is an element which, while pervading and completing the particular-categorial conduct, does not determine its content. The question therefore remains, whether the categorial content of the morality of Christians—their concrete moral conduct— is distinctly Christian, different from the morality of the human person as such, different also not only from a morality which is infected with error or malice, but different also from the purest and noblest, most deeply human morality. This is a fundamental question, independent from the question of when, where, and how Christians and non-Christians discover their morality in authenticity and truth.

Our answer to the question about the Christian nature of a categorial morality of Christians — that is, of their concrete conduct — is basically as follows: if we abstract from the decisive and essential element of Christian morality, of Christian intentionality as transcendental aspect, Christian morality in its categorial orientation and materiality is basically and substantially a *humanum*, that is, a morality of genuine being-human. This means that truthfulness, uprightness and faithfulness are not specifically Christian, but generally human values in what they materially say, and that we have reservations about lying and adultery not because we are Christians, but simply because we are human. This does not, however, deny that there is in Christian morality a specifically Christian element also; rather, it affirms it. Our reflection about the genuinely human and genuinely Christian dimensions of Christian morality derives basically from the fact that believers must translate their living faith — that is, their Christian intentionality — into concrete living and manifest it in their lives. This is the reality of the human person, but the human person in the manner and situation in which that person experiences and knows himself as believing. We must therefore speak in turn of the *humanum* and the *Christianum* of Christian morality, of its norms and values.

II.   THE HUMANUM OF CHRISTIAN CATEGORIAL MORALITY

1.   Since the 1920s and 1930s a strong tendency has been present in Catholic moral theology to move from the predominantly human study (or natural law study) of Christian ethics of a past era to the *Christianum* of Christian ethics. This movement has led at times to a one-sided Christianization, along with a levelling off of the *humanum* of Christian morality. Not only was the Christian intentionality that pervades all morality discovered, but it was also believed that a purely Christian valuation of the categorial morality of concrete living must be opposed to a "human" valuation; the Sermon on the Mount was seen as being in opposition to the *humanum.*

More recently, moral theology, under the impact of secular, even secularistic tendencies in theological and moral thought, has seen itself challenged to take a new look at the *humanum* in Christian morality. The existentially believing Christian discovers, in the search for a lifestyle which can express his faith, his Christian intentionality, that it is the human person who believes existentially, that therefore this belief must be lived and expressed by the human person, in the genuine realization of being-human, of the *humanum.* Thus Christians are directed, as Christians, to understand their being-human and the corresponding *humanum* of a genuinely human morality. We should add that this does not exclude the possibility that, in the attempt to arrive at the understanding of self and of "human" morality, Christians may find help in the sources of revelation, help not only for a distinctively Christian morality, but for a genuinely human understanding of the person and of human morality.

2. What is the nature of this *humanum* of the Christian's genuinely human morality? Many will perhaps think of it as a purely immanent human reality, separate from or even in contrast to a transcendent morality, one which teaches men and women of flesh to do the will of a transcendent God. Such a distinction is based on a misunderstanding of the nature of "human" morality, but also on a misconception of the nature of God. God is perceived far too anthropomorphically if we think of him as Someone who exists somehow, somewhere, and with whom one must also (in addition to other people) reckon decisively. Instead, it is precisely God's otherness that establishes his immanence as sustaining the personal ground in everything and everyone, while he himself is not part of or within this contingent world. We must, therefore, not perceive man and his world — pantheistically or mystically — as either "divine", or as a world of humans on whom a detached God externally imposes a moral law — his "will". God's creation is not man (or humanity) with his world *plus* God's will for man (that is, a moral order), but quite simply, humanity and its world. If we wish to speak of God's will, this is nothing else than the divine desire that man might exist and live. This implies, however, that he live as man, that he discover himself and his world as well as their latent possibilities, that he understand them, that he shape and realize himself as genuinely human, as bodily-spiritual being.

It is, therefore, up to man to discover what kind of life is proper to him as one who is responsible to the Absolute and oriented toward his fellow human beings, responsible for human-worldly reality — so that his whole life may do justice to the nature and personal dignity of being-human. By so acting, he does God's will. It is the will of God that man himself draw up the "blueprint" of genuinely human conduct, that he take into his own hands the reality of man and his world, in order to lead it to its highest human potential, and turn himself and humanity toward a lofty, truly human history and future. If, beyond this, we speak of God's will and his commandments in the plural, we imply only that either revelation makes "fallen" man, who is so selfish and so easily errs, conscious of a number of necessary ways of expressing the genuine *humanum* — which he could also find out by himself — or that we ourselves, in society and church, believe we have found some essential values of the genuine *humanum* and have formulated them accordingly.

3. We may ask whether these thoughts are in agreement with the ethics of Jesus, of the Apostle Paul, and of Christian tradition. Jesus does indeed say that we must not be "of this world" (John

15:19; 17:16); but let us not forget that "world" here does not refer to that which is truly human, but to that which is selfish and inhuman — that is, the world of sin. Christ demands the morality of a true and pure being-human.

The same is true of the apostle of the gentiles, Paul. He does not speak in his letters of a morality of Christians in contrast to a morality of genuine humanness. The difference between Christians and non-Christians on which he does indeed insist is the difference between the true morality of the spiritual Christian and that of the egotistical sinner. According to Paul, the same material norm of moral living, a truly human norm, applies objectively to Christians and non-Christians, Jews and gentiles (cf. Rom. 2:1f., 6-11). That is why he warns Christians to live honorably, because non-Christians too, Jews and gentiles, can discern what is honorable and dishonorable, moral and immoral. He insists on this because dishonorable conduct on the part of Christians would bring dishonor upon Christianity (Rom. 12:17; I Cor. 10:32; I Thess. 4:12) in the eyes of Jews and gentiles — precisely because they, too, can recognize human morality (it is written "in the heart" of all). Paul thus presumes that the moral conduct of good Christians is identical, in its material content, with the moral conduct of good non-Christians. In the light of the teaching of Christ and his apostle, it is therefore also part of the tradition of Christian theology that Christ has not added new moral laws to the "moral codex" of genuine being-human (cf. Thomas Aquinas, *Sum. Theol.* I-II 108,2;II-II 147,4 ad 7).

It follows from this that Christians and non-Christians face the same moral questions, and that both must seek their solution in genuinely human reflection and according to the same norms; e.g., whether adultery and premarital intercourse are morally right or can be so, whether the wealthy nations of the world must help the poor nations and to what extent, whether birth control is justified and should be provided, and what types of birth control are worthy of the dignity of the human person. Such questions are questions for all of humanity; if, therefore, our church and other human communities do not always reach the same conclusions, this is not because there exists a different morality for Christians and non-Christians.

4. Let us be more concrete. The question then arises whether certain moral laws are not distinctively Christian after all. Has it not often been said that justice is indeed a universally human commandment, but love of neighbor distinctively Christian, and that this is true especially of certain forms of love of neighbor, such as caring for the

terminally ill, and, above all, love of one's enemies? One could interpret this view of the Christian essence of love of neighbor in the sense that without Christ's revelation it is not possible to comprehend its demands; to this we might respond in a variety of ways, but they do not concern us here directly. The same is true of the question as to whether these demands can be fulfilled without the inner grace that comes from Christ. What concerns us here is the following question: are these demands valid only for Christians, or are they demands on all true human beings? We reply that, on the basis of *humanitas*, neither Christians nor non-Christians may foster hatred in themselves and in others, not even hatred of their enemies; they are called upon to love, with all the consequences for daily life.

But does not the Sermon on the Mount (Matt. 5-7), which is often rightly praised as the charismatic summation of Christian morality, proclaim a morality that is far above any "human" morality? We cannot here enter into a discussion of the many different interpretations of the Sermon on the Mount. The true meaning of its individual demands must be drawn not from the literal text, but from interpreting hyperbolic ways of speaking; then they will be understood not as legal obligations, but rather as daring "ethical models". In this perspective it becomes clear that the Sermon on the Mount is not at all directed against a genuine human morality but, on the contrary, against the profoundly inhuman conduct of the creature who is mired in egoism, that is, of "fallen" man. This Sermon rejects man insofar as he is selfish and sinful, but not insofar as he is human in the best and truest sense of the term. The grace of the Kingdom of God which Christ brings is able to overcome selfishness in human beings. Insofar as we renounce our egoism in grace, we will understand the demands of the Sermon of the Mount — which are the demands of love — not as negating our being-human, but as its purest expression. The newness that Christ brings is not really a new (material) morality, but the new creature of grace and of the Kingdom of God, the man of divinely self-giving love.

This may give us an insight into the belief that the cross of Christ as Christian challenge reduces to naught all merely human morality, standing in radical opposition to it. Let us first of all point out that non-Christians and atheists also have a certain understanding of renunciation, self-denial and the cross. For they, too, experience their egoism as "fallen" men and are able to understand that in this situation renunciation and self-denial, hence the cross, may be part of authentic being-human. They know that without such renunciation neither the harmonious shaping of one's own self which true being-human demands, nor the just and kind treatment of one's fellow human beings, is possible. It becomes clear right away that the view of the radical opposition between the Christian cross and human morality should not be accepted without further qualification. For while it is true that the cross of Christ is our salvation, this is so not primarily because it is denial of life, destruction and sacrifice, but rather because it is totally giving love, a love that does indeed lead to the cross, since it takes up its abode in the world of selfish "fallen" human beings. That self-denying love which translates itself into caring for the terminally ill or the needy, or into forgiving one's enemies will also be cross or experienced as cross, insofar as the egotistic tendency of "fallen" man is still alive. It is, however, precisely the insight into the inhumanness of egoism and into the humanness of love that can help us understand that the overcoming of egoism in the concrete, and hence the cross, represent for "fallen" man a basic requirement of authentic being-human. However, only the Christian teaching of the redemption of "fallen man", ultimately the form of the crucified and risen God-man, enables us to fathom the full depth and riches of the Christian doctrine of the cross. This doctrine also – and especially – enables us to understand more deeply the meaning of the cross in the sense of free renunciation (such as freely chosen poverty) in the world of "the fall" (and of redemption).[2]

5. We encounter one last obstacle to the fine Christian thesis that Christian conduct is substantially truly human conduct. The problem is frequently formulated as follows: A human morality is necessarily an "essential" morality – that is, it is static, impersonal. For man in his nature is a given, to be understood as such; human morality, therefore, calls for the realization of this nature. Christian morality, on the other hand, is an existential, dynamic, personal morality; for in the Christian order of salvation man is not fulfillment of his own self, but total openness to the call of the God of our salvation that is given in divine freedom.

This fascinating concept needs further precision. First, the relationship to God and hence also the radical openness and availability toward him belong to the *humanum*, to human nature. Were it not so, we would have no categories with which to understand Christian revelation about man's dynamic and personal openness. Secondly, Christians do indeed know themselves to be open vis-à-vis the always possible and never fully predictable call of grace of the God of our salvation. This does not cancel out the truth, however, that the call to salvation is directed to man, hence is always also a "human" call, pointing toward a morality of man – and not in the opposite direction. The "Christian-ness" of radical openness vis-à-vis God's salvific call may therefore also be explained as follows. First, the clear and explicit awareness of man's true relationship, as man, to God cannot be achieved easily by him — the "man of the fall" — without Christian revelation; Christian anthropology provides an excellent help for man's deeper knowledge about himself. Second, only in faith in the God who reveals himself do we experience that God's personal call to us is indeed a call to salvation.

III. THE CHRISTIANUM OF CHRISTIAN CATEGORIAL MORALITY

1. If we have show that "Christian intentionality", namely, living the Christian faith, exists and manifests itself in a concrete categorial way of life which is basically and substantially human, we must in no way lose sight of the distinctively Christian element in the concrete categorial conduct of Christians. The study of the *humanum* of (categorial) Christian morality must be followed by a study of its *Christianum*. It goes without saying that Christian intentionality must live and express itself in the total reality of the concrete being-human, that is, of its *humanum* as well as its *Christianum*. This should not make us afraid that the *Christianum* might come to contradict the genuine *humanum* (and not only the *inhumanum)*, and displace it. For the existence of the *humanum* as *humanum Christianum* should enable us to discover that the *humanum* is of its very nature open and related to Christian existence.

The realities that constitute the *Christianum* of the *humanum Christianum* are those such as the person of Christ, the Spirit at work in us, the Christian community, the hierarchical Church, the sacraments, Christian anthropology. Our relationship to these realities, which we recognize and accept in faith, is part of our very being. Therefore it must be taken into account and also become concrete in our lives; otherwise we would fail to live our truth as believers. We should not forget, however, that this relationship to the "Christian realities" is also the relationship of "man", hence a *human* relationship. And therefore, the Christian realities will not be the basis of a morality different from truly human morality.

2. We should try to understand how the distinctively Christian realities can determine our concrete (categorial) conduct over and above the "merely" *humanum*. The meaning of the *Christianum* for our concrete living is to be found in its motivating power. Christian motivation provides human conduct with a deeper and richer meaning, which is subjectively part of the action itself.

Two examples of such Christian motivation may be found in the letters of Paul. When Paul exhorts Christians to do and speak the truth, he does not base himself on the *inhumanum* of lying — this is presupposed — but on their shared existence in the one mystical Body of Christ that is the church (Eph. 4:25). When he warns the Christians of Corinth against prostitution, he presupposes the *inhumanum* of such conduct, explicitly reminding his readers that their bodies belong to Christ, are holy as temples of the Holy Spirit, and that the body's goal is to be glorified with the risen Lord (I Cor. 6:12-20). We do not deny that Christian motivation at all times animates much of the human conduct of Christians, such as almsgiving at one time, concern for social justice at another, or the readiness to work for a just distribution of goods and for economic aid to the developing nations. Moreover, Christian motivation has undoubtedly not only given a richer meaning to the human conduct of Christians, but also, as is expressed in Paul's warning, has frequently caused and inspired a truly human life.

This brings us to a second meaning which the *Christianum* has for the Christian's concrete (categorial) conduct. It not only motivates human conduct more deeply and inspires it, but it will also determine the *content* of our conduct. Whoever lives truly in faith within the community of believers and the hierarchically led church will not remain, in his way of life, outside the influence of the ethos of the community and the church; that ethos will fundamentally be an ethos of the *humanum Christianum*. The believer who is familiar with the person of Christ and his work and with the basic elements of a Christian anthropology — with the man of "the fall", of redemptive grace, and of an eschatological destiny — will acquire a specific and concretely effective understanding of the meaning of renunciation and the cross. The believer alone will understand the meaning of Christian virginity (which should be distinguished from the single life) and may even be able to live it in response to a charismatic calling. What we said earlier about the Christian's radical openness vis-à-vis God's continuing call to salvation can also be understood and realized in its concrete Christian form only on the basis of a Christian anthropology accepted in faith. The traditional doctrine of sensitivity to personal guidance through the Spirit of God in us, and the teaching of a Christian existential morality — such as that developed thematically by Karl Rahner — perceive man simultaneously in his *humanum* and in his existence in the Holy Spirit; both together determine the concrete (categorial) conduct of Christians in the plenitude of their personhood.

Third and last, let us not forget that man's explicit religious and cultic relationship to God is also *moral* conduct. It goes without saying that this conduct is largely determined, in its concrete Christian form, by the Christian's *Christianum*.

IV.   CHRISTIAN AND HUMANISTIC MORALITY

In speaking of the Christian-ness of Christian morality, we should not simply ask to what extent Christian morality is distinctively Christian, and to what extent it is universally "human" or humane. Rather, we must also ask how Christian morality relates to the morality of non-Christians. We shall speak only of the "humanists". And, since there are many types of humanists, let us take those who live lives centered wholly upon this world, although they sincerely seek to pursue a lofty "human" ethos.

1.   In our attempt to analyze Christian morality, we distinguished first two different aspects: the transcendental dimension of "Christian intentionality", which is distinctly Christian and permeates any particular conscious conduct of Christian life, even if it does so ordinarily without thematic reflection; and the categorial dimension, to which corresponds the concrete moral conduct of particular objects, values, virtues and norms. We noted, however, that the Christian's *Christianum* may also influence his particular (categorial) conduct, especially through Christian motivation — which may awaken not only philanthropy, but Christian love of neighbor — and lead to a religious and cultic life.

While the humanist as non-believer does not have access to the *Christianum* and hence to its influence on particular categorial conduct, access to the *humanum* and its ethos is open to him. With regard to the moral determination of our concrete conduct, then, Christian and humanist stand basically on the same plane. Both must seek to understand the phenomenon of man, in order to discover, on the basis of the criteria of an ethical epistemology, what conduct is worthy of human dignity in a given case; but also, which ways of acting are generally to be called moral or immoral. Whether Christians and humanists have yet worked out sufficiently such an epistemology and such criteria is another matter. The numerous discussions of moral questions among Christians as well as humanists show clearly that all of us, Christians and humanists, are still en route to recognizing moral truth more accurately and in a truer relationship to the given historical situation. We are not likely to reach the goal in the near future.

If Christians and non-Christians do indeed agree on many questions of a "human" morality, it remains true also that on many other questions there is no agreement. Let us not forget, however, that lack of consensus exists not only between Christians and humanists, but also between Catholic and non-Catholic Christians and, to some extent, even between Catholic and Catholic. This should not surprise us. For moral questions are not resolved through logical and clear deductions from the concrete being-human. Rather, moral "solutions" are an evaluative insight and understanding capable of corresponding to the concrete conduct of being human in each specific situation. Therefore it is not possible to "prove" such "solutions" in the strict sense of the word; we can only explain and describe them, make them intelligible. While it may happen that our partner in dialogue will arrive at the same insight and understanding, total agreement is an ideal that is hardly ever attained.

It is true that Christians receive help, in their quest for a human morality, within the context of revelation and its transmittal in the Christian and ecclesial community. We are aware today, however, that in the course of time non-Christian influences have become part of Christian moral teaching, and some of them do not even represent a genuinely human morality (we need only recall certain questions relating to the body and sexuality). Christians should always be concerned to eliminate such influences. Occasionally, humanists may be of help in this endeavor, because they are less burdened by the weight of tradition.

The most difficult aspect of dialogue about morality between Christians and humanists will be the question of the religious implications of a purely human morality. For while it is clear that the Absolute of moral living must ultimately have a religious interpretation to be valid — that is, in relation to a personal God — this cannot be convincingly proved. What is essential here, perhaps, is that in the course of dialogue the absolute character of the human, moral value be understood as deeply and completely as possible. The humanist partner in dialogue may perhaps never arrive at an explicitly religious interpretation of the moral Absolute; but it could happen that God will be experienced and affirmed by both partners more intensively and in greater fullness at that deeper level of unthematic consciousness mentioned earlier.

2.   The humanist, then, can be dialogue partner in the realm of the categorial human morality of Christian ethics, even though — as long as he remains a world-centered humanist — he has no access to understanding the *Christianum* of categorial Christian morality. This leaves open an important question concerning, not the possible dialogue, but our full understanding of the humanist's morality. What role does what we have called "Christian intentionality" play for him? It goes without saying that he is not aware of it in the realm of reflexive, thematic consciousness. Did we not say, however, that this Christian intentionality remains, for the Christian also, essentially in the realm of unreflexive, unthematic consciousness? May we not assume that in this realm of consciousness the Absolute is present ultimately as the living God, though not thematically and conceptually? May we not, then, also assume that it is in this same realm that the offer of salvation and the salvific call addressed to every person is experienced?

If this is so, we would have to assume that the humanist too, in his deepest nature, responds at this same level to the gift of grace and to the salvific call, and that his response animates and permeates his categorial moral conduct. It does not matter here whether or not we call the transcendental intentionality of moral conduct "Christian" or not. Beyond doubt it signifies true acceptance of that salvific call which comes to us in Christ from the Father of our salvation.

NOTES

1.   As we have already said, we are concerned with the *content* of an authentically Christian morality. This must be kept in mind because a morality which is called "Christian" or which is proclaimed in the Christian community is not necessarily infallible in every aspect or above correction. The question concerning the "Christian" or "human" *content* of Christian morality must be distinguished from another question: how do we, in the Christian community, come to an awareness of this content, at least insofar as it is purely "human" and not simultaneously contained in the scriptural revelation? Neither individual Christians nor Church authorities come to the knowledge of moral truth through some sort of private revelation. It may indeed happen that the context of Christian revelation may guide individual believers and the community in a direction where certain aspects of human morality become more clear. For this reason, and thanks to the constant assistance of the Holy Spirit – who does not, let us remember, guarantee the truth of each specific question – the Christian community, with the Church in its official interpretation, is a "place" in which the presence of a genuine awareness of "human" morality may be somehow presumed. We can therefore say of this ethical awareness of the Christian community, insofar as it does not stem from scriptural revelation, that

i.   the content of this morality is "human", not distinctively Christian;

ii.   the moral consciousness of the community is derived from a "human" understanding;

iii.   in the attempt to understand "human" morality, the believer will have to take into account the moral consciousness of the Christian community according to the theological validity of the community's understanding.

2.   Let us not forget, however, that the cross of selfless engagement in this world is no less a Christian cross than the cross of free renunciation. Both forms of carrying the cross correspond to a calling; both are legitimate and meaningful in the midst of "fallen-redeemed" humanity. See also what follows below.

5. Is There a Normative Non-Christian Morality?

In a recent article N. J. Rigali notes that the American moral theologian Charles Curran holds the thesis that, as far as content is concerned, there is no specifically Christian morality, while his fellow countryman and ethician, Richard McCormick, holds that there is only one moral order—i.e., the Christian. Rigali observes that despite differences of formulation, both theologians are of the same opinion.[1] Similarly, just as in the last few years one could formulate the question, "Is there a (normative) morality which is distinctively Christian?", so today one could also ask the question, "Is there a (normative) non-Christian morality?" To both of these questions one could answer with a "yes" and a "no". The possible answers will, in any case, be important,[2] provided that one did not wish only to ascertain that Christians and non-Christians have, in some way, each their own morality.

The problem of the *specificum* or the *proprium normativum* of Christian morality in the past few years was the result of certain tendencies of secularization which compelled the moral theologian to insist on the identity of Christian morality without excluding the possibility of moral solutions, common to Christians and non-Christians, to the actual problems of humanity. The latter is a possibility dear to *Gaudium et spes*,[3] and was reaffirmed in a recent letter of Cardinal Villot.[4] To the degree that common solutions are possible, Christian morality is evidently not, in this aspect, distinctively Christian, and the solutions given by non-Christians are certainly also "Christian". It is clear that similar formulations require a mode of speaking that is very precise and abstract. But such modes of speaking are absolutely necessary, if one does not wish to make merely global and consequently inexact affirmations.

From what we have said it follows that the question "Is there a Christian morality?" can also be phrased as "Is there a non-Christian morality?" Evidently, the answer to this last question tends to affirm that every truly serious non-Christian morality participates in some way in Christian morality, and in this sense is not simply non-Christian. Such a consideration can be important for a better understanding of Christian and non-Christian morality.

I.   NON-CHRISTIAN MORALITIES

There is no doubt that there is a normative non-Christian morality, and not only one. Different types of humanism have their
moralities. There is a (only one?) Marxist morality. The great world
religions have their moralities as do different cultures and subcultures. Many of these groups not only know some of the fundamental
principles of human behavior, but think that they possess answers of
a sufficiently concrete nature to many particular questions. Behind
such principles and moral norms often lie entire anthropologies, as
well as the teachings and sayings of great men and of prophets of
particular religions and cultures.

While a great knowledge of moral values can be found in such
moral doctrines, mistaken evaluations may be made in certain answers. But this apparent contradiction is found to a certain extent
even in Christian moral teaching.

The various non-Christian moral doctrines have certainly not
been planned as arbitrary systems. They attempt, rather, an interpretation of concrete man as he is known to them, under a moral aspect. We may express this in different words by saying that they are
an attempt at a "human morality," i.e., a morality of "natural moral
law". This attempt is more or less successful and in one point or
another it takes a particular cultural situation into account precisely in
order to correspond objectively to reality. To the extent that a non-
Christian morality is successful, it is a natural moral law which has
been formulated, a truly human morality. Within certain limits we
cannot exclude the possibility of a more or less truly successful attempt; this, at least, is what the Catholic teaching on natural moral
law means. Ideally, a non-Christian moral doctrine is of natural
moral law – i.e., it is, according to Aquinas, *recta ratio* in the area of
morality. Ideally, then, the question of a non-Christian morality becomes the question of human morality, or of the natural moral law.
We say this only "ideally" because we know very well that an historical non-Christian morality will never perhaps be *recta ratio* in all its
elements, that is, a true natural morality; but perhaps even Christians
never succeed in attaining this ideal.

Certainly, the ideal would not be an ahistorical or metahistorical
human morality or natural law – i.e., one which is totally independent of the historical data or culture of a given epoch. It is rather a
matter of realizing that different non-Christian moral doctrines dis-
play certain differences. A certain plurality of solutions for situations
which are only apparently equivalent is the price natural moral law
ought to pay for the predicate of honor, *recta ratio*. A total lack of di-

versity in normative affirmations would nourish the doubt that these affirmations, if they truly take into account historical and cultural differences which are ultimately very important, lack a certain objectivity, without which there is no *recta ratio*.

Ideally, the question of non-Christian morality becomes a question of human morality, and this conclusion has its own special importance, since the question "Is there a Christian morality?" is concerned with the material identity between Christian morality and human morality – and not precisely with the identity between Christian morality and any non-Christian morality whatsoever. On the other hand, it should be made clear that the affirmation of material identity between Christian and human morality does not presuppose an ahistorical morality but rather the *recta ratio moralis*, which as such must always take into account specific elements of the historical reality of man.

Let us note that here we are interested primarily in the material content of morality. Other questions – e.g., what the theological implications of a specific moral doctrine are, what the psychological possibility of a free fulfillment of moral norms is, what the degree of true and certain knowledge of morality is, etc. – are not the object of these reflections.

II. HUMAN MORALITY

It is clear that the problem of non-Christian morality is not resolved simply by confronting non-Christian morals with a Christian morality. The problem of human morality, i.e. of natural moral law, also needs to be considered. The latter, certainly, cannot be identified with any historical, non-Christian morality. In the past, it was also the case that historical non-Christian moral doctrines were not identified with the natural law, except where the concept of natural moral law was restricted and seen only as the sum of these few moral principles which all men acquire easily and without problems. I myself prefer the phrase "human morality" to the phrase "natural moral law" (or "natural law") because the latter is open to many misunderstandings today. Everything which is accessible to us without revelation as *recta ratio* belongs to human morality (natural moral law) as does, for example, right moral judgment or the evaluative intelligence of man.[5] The possibility of a human morality is, for its part, a condition for the possibility of faith by man and for the understanding of the moral affirmations given us in revelation. This is because only a person who is capable of such understanding is capable of receiving revelation which would not make sense without the human capacity.

The concept of human morality is not contradicted by the fact that certain moral truths are in themselves accessible to man's intelligence but are, in fact, not recognized by him.[6] This is the same distinction which Vatican I made with regard to natural knowledge of God (and thus, implicitly, natural knowledge of morality), between *ratio* (human) and *homo* (rational) in his situation of "fallen man".[7] If many men, for example, do not know the precept of love of neighbor and even of one's enemies, this does not prove that these precepts do not belong to what is truly human, i.e., to human morality. Nor is the concept of human morality contradicted by the fact that moral knowledge always takes place under the influence of grace and perhaps also under the influence of an athematic[7a] knowledge of God and even perhaps of an initial athematic faith in God who reveals and communicates himself as love. The reason for this affirmation of ours is that the medium of moral knowledge, even in the light of the conditions we have indicated, would still always be the evaluative *ratio* as such. Thus, the concept of human morality is not contradicted by the fact that the Christian believer cannot set aside his Christian faith, in his natural knowledge of human morality. Even for the Christian believer an intellectual reflection on the moral realization of himself always remains possible, although he knows so much because of his faith. Indeed, because of his faith he remains conscious in an athematic way of the true and more profound significance of his moral self-realization.

The full moral self-realization of man — as knowledge and as decision — is not human morality as such but rather Augustine's *"Deo caritate (Christi) adhaerere"*.[8] This *"Deo caritate adhaerere"* is realized in the medium of human morality — i.e., in the realization of interpersonal relationships and of solidarity in the formation of humanity and the world. Consequently, one ought to say that the most profound and transcendent and, notwithstanding this, the most appropriate meaning, of human morality is life according to faith in the Christ event and according to the fully realized formation of humanity and of the new world because of this event.

What we have said about human morality holds, *mutatis mutandis*, independently of the fact that the attempt at a human morality is made by Christians and non-Christians.

III.   CHRISTIAN MORALITY

No one doubts that there is a truly Christian morality, not only in the sense that we can present a morality acceptable to and to be accepted by Christians, but also in the sense that Christian morality has its specificity, its *proprium*.[9] The problem can only lie in what sense one can respond "yes" or "no" to the question, "Is there a Christian morality?" If the question refers exclusively to the material content of morality, i.e., to that which Christian theology has through the ages called *praecepta moralia*, it will be evident that the comparison is not between Christian morality and any historical non-Christian morality,[10] but rather between Christian morality and the reality which we call human morality or natural moral law, moral *recta ratio*. Christian morality, then, is compared to a morality which of itself is accessible to human reason[11] and is therefore also accessible to the *ratio* of the non-Christian, although his attempt to get the moral knowledge — like the attempt of Christians and of Christianity — is not always successful. In asking for the Christian moral norms which are different from those of moral *recta ratio*, of human morality, of natural moral law (although these may not be perfectly known by Christians and non-Christians), one may not realize that he is closer to a one-sided Christocentrism (although it may not be in the form presented by Karl Barth, for example) than to the centuries-long tradition of Catholic theology.[12]

Through the centuries Christian theology has treated the problem of the content of Christian morality primarily in the context of the problem of the "new law of Christ" in its relation to the old law (and sometimes to the natural law). Aquinas has done this especially in his *Summa Theologiae* I-II, 106-8, in particular, 108. In article two of this question he speaks of operative norms. St. Thomas clearly distinguishes between moral norms and norms regarding *credenda et sacramenta* (and worship).[13] This manner of phrasing the question is very important.[14] The following explanations of Aquinas should be understood in the light of it: "works of charity...which of necessity belong to virtue, pertain to moral precepts (*praecepta moralia*), which are handed down even in the old law. Hence, with regard to this, the new law did not have to add to the old anything about exterior actions which must be done" (108, 2c); "we are directed to works of virtue through natural reason... and therefore it was not necessary that some precepts be given beyond the moral precepts of the law, which come from the rule of reason" (ibid., ad 1).[15] The operative moral norms of the new law of Christ are then, according to Aquinas, determined by reason. They are therefore, in their materiality, human morality (natural law), and in a certain sense were already contained in the old law. There does not exist a moral law added by Christ, which in its material content would be "specifically"

Christian. The long and parallel explanations of Suarez in his tenth book of the famous treatise *De legibus* are well known. These usually deny that there is a moral precept added to natural law.[16] Let us cite a German author of the late eighteenth century: "Are not the two great commandments of love in Matthew 22, which are the first principles of natural law, at the base of Christian morality?...And from this concordance of natural law with revelation flows that most famous theological principle, that in the law given us by our Savior there is nothing which is not of natural law except those things which pertain to faith and sacraments."[17] The formula of Vermeersch, in this century, briefly says the same: "the new law, however, imposes no other precepts except those of faith and sacraments."[18] Zalba agrees with Suarez: "Christ added nothing purely positive to natural moral precepts... In positing some facts, however, such as the revelation of certain dogmas, the declaration of penitence, etc., he thereby extended the area covered by the obligations of natural law."[19] With regard to the double precept of love, he clearly says, "The command of love of God and man, in which is summed up the whole positive-divine law...was not introduced or enlarged by Christ, but was brought back from oblivion and obscurity and furnished with new reasons."[20]

The distinctiveness and newness of Christian morality (the new law) are consequently found, according to the tradition of Christian theology, neither in a specificity of material content of operative moral norms in comparison with human morality, or natural law — *recta ratio* — nor in the precept of love of neighbor and enemies, in renunciations (called the "cross" by Christians), in curing the incurables, in the disposition to nonviolence, in marital fidelity, etc. It is difficult to understand how one could deny that non-Christians "ought to love their enemies, renounce egotism, accept renunciation, sacrifice, and the cross."[21] If they did not have to do this it would, in other words, be morally licit and good for them to provoke chaos in human society. If certain non-Christians unduly defend every type of violence and sexual "freedom" and dubious forms of political and economic behavior, all of this, which is not morally licit for Christians, is objectively and similarly not licit for non-Christians, precisely because it is contrary to a truly human morality, i.e., natural moral law. The same may be said of a social ethic unacceptable to Christians.

Other questions ought to be clearly distinguished from what has been said thus far. For example, if the person of Christ and the word of Scripture, as well as the fact of an ecclesial community and the activity of an ecclesial ministry, have contributed to knowledge of the norms of human morality, and in some matters to such an extent that perhaps outside the ecclesial-Christian community certain norms are in fact sometimes not known or at least not known with the same ease and certainty, still, these norms are, even then, truly norms of a human morality. It is not without importance that today the biblical sciences can show that the high moral demands made by Jesus could in fact be found in several places in the world of Christ's time.[22] Finally, another question ought to be distinguished from the one regarding the material distinctiveness of Christian morality: the question as to whether the knowledge of certain moral norms and their fulfillment are conditioned by the grace of Christ. Certainly, our norms are conditioned by grace, but grace itself is not only a medium of knowledge. Furthermore, the grace of Christ is also at the disposition of those outside the Christian ecclesial community.

In the field of religion,[23] which in theological tradition is also clearly distinguished from the properly moral field (cf. above, Aquinas and Suarez), there are certainly specifically Christian realities. If a person accepts in faith the reality of the person of Christ and his word and life, and the reality of the Church with her sacraments and teachings, and of the Christian community, and the inspiration which the Spirit of Christ works in us, etc., he should take these realities into account in his religious life. He will also have some specifically Christian motivations for his moral behavior (human morality). Indeed, he will often feel himself moved by these motivations to a just and moral behavior with its proper values. And more than that, in the area of earthly realities and their moral realization he will give evidence of religious life, ultimately in the form of religious behavior, e.g., Christian virginity, sacrifice as the sign of the love of Christ crucified, etc.

More profound than the categorial religious life is the fundamental option of the Christian, his intimate faith, love, and following of Christ. It is present as transcendentally intentional and athematically conscious in every moral decision and activity as their most profound Christian nucleus.[24] Let us not forget that Christian intentionality, as well as Christian motivation, insofar as they penetrate all moral behavior, have to that extent a certain content, and certainly a specifically Christian content,[25] which as such is actively and personally lived together with moral behavior. However, they do not determine the material content of behavior, although they totally penetrate it and thus give the most profound and specifically Christian value to decision and behavior.

How do we explain the difficulty which many have in accepting the traditional teaching of the relation between Christian morality and human morality (natural moral law)?[26] We fear that Christ is seen in a rather one-sided manner — contrary to sacred Scripture and the Catholic tradition — as a teacher of morality instead of as the Redeemer of man the sinner.[27] Correlatively, we fear that the task of teaching morality is more apparent in the Church than the task of announcing and communicating salvation. The newness[28] which Christ brings to us is not so much a new moral doctrine but rather a new man, the man of the kingdom of God instead of the man of sin, the man who is *pneumatikos* instead of *sarkikos*. Certainly the new man, as such, will take care to have a more profound concept of true morality than had many Hebrews of Jesus' time. Christ shows the way with his example and words. The new man will then take care to live a life which truly corresponds to this understanding of morality, in grace and in the following of Christ. Thus we think it becomes clear in what sense we ought to understand the importance, so often cited, of the necessary correspondence between specifically Christian being and specifically Christian action.[29] It is not a new content of a new morality (in the sense of new moral precepts) that corresponds to Christian being but rather the content of the new man who does not remain in the life of the sinner (*sarkikos*) but rather is converted to the grace of being redeemed — in faith, in love, in the following of Christ — and who expresses his being redeemed by living true human morality and Christian religious life as a new man, in a Christian manner. It is precisely in this way that Christian action corresponds to Christian being.

IV. NON-CHRISTIAN MORALITY, HUMAN MORALITY, CHRISTIAN MORALITY

Non-Christian and Christian morality, considered in their material content (precepts) clearly meet each other in human morality (natural moral law). In fact, we reach the concept of Christian morality from the concept of non-Christian morality by means of the concept of human morality. The Christian meaning of human morality is communicated to non-Christian moralities to the extent that these are truly human.

Under this aspect of material content (precepts) Christian morality (or the law of Christ or the law of grace), founded on the Christ event, is made historically concrete in the medium of human morality, or of natural moral law. Thus natural law is understood as an extension of faith, i.e., of that which Christian revelation communicates to believers.[30] For its part natural moral law, as human morality, is shown to be an anticipation or analogous participation in Christian morality, or in the law of Christ or grace. Thus human morality has, as we emphasized above, its own complete, transcendent significance. This is truly its own, in Christian morality, insofar as it is truly, and in the plan of the Creator and Redeemer, the historical medium of the law of Christ. Considering the question in this way, we do well to affirm that — in its deepest meaning — the natural moral law is the law of Christ, and that human morality is ultimately Christian morality. Precisely for this reason it does not make sense to distinguish between the precepts of Christian morality and those of human morality,[31] with the exception (if one wishes to phrase it this way) of the "natural" obligation of humanly realizing man's beliefs, e.g., his religious practices, sacraments, etc.[32]

These reflections help us to understand better the various attempts of theologians today who wish to enhance the life of man and society by taking as their points of departure revelation and Christian anthropology, respectively. There is a conviction today that faith should have its meaning and its consequences not only in one's private practice of it as between a person and his God, but also in the formation of society and the world. In the attempt to put this into action, however, revelation and faith do not of themselves give concrete solutions. The truths of faith do not give concrete results except in the medium of human morality (natural law), which thus reveals itself to be basically "Christian". Is this not what the repeated formula of *Gaudium et spes* means, according to which the Christian will have the solutions to the problems of humanity from his experience of the world and in the light of the Gospel?[33] For the solution of moral questions and problems of social ethics, it is rightly emphasized today that insofar as one is Christian, one ought to begin from the data of faith, e.g., that this world of sinners has been definitively accepted and loved by God.[34] Even the ideas of the political theology of J.B. Metz, i.e., the fact of the "eschatological reserve" (the true perfection of humanity will be a *gift*; perfect and definitive solutions on the part of man are never given to us, not even with the help of grace) and the promises of reconciliation, justice, peace, etc., which have been given to us, demand from us constantly renewed attempts to seek solutions to the problems of human society which correspond more closely to the ideal of the eschatological promises. Something similar should be said with regard to the various attempts at a political theology made by some Latin American theologians. e.g., J. Segundo, G. Gutiérrez, and U. Assman. Metz, in answering some objections put to him, did well to admit that political theology cannot of itself give concrete solutions to concrete problems, e.g., to the problem of the so-called "third world"; for these solutions political theology must turn to political ethics,[35] must turn on a practical level to those who are competent in the matters at hand, to whom alone falls the task of finding the best and most concrete solutions possible. This is done by evaluating all the elements involved in the light of man's personal dignity and communal vocation. Only thus do we discover what is to be achieved. It will be a human achievement, but a medium of the Christian achievement, and thus it will ultimately be a "Christian" solution. Once again we see that the human thing to do and the Christian thing to do are not distinguished by their material content.

From this it follows that non-Christian moralities, to the extent that they are truly human, are an anticipation of and an analogous participation in the *lex Christi*, and that their deepest meaning is Christian. We should not forget that outside of Christianity the grace of Christ is also working in knowledge and fulfillment of human morality.[36] Nor should we forget that the search for and fulfillment of human morality can be, according to a very Catholic theologian (K. Rahner) athematically penetrated by an intentionality which is in a certain sense Christian,[37] insofar as the interior acceptance of grace, on the part of the non-Christian, would also be the athematic acceptance of an initial revelation.

From this it follows that Christians and non-Christians have the task of seeking always to individuate the concrete *humanum*. This *humanum* can and must be the general norm or concrete solution to human problems, and is in its ultimate meaning "Christian". Indeed, it is possible and desirable that Christians and non-Christians seek to do this together. Thus *Gaudium et spes* proposes that Christians and non-Christians, according to the degree of their specific competence, work together,[38] thus avoiding a ghetto culture and morality and creating one which is truly "human" and, by an analogous participation, "Christian". Or according to Cardinal Villot, the Secretary of State, in the already mentioned letter: "[Moral theologians] ought, together with non-Christians, to make an attempt to individuate those solutions to contemporary human problems that best correspond to the reality and dignity of man...Catholic moral theology, precisely because it is irradiated by the light of the Gospel and is destined to enlighten all nations, claims to give an authentic contribution, one which is acceptable to all men of good will: it is not, therefore, a morality for Catholics alone."[39] Clearly, what is being discussed here is an authentically Christian realization in this world, but a realization which, in its human materiality, is of itself accessible to and acceptable by all, Christians and non-Christians alike. With regard to the formulations of *Gaudium et spes* and the Cardinal Secretary of State, it is good to observe that *Gaudium et spes* itself connects the fundamental "Christian" commandment of love of God and neighbor, the foundation and summary of all moral precepts, with *humanitas*, and sees it as a genuinely human exigency based on the fact that all are created in the image of God.[40] This, then, is a "human" precept. It is "new" not as it relates to the "human" but rather as it relates to the "old man", the unredeemed man — "new", consequently, according to the example of Christ and of his grace which helps us to understand this commandment profoundly and to put it into effect.

If human morality, i.e., the natural moral law, is the meeting point of Christian morality and non-Christian moralities, and if it is the historical medium of the law of Christ and is, under this aspect, profoundly Christian, then another consideration follows. This consideration is common to serious moral efforts, whether they are Christian or non-Christian. It is this: human morality — as natural law — is not a codified morality, nor even totally codifiable. It is, rather, as long theological tradition says, an internal law, i.e., a right manner of acting, *recta ratio*, as the medievals said. It is not, therefore, an already formulated law, but a *recta ratio* to be found by men themselves, by humanity. It is men themselves who ought to seek to understand man and his world "in their process of evolution" in order to "make of themselves projects of human life", and to do this "for the man of today, and, insofar as it is possible for men of different cultures", as Cardinal Villot says.[41] Whether Christian or non-Christian, man can — at least ideally — arrive at some general norms for life and even at some specific norms aimed at realizing concrete aspects of his being which arise as the determined yet diverse levels of human, cosmological and cultural evolution present themselves. This is an idea dear to *Gaudium et spes*.[42] In doing this, however, man (humanity) searches for the historical medium of the law of Christ (or the law of grace); and he finds the historical substratum and the historical body for the law of Christ. This is the substratum which the law of Christ presupposes for itself. Thus both the Christian "in the light of the Gospel" and the non-Christian can seek that *recta ratio* and therefore that human morality or natural moral law which is an element and indispensable aspect of the law of Christ, of Christian morality. They can even do this together.

The formula used by Pope Paul VI (September 6, 1972) is very apt and perfectly consonant with *Gaudium et spes* when it states that in our secularized world there exists the temptation to "lower arbitrarily the level of moral law, to place in doubt its exigency or even its existence, by extending the range of what is allowable beyond that of what is upright and by substituting permissive liberty for dutiful liberty." In saying that "what is upright" is the measure of what is licit he came very close to using the mode of speech of St. Thomas, which was cited earlier. It is very true that the Church, which proposes "what is upright" as a "moral program" to her children, i.e., "the new man" instead of "the old man", today meets "much aversion and hostility in the exercise of her ministry as pastoral guide" (Pope Paul VI, ibid.). The Church experiences this difficulty with Christians and non-Christians alike. He who is upright, then, is "truly human" and — as we have seen — is ultimately "a Christian" who finds his historical fullness in historical Christianity, i.e., in the person of Christ, in the light of the Gospel, in the grace which helps him to believe, hope, and love. It is this which frees from the egotism of the "old man", the real obstacle to living uprightly. That same grace helps him live, in a truly upright manner, that expression of faith, hope, and love which is Christian morality, "a manner of living which deserves to be called Christian" (Pope Paul VI, July 26, 1972). Uprightness as such, human morality or natural moral law, is an anticipation or analogous participation in Christian morality. Moreover, according to Catholic teaching on natural moral law, "what is upright" can by itself — although with difficulty in the world of sin[43] — be known by all men and can even be lived by them to the extent that they accept the grace of Christ offered to all.

NOTES

1.   N.J. Rigali, "New Epistemology and the Moralist", *Chicago Studies* 11 (1972), 237-44.
2.   The following Italian studies have given rise to this present article: "Esiste una morale cristiana?", *La Civiltà Cattolica* III (1972), 449-55; D. Tettamanzi, "Esiste un'etica cristiana?", *La Scuola Cattolica* 99 (1971), 163-93; G.B. Guzzetti, "C'è una morale cristiana?", *Seminarium* 11 (1971), 536-63; F. Compagnoni, *La specificità della morale cristiana*, ed. Dehoniane, Bologna 1972; A. Di Marino, "Criteri e crisi nel rinnovo della morale", *Rivista di Teologia Morale* 3 (1971), 429-42.
3.   Cf. my article, "Vocazione e speranza. Indicazioni conciliari per una morale cristiana", *Seminarium* 11 (1971), 491-510.
4.   This affirmation may be seen in the letter of the Secretary of State, Cardinal Villot, to Cardinal Ursi on the occasion of the celebrations in honor of St. Alphonsus, doctor of the Church, in *L'Osservatore Romano*, 30/31 October 1972.
5.   We think it only too evident that in speaking of man one does not speak of a purely natural reality, i.e. one not inserted in the supernatural order; but neither is this reality necessarily lay or atheistic.

6. It seems that this difference escaped the author of the editorial which appeared in *La Civiltà Cattolica*, September 1972, especially on pp. 449 and 453.

7. Vatican I, DS 3004ff; *Humani Generis*, DS 3875.

7a. The distinction intended by the use of the words "thematic" and "athematic" (= "nonthematic") is generally well-known in present theological circles, above all among those familiar with transcendental theology. "Thematic" refers to objective *knowledge (Wissen)* of a *particular object* as an explicit *theme* of such knowledge; thus a person can speak about the thematic knowledge of his own self as an *object* of this type of knowing. There is, however, a deeper, "nonthematic" awareness *(Bewusstsein)* of the human self as a *subject* in his *totality* as person; according to Aquinas, the human being is always consciously present to himself as a personal whole *(Summa contra Gentiles*, P. 4, q. 11; *Summa Theologiae*, Ia, q. 78, a. 1). This awareness, since it involves the person as a *total* entity, is necessarily an "unreflective", "unobjectifiable", and thereby "unthematic" awareness of the self as *subject* and not as object. For a description of the same distinction in different terminology, cf. J. Fuchs, *Human Values and Christian Morality*, Dublin 1970, 104-8; 131-4.

8. Cf. K. Demmer, *Ius caritatis. Zur christologischen Grundlegung der augustinischen Naturrechtslehre* (Analecta Gregoriana 118), Rome 1961.

9. Pope Paul VI spoke thus, 26 July 1972.

10. It is necessary, therefore, that anyone who uses the phrase "human morality" clarify whether he is speaking of natural moral law or the morality of any particular group of men.

11. In fact, in a recent discussion, the word "natural" was equivalent to "accessible to human reason" or "intelligible". Therefore the distinction between *natura ut sic* and *natura ut hic* becomes less pertinent.

12. At this point we recommend the article of A. Russo, "Principi ispiratori di un rinnovamento in teologia morale", *Rivista di Teologia Morale* 2 (1970), 29-53.

13. Parallel texts are *S.T.* I-II, q. 99, a. 3 ad 2 and q. 99, a. 4c.

14. F. Compagnoni insists far too little on this distinction. Cf. his *La specificità della morale cristiana*, Bologna 1972, 122.

15. Some recent authors contradict this text of Aquinas.

16. F. Suarez, *De legibus*, 1. 10, c. 2, n. 5-12.

17. P.J. Weber, *Dissertatio theologica inauguralis de genuina idea moralis christianae*, 1778, cited by F. Böckle in his article "Unfehlbare Normen?" in *Fehlbar?* (ed. H. Küng), Zurich 1973, 287ff, n. 19.

18. A. Vermeersch, *Theologiae moralis principia-responsa-consilia*, I, no. 154, 4th ed., Rome 1947.

19. M. Zalba, *Theologiae moralis compendium*, I, no. 355, Madrid 1958. The author further explains this according to the system of Suarez: "This also holds with regard to the *lex credendi*. For the *lex credendi Deo revelanti* is ultimately natural; and from the nature of the matter extends also to those things which are to be professed from Christ's revelation. This must

likewise be said with regard to the obligation of entering the Church, of receiving the sacraments, of obeying the hierarchy, etc." (Ibid., n. 28).

20.   Idem, op. cit., n. 355. It seems that not a few theologians spoke in this sense during a week of meetings convoked by the Italian Biblical Association, cf. Carlo Martini, "Fondamenti biblici della teologia morale. Riflessioni di un biblista", *Rassegna di Teologia* 14 (1973), 1-9; G. Giavini, "Le norme etiche della Bibbia e l'uomo d'oggi" II, *La Scuola Cattolica* 100 (1972), 83-97; G. Girardi, *Cristianesimo, liberazione, lotta di classe*, Assisi 1971, 27. It is interesting to see that today many Protestant theologians have begun to admit that the content of the moral demands of Christians are not distinguished from those of other men, that the specificity of Christian morality (on which they insist) does not consist of its content; B. Schüller, in "Zur theologischen Diskussion über die lex naturalis", *Theologie und Philosophie* 41 (1966), cites on p. 495 various texts of Bultmann, H. Greven, O. Cullmann, R. Liechtenhan, E. Dinkler.

21.   Cf. *La Civiltà Cattolica*, art. cit., 452.

22.   R. Schnackenburg, "New Testament Ethics", *Sacramentum Mundi* IV, London 1969, 212-6.

23.   Cf. J. Fuchs, *Esiste una morale cristiana?* Rome-Brescia 1970, 29-31; and Chapter 4 of this book.

24.   Ibid., 14-20. There are some who think that I ignore what is specific about Christian morality and end up with pure nominalism and aprioristic subjectivism. But this is true only if one does not take into account the category and profound reality of athematic consciousness, which is quite different from unconsciousness! It should also be noted that, in my view, "the Christian intentionality of Christian morality" (pp. 14-20) is not the only specifically Christian element: "that which is specifically Christian about Christian morality" (pp. 29-31). Besides, if someone shuns the category "Christian intentionality", thinking that it is nonverifiable, we ask: is God more verifiable?

25.   Tettamanzi, art. cit., 193, rightly uses this phrase, too.

26.   Let us mention only three facts: i) we are inclined to think that it is not accidental that in *Seminarium* 3 (1971), dedicated to moral theology, there is the article "C'è una morale cristiana?"; ii) the editorial in *La Civiltà Cattolica* (September 1972) could give the impression from its title ("Esiste una morale 'cristiana'?") of being the work of the entire editorial staff of the periodical — even of being a work desired by a higher authority, while it is evident to us that neither supposition is true; iii) the "premise" of the previously cited work of F. Compagnoni, who refers to *La Civiltà Cattolica* and Tettamanzi, is eloquent enough.

27.   According to St. Thomas, *S.T.* I-II, q. 106, the "principal" element of the new law of Christ is the grace of the Holy Spirit; documents and precepts are "secondary" elements.

28.   Some theologians give an interpretation of the "newness" of the message of Christ different from ours, being based, rather, on St. Paul and St. Thomas.

29.   Cf. *La Civiltà Cattolica*, art. cit., 453.

30.   Cf. J. Fuchs, "Teologia morale e dogmatica" in *Esiste una morale cristiana?*, 77-111.

31.   Cf. K. Demmer, *Sein und Gebot*, Paderborn 1971, 223-34.

32.   See the doctrine of Suarez, mentioned above (note 16), of Zalba (note 19), and also my *Esiste una morale cristiana?* 29-31 (note 23).

33.   *Gaudium et spes*, n. 46; cf. also nn. 4, 11, 23.

34.   Cf. K. Demmer, "Moralische Norm und theologische Anthropologie", *Gregorianum* 54 (1973), 263-305.

35.   J.B. Metz, "Politische Theologie in der Diskussion", *Diskussion zur "politischen Theologie"*, Mainz-Munich 1969, 267-301, especially 281ff.

36.   Being "free from sin and the slavery of Satan" (wording of *La Civiltà Cattolica*, art. cit., 451), i.e. grace, can be found even in non-Christians.

37.   Cf. the thesis of the "anonymous Christians", held by K. Rahner, and also the application of this theologoumenon in moral theology, e.g. in K. Demmer, *Sein und Gebot*, Paderborn 1971; cf. also the suggestive formula in *Gaudium et spes*, n. 22.

38.   *Gaudium et spes*, n. 33; and also n. 4.

39.   *L'Osservatore Romano*, 30/31 October 1972.

40.   *Gaudium et spes*, n. 24.

41.   *L'Osservatore Romano*, October 30/31, 1972. F. Compagnoni, *op. cit., 122*, is a bit skeptical with regard to this formula, but it seems that his fear that God would thus leave "full liberty" to man is unfounded, precisely because man (with his intelligence) is a determinate creature of God. Otherwise, one again falls into a pure voluntarism.

42.   Cf. my article "Vocazione e speranza. Indicazioni conciliari per una morale cristiana", *Seminarium* 11 (1971), 491-510.

43.   Vatican I, DS 3004 ff; *Humani Generis*, DS 3875.

6. Autonomous Morality and Morality of Faith

The reason for my personal interest in the question as to whether there is an autonomous Christian morality was and is both a scientific and a pastoral one.[1] For me it is a matter of determining a normative morality and, above all, of delineating the normative content of such a morality with respect to man's concrete life in the world; it follows that it is also a matter of investigating the possibility of knowing such things. One can list many elements which characterize Christian morality as Christian. My question is this: does the difference lie in the nature of objective moral norms? Are there different norms for Christians and non-Christians, for example with regard to effecting justice, with regard to marriage, etc.? Or does the difference lie elsewhere, and can this difference, at least to some extent, be clearly demonstrated? Can one say that for good Christians, confronted with diverse secular issues, moral ways of behaving are objectively valid which are not so for good humanists? Do we Christians, legally speaking, form a ghetto with respect to other human beings in this world? Can we seek one common road along with other men toward a more just organization of humanity and the world (for doing so always involves moral questions), even if this attempt succeeds only in a minimal way? In any case, by promulgating *Gaudium et spes* Vatican II not only considered such an attempt possible, but in fact demanded that it be made. In a world which is dominated by humanism, secularization and secularism, we Christians are required to contribute to the process of building up the earth with as much moral insight as is possible; as men standing under the light of the Gospel, we are expected to possess such insight.[2] At least this is the position taken at Vatican II.[3] But this implies more than simply the possibility that Christians may speak in some commonly determined way about the morality of faith. The mandate of Vatican II also calls us to stress more firmly the autonomous character of normative (and also of Christian) morality. This task in particular necessarily raises two central questions. The first concerns the rationality of normative morality and the autonomous access to moral norms and reasonable judgments; in other words, is it possible to come to such norms and judgments in a way other than that made available through Christian faith? The second question concerns the importance that faith has for such an autonomous approach to morality.

I. THE PROBLEM: "HUMAN" AND "CHRISTIAN" MORALITY

1. The One and the Many Moralities. If I am to make an introductory remark about the topic which is to be treated, I must obviously say something relevant to both questions which have been posed. I must describe the content of a genuinely autonomous-human morality and I must explain how it is possible that we can come to know such a morality.

As far as content is concerned, there are moral systems and moral codes in different parts of the world which de facto are, in part at least, quite different from one another: there are those that have risen up spontaneously in various groups and peoples; there are those that are grounded on philosophical-ethical arguments; and there are those which are based on religion. Besides, there are and always were, even among Christians, including Catholics, certain differences which are quite significant,[4] not to mention the personal morality of individual Christians. Religiously grounded moral systems are, according to the opinion of many, more a matter of religion than of morality.[5]

But various moralists are convinced that they possess the truth about man and thus that moral code which is genuinely human. Are we not really dealing here with a rather general human consensus which is implicitly maintained even when it is explicitly denied – and is maintained precisely in the denial, if the latter is to be taken as meaningful and sincere? There is a **de facto** consensus that there is one true moral order aimed at the concrete realization of man, society and world, and that this order corresponds to human nature, no matter how varied are its manifestations. Furthermore, there is agreement on the tenet that this moral order can be discovered. In the most varied ways people believe either that they possess this moral code or that they are steadily searching for it. Even the moral relativist and the convinced skeptic hold to a moral norm capable of guiding correct human behavior in this world, though each may formulate such a norm in a relative or in a skeptical manner, respectively. It is, of course, obvious that there can be only one objectively genuine *humanum* that implies corresponding moral consequences. This is true even if one takes concrete factors into consideration.

It follows that in various cultures and subcultures certain divergent moral patterns of behavior are not absolutely excluded, for correct human behavior, precisely because it is to be appropriate for the concrete human person in his totality and in view of all the factors of his existence, must not only judge the entire concrete situation to be a *human* one, but also actualize or bring to light the human. Furthermore, the sinful but at the same time graced condition both of the individual person and of all mankind does not contradict what has been said thus far. The man who finds himself in the kind of situation we have just described can only experience himself as such, and as such must realize himself in the best possible human manner. It is apparent that behind these statements there is at least the implicit certainty that at his deepest core the human person is present to himself (*bei sich*) — that is, conscious of himself and of his nature. For this reason, he is also aware, even if only athematically, of the requirement to recognize a moral code of behavior. And he knows that he must be absolutely faithful to this code. Whoever sees a distraught man clinging to the parapet of a bridge is conscious of the moral prohibition against passing by him without a sufficient reason. Such a prohibition may be only an intuitive one, to the extent that its binding force cannot be explained theoretically. The latter problem, namely that of theoretical explanation, is particularly relevant to the topic being discussed.

Christianity which, because of faith, is certain of its understanding of man, necessarily comprehends the genuine human moral code to be the Christian one. For, it is the human person who believes. Christianity may allow the human person to acquire information about how to be human in the world and also about how to be humanly related to God; Christianity may allow him as well to be in possession of new strength and to be aware of the truth of things. Even so, the Christian understands himself as a *man* and as such has to realize himself. This is his primary task as man (*primum quoad nos!*). For this reason, he has to incorporate the data of Christianity into his human reality. This fact does not deny that the "human-Christian" in its fullness is, objectively speaking, the prime reality (*primum quoad se*) and that as such it contains the *humanum* within it.[6] The full realization of faith is always a full realization of the human person. The Christian possesses the Holy Spirit and the light of the Gospel, which present him with a significant aid in his search for moral value judgments. Yet the Christian himself, like other human beings, must discover in the world the true realization of his particularly determined human nature. This obligation is not diminished by the presence of the Holy Spirit or by the validity of Christian insight. Given this situation, the Christian is never totally exempt from uncertainty and error either by the content of revelation or by the inner grace of the Holy Spirit. Non-Christians and Christians alike have the task of coming to an increasingly adequate and certain knowledge of the *humanum* and of its moral demands, which are conditioned by constantly varying situations.

Thomas Aquinas knew of no Christian morality which differed in content from *virtus humana* (virtue) and *ratio humana* (reason).[7] As far as material content is concerned, is it not perhaps typical of Christian normative morality (even a religious essential) that one break the power of the inhuman?[8] And is this not true less because of individual moral doctrines or because of Christ's concrete example than because of the totality of the Christ-event? Therefore, it is not so much a matter of moral teaching as it is of liberating redemption! For, the inhuman was and is not only ignorance and error but, more importantly and above all, also the implicit attempt at absolute autonomy, denial of the Absolute, godlessness. With this in mind, it is clear that even the valid truths about the cross contained in the Sermon on the Mount would not be absolutely foreign to the human being who finds himself sinful and graced at the same time. Therefore, Christ's coming seems to be less a question of morality than it is of salvation. Indeed, the moral question remains a burdensome and demanding one for man's autonomous reason, even if Christianity aids him a great deal and sheds considerable light on his situation. And it cannot be said that the act of faith itself replaces man's obligation to search for moral norms, as long as he bears his responsibility honestly and does not fall into an egoistical desire for happiness. The latter is not due to man's need to discover autonomous norms but to his weakness and his refusal to take on moral responsibility; both these dangers incessantly confront the Christian as well. Erich Przywara was indeed correct when he stated many years ago that man's path would have to lead from moral "sacralism" to moral secularism.[9] What he meant was the direction established by the Creator for the ever greater development of man as creature; this is the human autonomy set down by God himself (theonomistic autonomy), so that man could unfold his potential as God's image. I believe that this observation is totally consonant with the above-mentioned position of Aquinas.

2. Some Conclusions. Can we formulate some conclusions based on what has been said so far?

A. Quoad nos there can be no moral code which does not have a human-autonomous starting-point. There is simply no other source. Even the gift of faith can be real only if it is accepted in a human and autonomous fashion with the help of grace. If revelation is accepted in this way, it is then, to be sure, the starting-point of a scientific theological morality, since the moral question is posed to the Christian who is confronted by faith. Christian morality, therefore, cannot be essentially distinguished, as far as its material content is concerned, from a human autonomous morality. Yet one must realize that man, precisely because he is human and autonomous, has necessarily to take into consideration and include in moral judgments all available data, even the most variable and circumstantial cultural and religious factors. All these belong to his concrete being.

In this way, and often only in this way, can a human-autonomous morality meet the possible objection that it is by its very nature unhistorical and undynamic; in effect, this means that it does not correspond to reality. This charge could be answered only if one does not restrict human-autonomous morality, which is also called morality based on natural law, to a very few broad statements rather than viewing it as practical reason and attributing to it the moral judgment of the entirety of human behavior, which is not written down anywhere and which cannot be totally captured in words. In this sense, if someone were to observe the matter *quoad nos*, he could define our Christian de facto morality as human-autonomous morality with regard to its normative aspect. This is still the case, even though and precisely because Christian morality has, in a human way, to take into consideration the totality of the Christ-event and its significance for the moral life. It is in the Spirit and in the light of the Gospel that the Christian has to carry out this human task. But even though this is true we would still be dealing with a truly human morality: as far as their material content is concerned, the demands of justice and of behavior within marriage are for both Christians and humanists objectively the same.

B. *Quoad se*, the situation is quite different, for in this light Christian morality will have to be seen as *the* morality par excellence. This is because Christian morality as the human enterprise of those who believe contains in itself the total horizon of meaning and the religious (!) orientation which has been revealed in the Christ-event. I lay stress on the words "religious orientation" because, as such, they cannot change the material content of morality as a human task. For this reason, everything which is sought and found to be genuine human morality in different moralities must be regarded as an objective part of (or participation in) Christian morality based on the Christ-event. At another point, we will have to discuss the Christian dimensions of the one human-autonomous and yet Christian morality: the Christian sense of meaning, the Christological foundation, Christian intentionality, Christian motivation, etc.

C. The Christian's full self-realization-through-faith is that of a human being, and is therefore always the fulfillment of human morality at the same time.[10] It is the full self-realization-through-faith of the human person who is always realizing himself as a subject through moral activity. Thus Christian faith and human-autonomous morality are inseparable, but nevertheless different and to be differentiated. It is only by way of treating each in a decidely abstract manner that Christian moral theology can be applied without causing unnecessary confusion.[11]

In this initial treatment of the *status questionis* the answer is already indicated; it remains now to elaborate it further.

II. ETHICAL EXPERIENCE

Ethics and moral theology cannot be pursued in the same way as metaphysics and dogmatics. For, the former essentially presupposes not only an emotive but above all a cognitive moral experience which has an always evaluative, often intuitive and ultimately athematic-transcendent character as well.[12] This thesis demands a brief reflection; for, unless one considers the relation of these facts to one another, morality — and also the question of norms — cannot be understood.

1. *"Is" and "Ought".* The difference between metaphysics and dogmatics on the one hand, and ethics and moral theology on the other, is made clear simply by examining the quite diverse terminology employed in the field of philosophical ethics. It should be noted that different terms do not always and in every respect indicate the same thing! As an example, we might take the term "original conscience" which presumably approximates to what Thomas Aquinas meant by "synderesis." It is a conscious self-evident "given," a moral-religious and indestructible factor of the human subject's existence; thus it is ultimately an athematic and transcendental reality, which means that it cannot be known as an object. This self-evident factor is oriented toward God and contains in itself the ultimate and essential "given-ness" of moral responsibility. Even when it exists in a state of confusion or of protest, the "original conscience" still affirms itself. People also speak of "conscience" as cognitive "percep-

tion", whether athematic or thematic moral experience. Thomas Aquinas[13] knew of a totally experiential (and also cognitive) transcendental "presence-to-himself" of the human person as a subject in the moral sense as well. Furthermore, he spoke of first, irreducible moral perceptions-evaluations-experiences, and attributed a thematic character to them. Being a *good* human person can be directly experienced, on the basis of evidence, as the very meaning of life and as an "ought", to introduce Hume's terminology. This is true even if one's fundamental athematic consciousness is, according to Romans 1:18ff, malevolently being "suppressed". Without "the experimentally and directly given obligation to affirm values, especially the personal dignity of the human beings", [14] there can be neither autonomous morality nor faith ethics.

If one does not intend to fall prey to irrational fideism, one will have to admit the spontanteous and independent ground of human values. Scholars have often remarked, appropriately, that man's athematic-transcendental and direct experience of his senses (and this is, as was mentioned, also the experience of morality) first makes possible the different types of his categorial sense experiences and with them his moral experiences. The former experiences are always present in the latter as in their ultimate source. From what has been said it follows that the experience of morality, as an original experience, can take place and actually takes place without an explicit knowledge of God. The philosopher Joseph de Finance has made the very apt observation that human reason bears in itself a trace of its "deputyship" for the unknown God.[15] This means, however, that openness to the personal Absolute is always concomitantly given with the awareness of moral experience. This is true even in the case of thematic atheists and of sinners (therefore also in the case of the guilty atheist).

Another consequence of these observations is that Hume was correct in stressing that from the "is" no "ought" should be deduced. Man cannot deduce any ethical categories from categories of being. The experience of light and that of sound represent, at any given time, original experiences. This independence does not exclude the fact that there is a correlation − not only in transcendental but also in categorial experience − between being and obligation, between the experience of being and that of ethics. The "ought" always contains a categorial content which in turn is always an ethical one. If someone were to lack the ability to make value judgments and the capacity to undergo ethical experiences, then it could not be made intelligible to him what an "ought-statement" or what an "ethical-statement" really means.

2. Moral Experience within the Context of Faith. The foregoing considerations already make it perfectly clear that moral experience has to do with the experience of God. In current theology (and not only in the introductions to theology written, e.g., by Ratzinger, Kasper and Rahner), we find the thought that it is essentially God who is believed in by the human person; if anything at all is believed in, then above all, God. This fact does not contradict the defined teaching concerning the possibility of a natural knowledge of God. Since, by his very nature, man *is* the question concerning his meaning, he fundamentally cannot escape the possibility of finding in some human way a correct answer to the question which he himself is. This happens not only in the case of concrete individual questions, but also in the case of the underlying *origo-finis* question, hard as it may be to attain de facto clarity and certainty in this matter. If, however, the answer is given in faith, then on the one hand, faith must indeed presuppose for itself in some way the possibility of understanding; this is done through reason's "representative" function. On the other hand, moral experience (as well as the obligation to believe in God) is always, at least implicitly, also the experience of faith.

At the conclusion of a Christological contribution in a theological journal, M. Serenthà takes a position on the problematic relationship between Christology and anthropology. He formulates his understanding of the issue somewhat as follows: the question which man himself is and the answers which in the course of time he works out for himself through critical reflection are not, as they are taking shape, indifferent matters to which he subsequently adds a theological reflection. Rather, these questions and answers proceed from Christology − certainly not in such a way that the latter itself provides the response to the query, "What is the human person?" But Christology does present us with a positive, salvific meaning to the constant and ever new question, posed throughout history, about the human person. For this reason, Christology becomes an inner moment of theological anthropology, but does not constitute it as such. Instead, Christology allows to anthropology a thoroughly independent development, even one which varies according to different periods of time and according to different personal preferences. This position of M. Serenthà is introduced here so as to enable us to remark that a similar relationship can be said to exist between Christian faith and anthropological self-understanding; this holds true also of an anthropological vision which is developed from an ethical perspective. Precisely for this reason faith in God necessarily demands a human, and thus partially variant, means of expressing itself.[16]

It should be stressed again that the moral experience arising from within the experience of faith as a form of self-understanding clearly connotes the absolute binding force of one's attempt to order one's life correctly. Yet the possibility of finding correct solutions to moral problems undoubtedly often depends on diverse factors which condition the rational knowledge contained in the moral experience. Moreover, the correct solution is to a great extent and primarily conditioned by whether the *fides qua* is really a graced *optio fundamentalis*—that is, openness and self-surrender. The reason of the explicit believer is furthermore one that has been enlightened by the *fides quae*. But it is in reality the practical reason itself which must come to moral insight and experience. Therefore, nothing has been said here about whether and to what degree the *fides quae* mediates moral knowledge or guarantees that it is correct.

Every human person meets with situations which demand moral reaction. Whether a believer or a non-believer, one enjoys an absolute, even if also intuitive, knowledge concerning what one ought to do in such situations. Of course, an exception would be the case of someone who is so overcome by sickness that he is incapable of moral experiences. Even atheists, who claim that moral norms do not exist for them, still choose to direct their lives by some standard such as the human achievements of modern science. Is such a decision to guide one's way by human reason simply a statement of fact or is it perhaps both an implicitly admitted, morally binding experience and a conviction, rooted in an athematic faith-experience, that one must fashion one's life in a certain way and not in another? Even if they do so without *fides quae*, many people act responsibly and apparently arrive at moral insight and experience. They seem to live from a morality of faith (an athematic *fides qua*) in the sense in which this was explained above; yet the morality of faith is bound to an intuitive experience of morality.

3. "Philosophical Ethics". There are many who also pursue what is called philosophical ethics; this is not metaphysics, but should be nourished by metaphysics and logic: in this sense philosophical ethics is related to these other branches of philosophy. This is the proper way to put ethics in perspective.

A. The fact that various branches of philosophy are closely related should not mislead one to the point of forgetting that ethics simply does not have its origin in metaphysics. One should not venture to derive first ethical insights from metaphysics and then try to handle very concrete and practical ethical questions in a totally metaphysical framework. The ethical experience is the starting-point of personal morality! Ethics ought to reflect in a scientific manner on such an experience in order to create more clarity concerning the nature and significance not only of ethical experience but also of ethical conscience, ethical norms, ethical decisions, etc. It should be repeated that ethics is not concerned with deducing the "ought" from the "is" but invariably with coming to a correct understanding of the adage *agere sequitur esse*, a phrase which in various respects has often been falsely interpreted. There is a normative (!) aspect to such ethical reflection, since it investigates not only the understanding of one's athematic-transcendental ethical experience (the transcendental experience is by its very nature athematic), but also the understanding of categorial experience or of concrete problems. The ethical experience frequently takes place along with a simultaneous reflex consideration which is meant to serve as an assurance that the content of the experience is valid; but it also takes place in a purely intuitive manner which is not explicitly taken note of, and for this reason it could also be called athematic. The thematic reflection on ethical experience, however, can also begin when a person is confronted with apparently contradictory ethical experiences which are conditioned by a variety of influences and particularly by different persons, groups or societies. Ethical reflection is also sparked by a situation in which several ethical experiences of the very same person seem to contradict one another. Even ethics enjoys an affinity to logic!

Due to the difference between metaphysics and logic on the one hand, and ethics on the other, it is also somewhat paradoxical to want to clarify ethical questions in a thorough way when one is involved in the process of devising a proof or in the midst of a logical discourse. The source of ethical insight is not a metaphysical or logical thought-pattern, but a form of reasoning which experiences and evaluates. But it is also the case that the human interpretation of facts is measured by the evaluative function of reason (*die wertende Vernunft*). The first flight to the moon, in its planning stage, was a question of fact; but the meaning of the chance and risk involved for human beings demanded that those responsible make evaluative computations and judgments. An ethical discernment of the undertaking could not be proved simply through metaphysical or logical reflection which was exempt from ethical (cognitive) experience. Ethical proofs are not demonstrations in the strict sense; this is especially true when it is a matter of treating ethical questions themselves and not only of presenting logical or metaphysical reflections on ethical proofs. For this reason, many ethical dialogues are doomed to failure from the very start. Yet, the party explaining his ethical "grounds" can possibly help his partner to arrive at a very different ethical experience from what he is accustomed to, precisely by means of these so-called grounds.

B.   It was mentioned above (II, (2)) that moral experience is essentially open to an Absolute, and indeed ultimately to a personal one. Put differently, it can be said that this Absolute is implied even in the case of an explicit unbeliever or sinner. The *optio fundamentalis* which is made by every human person constitutes either a fully accepted self-surrender to or a self-despairing rejection of the personal God. Many adopt the solid theological position that in the de facto order this acceptance or rejection takes place as an acceptance or rejection of an original intimate revelation of grace on the part of the God who communicates his very self. But the acceptance or the rejection occurs athematically, since it comes about through the self-fulfillment of the subject as such. This interior, self-surrendering acceptance or self-despairing rejection should certainly have an influence on the theory of ethics of a philosopher. The so-called philosophical or natural ethics, which is carried out by human reason as it experiences and evaluates reality, is always pursued in the presence of the Absolute and, what is more, of the self-revealing and self-communicating Absolute. The engaged ethician believes and loves, or he refuses to do so and denies himself. In spite of the sheer (unreflective) implicitness and the athematic character of the religious dimension of ethical experience, one can still speak of a "philosophical" and "natural" ethics. This means an ethics of the human person as we find him existing without thematic consciousness of revelation, since the implicit and athematic are not manifest in him in an objective fashion. Ethics does not happen by itself; the ethician *does* ethics — without necessarily referring to the God who has been proven by metaphysical arguments to exist, or without referring consciously to revelation or explicitly to faith. Thus the ethician is appreciated precisely for his "being-a-man" and "being-a-philosopher"; the ethics he examines is called "natural". This is how it should be, since in doing so the ethician and his philosophizing are viewed only in a thematic way. Yet this does not deny that he and his field of study are imprinted at their core with theological significance, and as such they are marked with freedom. Thus we speak of the "philosopher" and the "ethician", and not of the "theologian" and the "moral theologian". In doing so, however, we should also *not* claim that the ethician is an absolute rationalist, as long as he essentially (as a philosopher) keeps himself open to higher forms of knowledge and criteria. What has been said here should be of obvious importance with respect to the themes "theological autonomy" and "the morality of faith".

III. THE RATIONAL AUTONOMY OF THE CHRISTIAN

From the foregoing considerations arises the question of the extent to which moral theology as normative — that is, with respect to its material content — does make use of philosophy or must do so. Perhaps this question could even be extended to include the whole span of moral theology's material norms (autonomous morality). This question requires that the following topics be treated: (1) the necessarily rational character of moral norms — that is, their character as cognitive experience — and (2) the autonomy of moral norms and judgments.

1. Moral Rationality. "In discussing acts of moral behavior, we will be guided by natural reason *(per rationem naturalem)* which is the standard of human behavior." These are the words of Thomas Aquinas.[17] In a logical fashion he considers even the moral directives of the Old Testament to be commandments of reason. This explains why Christ does not have to append to the tradition any further moral commandment.[18] Thus, Christ has left moral teaching to human reason.

Moral rationality implies that it is man himself who has access to and can arrive at insight concerning the domain of moral norms. It is man, as the work and image of the Creator, who has the task of acknowledging that his behavior must not be indifferent but must lead to his self-realization. Either through intuitive experience or through scientific reflection on ethical experience, man is obliged to search out the implications of moral non-indifference and to understand this phenomenon. The moral and cognitive fundamental experience of man as a person — that is, as a totality — as well as the inevitable cognitive consciousness of first, entirely irreducible principles, can, to a certain extent, also be reflected on in a scientific manner. The same is true, in a different way, of the multiplicity of possible synthetic moral norms and judgments (these, by the way, are synthetic a priori, in accord with experience's evaluative-cognitive uniqueness, which has already been presented). The binding force of morality would be nonsense if it did not enjoy a fundamental ability to be perceived and understood. This truth is not denied by another —

namely that, faced with some questions, many persons do not de facto consider themselves capable of producing a sufficient moral insight for themselves (in a society); nevertheless, as human persons essentially oriented toward others and toward society, they indirectly arrive at a consciousness of rationally grounded moral obligations, without, however, understanding values as such.

Once again, what has been said is not contradicted by the fact that human persons, as experience proves, come to the most divergent moral attitudes when confronted with many moral questions, or, indeed, even with the central insights or the fundamental options which serve as the basis of concrete norms and judgments. For, in spite of all the divergence, three factors remain constant. (a) Generally, it can be said that at least in an implicit fashion agreement prevails with regard to the first moral insights which human beings attain. (b) The rational insight into morality can be regarded as accepted by all men on the basis of an at least implicit consensus (as was already determined above); in border cases it may be that the only consensus is that "meaninglessness" is accepted as meaning! (c) A testing of the questions which arise can be carried out in the case of divergences – and not only in the case of those which concern concrete norms and judgments, but also those which deal with decisive fundamental standpoints. Furthermore, this testing can, as a rule, take place on the level of rational discussion, so as possibly to come to similar (or divergent) evaluations; fundamental positions or particular evaluations certainly are not arrived at in a random fashion – at least not when genuine moral responsibility is involved. In fact, what is in question is the correct insight of practical reason and the corresponding option which it entails. What has been said does not exclude the fact that, even in scientific discussion, the problem of determining normative morality is de facto brought closer to some common insight only within certain limits – and this is due in no small part to the many circumstances which condition the individual participants. This does not deny the fundamental rationality of normative morality, but once again affirms it in spite of all the difficulties which remain.

In passing, it might be noted that, owing to a basic inability to arrive at a common insight into correct moral behavior, morality can be degraded by being understood as sheer obedience in the presence of an absolute. Morality might then be given the role of a merely executive organ and denied its more important tasks of realizing values as such (since the latter cannot be comprehended) or of being responsible for fashioning human life and the world as a way as actualizing their meaning. Yet obedience does not mean moral positivism, although many understand morality this way and although many non-Christians (and perhaps many Christians who maintain a primitive understanding of the issue) often think of moral theology in such a fashion.

Moral theology simply does not permit such positivism to influence it. A God who would set down laws arbitrarily and who would impose on his spiritual creatures whimsical and meaningless "commandments" would be an all too anthropomorphically conceived God, a "non-God". The human being who is created by the true God must necessarily have clear access to the meaning of his free self-realization and to the meaning of the ways in which he expresses the latter—as an individual, as a member of society, as a person who steers the world; otherwise he would not be the image of God. There is a basic difference between ethical norms determined by means of man's free self-realization, on the one hand, and revealed mysteries, on the other; the latter are by their very nature thoroughly inaccessible to man, whereas the former are not.

Even where revelation speaks of moral values and behavior, the possibility of moral insight must per se enter into what has been said; if this were not the case, we would not be dealing with an injunction. If the information which is given to us in revelation is to be ethically meaningful — be it information in the form of a mystery or in the form of anthropological implications which follow on a mystery — then the attainment of insight into the relationship between the information and moral behavior must be possible. If, on the one hand, God's Yes to the sinful and redeemed world is to have any meaning for morality, and if, on the other hand, revelation's message about the special worth given man by the Christ-event is to become significant for interpersonal moral behavior, then these consequences have to be perceptible. They are de facto perceptible, since not all moral experience concerning the relationship between human persons eludes man. The importance of man's ability to experience and know moral values is demonstrated by the following reflections on the extent to which a man may determine the fate of another human life: even after a believer has been exposed to a profound theological description of the worth and corresponding inviolability of human life, the question of the eventual limits of this respect can become acute. In such a case, the believer must proceed by using the resources of practical reason, moral experience and natural law, since none of these is taken away from him once he believes; instead, they are "taken up" (*aufgehoben*) into his life of faith.

The following statement pertains, mutatis mutandis, to what has been said here: "Whatever does not enter into the a priori horizon of understanding which human existence enjoys and whatever attempts at the same time to deceive him cannot become existential for the human person, that is, it cannot serve as the ground of his being."[19] This way of thinking is a familiar pattern in the Catholic tradition; it explains, for example, why Suarez and the School of Salamanca describe the ethical obligations that stem from the mysteries of Christianity as *quodomodo naturalia* or *connaturalia gratiae*. In this case, "natural" apparently means simply the appropriate ability of the human person to gain insight into the relationship between revelation and ethical behavior. This principle would apply as well to the human person's fundamental access to a concrete, though still limited, self-understanding with regard to the sayings of Jesus concerning the cross. The latter simply cannot escape the law of rationality which is operative in ethical cognitive experience. This must be maintained no matter how difficult it may be to come to an actual understanding of these truths without the aid of *fides qua* and *fides quae*. Even though Jesus' sayings are particularly meaningful in the Christian context, they are not for this reason totally impenetrable to human rationality.

2. Moral Autonomy

A. The thesis concerning the essential rationality of moral norms and judgments is similar to the differently formulated thesis concerning the moral autonomy of the human person. In order to counter from the very start the misunderstandings which have arisen with regard to the latter thesis, the accent in contemporary moral theology is often placed on the theonomy of autonomous morality. In this way, the autonomy is understood not only as a fundamental possiblity given to humanity by the God who has created and redeemed the world, but also as a task which has been entrusted to humanity. Man is commissioned to seek and to find a way of behaving which corresponds, in every one of his acts and deeds without exception, to his "being-as-spirit-in-a-body". This autonomy, as a possibility and task, ought to be capable of being experienced by every man, at least in an athematic way; it ought to be implied in one's faith in the Creator and Redeemer. We will return later to a reflection on how this statement touches not only upon the question of the relationship of faith and reason, but also upon that of the evidence for faith.

The "theonomy of moral autonomy" therefore means that, in creating man, God has not posited another absolute, a second God, who stands beside him, but an image of himself. Man has to search, find and experience a way of freely living out his being as image of God, and also has to bring such a life to its full completion in some meaningful fashion. In this sense, it is true that the created and re-deemed human person is the "measure of all things" since he di-rectly reflects the source of all things. God himself is the measure of all things in an indirect way, since he is their archetype, whom we, for our part, can know only as the one who is analogous to our own real-ity. Such knowledge is possible only if God has communicated him-self to us in history in such a way that his communication is primarily aimed at shedding light on our own real situation and also on the morality which is demanded of us. God's self-revelation neither al-ters the nature and structure of human existence nor infringes on man's obligation to seek, find and experience human-autonomous norms of behavior. Instead this obligation becomes still more press-ing in the presence of the divine intervention in history. Man is to seek his being-as-God's-image not through letting himself be told about it but through his own fashioning of right behavior, as well as through bringing himself to fulfillment.

In the light of these reflections, it becomes clear that Dorothée Sölle's decision to entitle a book "Fantasy and Obedience" was close to the point.[20] The extent to which sinful and graced man can in fact arrive at clear norms through the power of his own autonomy, and the extent to which God himself provides "assisting relief" is, as has been said above, still to be investigated. What is certain is that man has been granted a certain active creativity in his task of coming to moral norms and judgments since he is a participant in God's own being as Creator. The discovery of moral norms and judgments is an act of human culture. (The opposite can also be said: every culture, even when it is already formed, is challenged to surpass and develop itself; in doing so, a culture determines the content of those further moral judgments which are appropriate to its own growth.) Of course, one should not deny the fact that self-interest and even egoism can also play a role in this process if human groups or societies attempt, without serious reflection, to arrive at norms which are moral and binding. But we should view the human situa-tion as one determined not only by sin but also by efficacious grace; therefore, such a seeking-finding-experiencing, which can take con-scious form in any number of ways, also exists for the sake of man's worth and responsibility. It may be right to categorize contemporary humanism as "post-Christian" (though this would have to be proven in detail!), and it may be just as right to describe some aspects of it as post-Jewish, post-Roman and post-German! Such genetic classifying says nothing either about the nature of the genuinely *humanum* or about the fundamental autonomy of man who can freely understand it.

The elements which determine a concrete human person have come about historically (and are not the same everywhere and in all respects); these particular elements naturally have to be taken into consideration in the process of coming to concrete moral judgments and in directing moral experience toward the future. Man's good intentions, which are indeed endangered by his weakness and sinfulness but which are brought about by grace, deserve serious attention, as do the plurality of convictions (and eschatologies) which man creatively and autonomously produces: "What is the right behavior of the human person — given the way his existence is determined in the concrete? Without reaching a compromise between human goods and values, there is no correct discovery of a norm! Even the judgment which has been made responsibly — whether it is morally right or wrong — still determines the concrete existence of the human person and becomes his "final state". Thus, as far as norms are concerned, it is morally correct that man realize his human existence by responsibly forming his own conscience. In carrying out this correctness in and through the free acts by which he realizes himself, the human person fulfills his personal moral attempt to be good. This remark perhaps offers a slight nuance to the validly employed distinction between correctness of normative morality on the one hand, and goodness of personal morality on the other.

B. Now we should ask: what place does the meaning of the Christ-event have in what has been said here? We return to this question, even though we have briefly referred to it earlier in this essay.

The basic answer is that the Christ-event, in which man the sinner took part, does not destroy the essential structure of man's this-worldly existence, and therefore leaves intact the material content of the interpersonal moral order. The immanent and natural structure of the this-worldly, theonomous-autonomous moral order remains the same. The key point is that the Christ-event does not directly lie on this level — that is, that this event is not in itself concerned with the manner in which man arrives at a normative interpersonal morality. Rather, the Christ-event directly pertains to the essentially theological and religious domain. Thus the personal human being attains through the Christ-event a wholly new horizon and meaning which affects him in his totality, including, therefore, his morality. In considering this newness (which is indeed man's salvation), one should in no way lose sight of the sinful situation of the human being whom Christ calls home. The redeemed human person has to bring to expression the horizon of meaning for his life which he possesses as a gift; it is precisely through a continual discovery of the moral order which is immanent in him and autonomous as well that the human person can express his redemption. Insofar as man voluntarily lives according to this order, he realizes at the same time the Christian (theological-theonomous) meaning and horizon which were given in Christ as a gift to himself, to mankind and to the world. Moral reality and theological-religious reality are not two juxtaposed or supplementary entities. Rather, the moral dimension, by remaining totally itself, is penetrated, enriched and fulfilled in every respect by the theological-religious dimension which grants it a meaning that it did not properly possess. In a word, the moral dimension is taken up into the religious. Furthermore, since theological-religious behavior is not simply a matter of whim, there occurs in the moral behavior of the Christian, at least implicitly, something more than is explicitly expressed in moral norms and judgments.

What happens to us in the Christ-event is an objective reality. The believing Christian, however, can subjectively attain a certain categorial knowledge of the objective event. Yet the total human experience of the mysterious theological reality, in which the Christian partakes through faith, hope and love, is indeed made possible only in a thoroughly athematic fashion through the personal attempt to live out one's own existence (*Bei-sich-sein*). Therefore, it would perhaps be better to speak of religion, of its constituent meaning, values and acts, when one is referring to the categorial and thematic dimensions of Christian existence.

Thus, the athematic, theological experience of Christian existence is brought to full expression in and through the continual intentionality that one manifests in moral actions, and not only categorially nameable moral actions. But even the elements of *categorial* religiousness lend one's nameable moral and categorial actions a definite moral enrichment. Such elements might be, for example, knowledge of the person of Christ, the deeper sense of the worth of every man which is comprehended through faith, the significance of statements about the cross for the person who is turned in on himself and who previously could not grasp the religious meaning of his suffering and alienation. These elements, however, can be effective only to the extent that the human person, who also lives in an unredeemed dimension as well, can understand their import. It can also be said that these elements perhaps lead one from knowledge illumined by faith to the fulfillment of behavior patterns already correctly determined in some sort of autonomous fashion, though they now take on a deeper understanding. Should not such values, which have become thematically conscious for the first time because of the Christ-event, also be considered a motive for further correct behavior, arrived at in an essentially rational and autonomous way?

With respect to the virtue of religion, one should note that through the Christ-event new realities have occurred in this area which alter us significantly: a definite understanding of God, the person of Christ, the written Word, a Christian community (the Church) with its own religious and moral accents (and with its own ethos, which is not to be confused with normative morality), sacraments, etc. These new realities are of such importance because religion is an essentially perceptible virtue and one which must be taken into consideration in fulfilling one's moral duty. Nevertheless, religion and morality — this must be repeated once more — have to be conceptually differentiated. It may well be that a Christian allows himself to be motivated to a certain type of this-worldly behavior whose meaningfulness is grounded on purely religious factors which reflect the elements of Christian religion. An example of such would be Christian virginity which, in contrast to other forms of morally meaningful abstinence from marriage, is consciously motivated by categorial elements of Christian religion, just as are many types of behavior by Christians which reflect Christ's teaching on taking up one's cross. What must not be forgotten, however, is that such explicitly Christian acts can and, in fact, do prove to possess a certain human accessibility which is not Christian or religious.

My chief intention here has been to distinguish between definite modes of behavior. On the one hand, there are those which arise from Christian faith and from the religious horizon which corresponds to it; these modes of behavior all imply a deeper enrichment of one's moral life — even of the moral norms and judgments which are not conditioned by *fides* or *religio*. On the other hand, I have also tried to point out the existence of basic moral norms and judgments which are independent of faith. Several moral theologians have adopted the distinction which Norbert J. Rigali[21] has made: (i) *essential* morality (*Wesensethik*), whose immanent meaning is readily accessible to the autonomous process of searching and experiencing in which all persons engage; and (ii) *existential* morality of the individual (*existentielle Ethik des Einzelnen*), which makes possible a decision on the basis of Christian faith and of categorial Christian religion — even in cases which touch on one's immanent behavior in the world — for example, Christian virginity. There is one factor, however, which must be kept in mind as one formulates such a distinction; this is that in a Christian context the essentially autonomous nature of morality de facto always connotes something more than its own immanent meaning and something more than we are accustomed to think or express; this "more" has to do with the way the Christian arrives at norms and understands the meaning of existence. In other words, Christianity brings out the transcendent dimension which belongs to autonomous morality itself! Yet this "more", this new dimension, enjoys primarily not a moral but a religious character, so that it is truly the most profound aspect of moral behavior, even though it is "only" an implicit dimension of such.

IV. THE QUESTION OF EVIDENCE

In the ongoing discussion of the theme "theonomous autonomy — morality of faith," it has gradually become clearer that the so-called question of evidence, that question concerning the possible intellectual avenues for arriving at a normative ethics, is the central problem. Although this problem will cause us to deviate somewhat from the original theme of this chapter as outlined in the introduction and in section I, (1), it still deserves attention. The importance of this issue for our topic is further indicated by the fact that the editor of the *Wörterbuch christlicher Ethik* purposely chose not to include the heading "Autonomy" but decided instead on "Evidence".[22] In the reflections which follow, one ought once again not to lose sight of the scientific and pastoral starting point of this present essay: is a discussion with others concerning objective and correct moral behavior a meaningful possibility or are we necessarily doomed to live in a Christian ghetto? I have in mind discussions between Catholic moral theologians and learned people who either are becoming secularized or are already secularized, with humanists, atheists and other contemporary non-Christian spokesmen. This is a de jure approach to the question. However, there are also de facto approaches to a solution which, because they are essentially different from the de jure solutions, ought to be examined briefly.

1. De Facto Solutions. There are basically two distinct starting points to de facto solutions.

A. The first attempt starts with the unity of the moral act; this unity is understood to result from an at least athematic act of Christian faith at the deepest core of the self. The moral judgment, which is continually sought and found, thus belongs to the very nature of the act of Christian faith. Furthermore, the *fides quae* leads to certain fundamental anthropological implications which as such, or at least in their deepest sense, are only made possible because of faith (e.g., the Christian worth of every person, the definitive Yes of God to the still sinful world, etc.); these implications constitute the privileged laws which are then concretized by the Christian through his attempts at a rational morality (natural law). There is no doubt that this approach represents an impressive attempt to ground ethical norms (and also the norms of natural law) in Christian faith, so that these norms are Christian.[23]

B. Other theologians, both in the past and especially in the last few years, have chosen an essentially different, though not contradictory, approach. According to them, normative moral knowledge is absolutely unique, is rooted in the practical reason and therefore is not simply reducible to metaphysics and logic. Yet the various disciplines of philosophy have the task of reflecting on this original fact of cognitive moral experience.[24] (One might compare this position with that taken in this essay in section II.) Such a moral experience might athematically imply belief in God. What is certain is that it includes an athematic solution to the question of life's meaning; through an explicit or thematic acceptance of Christian, Jewish, Islamic (or other?) faith, such a moral experience is doubtless influenced by the particular thematic faith which is adopted.

2. *De Jure Solutions: Two Different Types.* The de jure solutions can do justice to man's "everyday morality" (*Alltagsethik*) which is normative but rarely reflected in a conscious way; above all, such de jure solutions can address the scientific grounding of normative morality which is so frequently discussed today.

A. *Normative "everyday morality."* I will say only a few words on this point. Many hold that *fides* — what is meant is really *fides christiana* — is absolutely essential for the ethical norms which determine one's daily behavior. But they also believe that faith in the form of *fides athematica* suffices for this purpose. Such a faith would solve the question of life's meaning as well as making the significance of individual human problems more readily intelligible. What is apparently meant here is the case in which a person comes to a positive realization of his fundamental option.

B. *"Absoluteness" and "evidence" in a scientific morality of faith.* The issue at stake is how, allowing of course for different nuances, one establishes a basis for normative morality, in a scientific way. The common thesis is as follows: without *fides quae thematica* it is impossible to establish a basis for morality in a scientific way. Although it is often *fides christiana* which is clearly intended, many arguments in fact presuppose only a faith in God — that is, theism. In the following section, these two starting-points are distinguished as much as possible.

(i) Theism as faith. The decisive questions in this regard are: what if there is no God? What if the human person is *homo absconditus* — that is, completely incomprehensible, especially with respect to the question concerning his origin and goal — and is this not possible precisely because of his sinful character? What if the much talked about "end of metaphysics" is true, and therefore true also the concomitant fact that a priori thought of any kind would only destroy the evidence necessary for morality. These are explosive questions.[25]

The question "What if God does not exist?" does not lie directly within the scope of the problematic concerning whether there is a Catholic "theonomous autonomy". The reason is that Catholic theology is clearly interested in this problematic so as to find rational and autonomous norms on the very basis of its Christian belief in God. Whether God exists or not touches on the problematic in an indirect way, however, insofar as an openly atheistic dialogue-partner perhaps might not expressly want to understand the norm question as a truly moral question. But it also may be that such a dialogue-partner does indeed live out — athematically at least — a positive or negative *optio fundamentalis*, and is therefore at the core of his being not untouched by the moral question. Must not the frequently admitted "pre-rational basic decision" (*vorrationale Urentscheidung* — H. Albert) necessarily be understood only as an "apparent" option — or would not the above-quoted formulation rationally presuppose that genuine certainty on the part of such a dialogue-partner is possible only if he enters into the process of discursive reason? A genuine and positive *optio fundamentalis* generally makes possible a more willing and more profound understanding of the moral problematic, and indeed it likewise already contains an inchoate self-revelation of the God of grace.

As compared with the theses favoring a morality of faith, Vatican I understands the issue concerning *homo absconditus*, especially with regard to the question of his origin and goal, in a somewhat more nuanced way.[26] The Council insists on the ability of reason to attain "natural" knowledge of God as *principium et finis* (this is also understood as moral knowledge). Yet the same Council, and even more so the encyclical *Humani generis*,[27] speak of a morally necessary aid to man's reason through revelation if *homo lapsus* is to arrive at the right use of his reason. How one might, here and now, possibly interpret the word "natural" — by using categories which were not yet at the disposal of the Council — has already been suggested above. Once again: the correct athematic *optio fundamentalis* would be able to turn a discussion about moral norms into one which genuinely treats morality as such. This route to moral discussion is surely more apt than the one which St. Paul took in the first chapter of Romans, where he presumed that atheists had made a culpable option. The human being existing-in-himself (*der bei-sich-selbst-seiende Mensch*) is not totally incomprehensible to himself. Yet one must remember that a person's deep self-consciousness cannot, for obvious reasons, become the objective theme of a dialogue.

What about the apparent "end of metaphysics" and the corresponding difficulty of employing necessary a priori arguments in ethics? It is certainly true that not all philosophers voice themselves in these matters with the same assurance that marks many versions of the "morality of faith"! Besides, as already pointed out, many ethicians, not only at present but in past centuries as well, do not view ethics as directly and necessarily dependent on metaphysics.[28] One could legitimately ask if the "is-ought" problem is not a false premise in may ethical treatises which depend on metaphysics. It could even be the case that metaphysics could gain a great deal from philosophical reflection on ethical experience. And is not the problem of ethical a prioris often overcome for many thinkers — in spite of the manner in which they justify this fact philosophically — in an existential and athematic way? Thus it is, after all, meaningful to speak about normative moral questions!

(ii)   The Christ-event as faith. The questions which arise here, more than in the previous section, touch upon the certainty one can gain with regard to particular categorial norms and judgments. Yet there is one fundamental question which should first be considered: does so-called good and virtuous activity have any meaning if we do not know whether God loves us—and especially if it is undertaken by the likes of us sinners? To what extent can we deal with this issue only within the context of faith? This type of question is one which is generally formulated by Protestant theologians. It is, however, still helpful today. It forces one to reflect in a more forceful way in the fact that (1) "love" can mean many things: is not the acceptance of "meaning" as a "whole" ultimately a certain basic experience of being protected and loved, even if this conviction is arrived at in a way which differs from that which we have experienced through the Christ event? and (2) we ought not confuse "love" itself with definite signs or works of love.

Now let us turn to the question of the certitude of particular moral norms: according to some, absolute certainty can be had only through faith. Yet no one says exactly where concrete norms for living are laid down for us with certainty. Even the recent book, *Acting out of Faith*, which was written from the perspective of an explicit morality of faith, does not manage to do so.[29] It is certainly true that acting out of faith is really living a concrete Christian experience, but *not* on the basis of the absolute, concrete norms which this book presents. On the other hand, many have written quite clearly about what the Bible—I am thinking chiefly of the New Testament—has to say on the matter.[30] Moral theology cannot regard the New Testament simply as a book of norms without employing some hermeneutical tool and method, and without distinguishing between parenesis, on the one hand, and teaching, on the other. This is not to say that the New Testament does not offer us the riches of revelation as divine self-communication, or that it does not contain anthropological implications which follow from such a unique act of God and does not attest to the continually unfolding reality of the Christian people of God (the Church). But when we make concrete the riches of revelation in norms and judgments, by means of anthropological and ethical reflection, and thereby discover a moral life which far surpasses in depth and value anything which we ourselves could create, we must not forget one important factor: what we have unearthed is certainly what the man "of flesh" does not want to recognize, but it is also something which makes the purely *humanum* into a Christian ethos. The latter is as such the same as the former as far as its material content is concerned, but it also what a human-autonomous morality, on its own, cannot grasp.

Furthermore, it can be said that an ethics − even a Christian ethics − does not demand metaphysical evidence for its particular norms and judgments. Moral theology has learned, even in the past, that in moral questions, a true moral certainty (*late dicta*) is the only type of evidence which points out to us a morally binding path in the presence of God and which does so with unconditional certitude. Greater evidence is not necessary for the particular questions which arise. Precisely for this reason there can occasionally be a "mutation" in our knowledge of norms.

(iii)   Dangerous elements and benefits of a morality of faith. The various starting-points of a theological morality, particularly with regard to its normative aspect, doubtless all have their pros and cons. The following remarks refer primarily to the scientific de jure solution which is generally called the morality of faith par excellence.

Let us begin with the dangerous elements. First of all, it is hard to see how that reality which is called the moral natural law or natural right and which can be understood in different ways, can be sufficiently protected in the context of a morality of faith. The danger is still present even when, as is often the case, one speaks of natural law in other terms: *ratio practica (recta)*, *ratio recta (aestimativa)*, *humanum*, human self-realization, etc. Human beings — and the Church — have a pressing need for such an instrument, both as "reason illuminated by faith" (*ratio fide illuminata*) and as "reason which must not be unduly restricted" (*ratio non indebite restringenda*)! Equally dangerous is a one-sided dependence on faith statements which lacks sufficient regard for human (enlightened) reason and anthropology. Even Christocentric theologians as prominent as H.U. von Balthasar recognize the possiblility of an extra-biblical ethics, which, however, he insists must be integrated into salvation history.[31] His well-known nine theses clearly depend to a great extent on his much earlier book on the *Theology of History*.[32] By being open to one or other of these dangers, the morality of faith might, at great cost, lose the ability to communicate with others in society, while we Christians give the impression of apparently enjoying absolute certainty with regard to many moral questions. All this is fine and good, insofar as it is true. As for the others: blessed are the poor, those who are searching diligently!

A word should be said, however, about a benefit of the morality of faith, one that proponents of this approach do not sufficiently make clear—and this fact alone is a disadvantage! I am referring to both the inherent worth and the considerable usefulness of those elements which faith, its implications and consequences can contribute: one who has been enlightened by the various truths of faith can then much more easily appreciate in its full autonomy the rightness and beauty of what he has discovered.

With this statement we have arrived at the positive insights which the morality of faith can furnish. They are, first of all, those elements of Christian reality which place normative morality in the light which is properly its own and for which it was eternally destined in the divine Logos and Redeemer. The morality of faith offers a way of rooting moral action in the self-fulfillment which is faith — a formulation which Fritz Tillmann and others have adopted so as to move from biblicism and fundamentalism to a theological deepening of morality. Finally, such a morality provides Christian values which are meant to promote the humanization of the world and of man himself. The advocates of a theonomous-autonomous approach to morality are well aware that this is the end to which they must commit themselves.

It is fitting that the conclusion of this chapter should call attention to a non-Catholic theologian's words which seem to be written in the very spirit of this chapter. In his introduction to the study of theology, G. Ebeling says: "There is one thing a theologian must be strictly warned about: he should not too quickly set the study of theology on the scales in an attempt to offset and outweigh philosophy, instead of patiently and constantly wrestling with the reasonableness of reason itself."[33]

NOTES

1.   The theme of this essay was suggested to me by the organizers of the 1977 meeting of German-speaking moral theologians. I have not altered it, despite the ample opportunity for doing so. This is because I am convinced that the "autonomous morality" of Catholic theologians is also a form of the morality of faith. The actual circumstance which led to my being invited to present this paper could have been the appearance of my article on this topic in *Stimmen der Zeit* (1970). This article was not written for moral theologians, but was the formal rendition of a talk to the Catholic student center in Zurich. I had never expected that my reflections on this theme, along with the thorough study by A. Auer (1971), *Autonome Moral und christlicher Glaube*, would have sparked so much theological debate in various countries. For the reaction in Italy, cf. S. Bastianel, "Il carattere specifico della morale cristiana; una riflessione dal dibattito italiano", *Quaderni di teologia morale* 13, Assisi 1975. For Germany, cf. also S. Privitera, *L'uomo e la norma morale; i criteri delle norme morali secondo i teologi morali di lingua tedesca, (Studi e ricerche)*, 21, Bologna 1975.

2.   Vatican II, *Gaudium et spes*, n. 46.

3.   Ibid., n. 33; cf. also nn. 4, 62, 75, 84, 93, etc. There are similar remarks to be found in the Decree on the Missions.

4.   N.J. Rigali, "New Epistemology and the Moralist", *Chicago Studies* 11 (1972), 237-44, especially 243.

5.   Cf. J.M. Gustafson, *Can Ethics Be Christian?*, Chicago-London 1975.

6.   This is essentially the thesis which H.U. von Balthasar presents in "Neun Sätze zur chrstlichen Ethik", in J. Ratzinger (ed.), *Prinzipien christlicher Moral*, Einsiedeln 1975, 67-93.

7.   Cf. E. Zenger, "Leib und Geschlechtlichkeit: Biblische und kulturges-

chichtliche Aspekte", in F. Böckle (ed.), *Menschliche Sexualität und kirchliche Sexualmoral. Ein Dauerkonflikt?*, Düsseldorf 1977, 51-73, especially 72.

8.   Cf. E. Schillebeeckx, *Glaubensinterpretation. Beiträge zu einer hermeneutischen und kritischen Theologie*, Mainz 1971, 97.

9.   E. Przywara, *Crucis mysterium. Das christliche Heute*, Paderborn 1933, 68, cited by A. Auer, "Die Autonomie des Sittlichen nach Thomas von Aquin" in K. Demmer and B. Schüller (eds.), *Christlich glauben und handeln*, Düsseldorf 1977, 45.

10.   Cf. various contributions of K. Demmer, e.g. "Moralische Norm und theologische Anthropologie", *Gregorianum* 54 (1973), 263-305, especially 267-71; "Kirchliches Lehramt und Naturrecht", *Theologie und Glaube* 59 (1969), 191-213; "Die Weisungskompetenz des kirchlichen Lehramtes im Licht der spezifischen Perspektivierung neutestamentlicher Sittlichkeit", in K. Demmer and B. Schüller (eds.) op. cit., 124-44.

11.   As a scientific and methodical reflection on the moral fulfillment which faith brings, moral theology likewise needs argumentation based on man's natural rights. Cf. B. Fraling, "Glaube und Ethos. Normfindung in der Gemeinschaft der Gläubigen", *Theologie und Glaube* 63 (1973), 81-105, especially 103.

12.   For a study of moral experience, cf. R. Egenter, *Erfahrung ist Leben. Über die Rolle der Erfahrung für das sittliche und religiöse Leben des Christen*, Munich 1974. For a study of the role of moral experience for morality in general, as presented by contemporary Polish moral theologians, cf. H. Juros and T. Styczen in *Theologische Berichte* 4, Zurich-Einsiedeln-Cologne 1974; T. Styczen, "Autonome und christliche Ethik als methodologisches Problem", *Theologie und Glaube* 66 (1976), 211-19. Cf. also the similar essay of E. McDonagh, in *Gift and Call: Towards a Christian Theology of Morality*, Dublin-St. Meinrad, Indiana 1975. Also important are K. Rahner's essays in transcendental philosophy and theology, especially "Ziel des Menschen" in *Sacramentum Mundi*, vol. 4, 1429-39 and by J.B. Metz, "Befindlichkeit" in *LThK* 2, vol. 2, and by K. Demmer, "Elementi base di un' antropologia cristiana" in T. Goffi (ed.), *Problemi e prospettive di teologia morale*, Brescia 1976, 31-84; cf. also W. Korff, *Theologische Ethik, Eine Einführung*, Freiberg 1975, e.g. pp. 30ff, and A. Auer, op. cit., pp. 38ff, who relies on W. Kluxen, *Philosophische Ethik bei Thomas von Aquin* (Walberger Studien), Mainz 1974.

13.   Cf. J.B. Metz, op. cit.

14.   H. Juros and T. Styczen, op. cit., 89-108, especially 104ff.

15.   J. de Finance, "Autonomie e théonomie", *Gregorianum* 56 (1975), 207-35, especially 230ff.

16.   M. Serenthà, "A proposito di antropologia teologica", *La Scuola Cattolica* 103 (1975), 256-68, especially 267f.

17.   *S.T.* I-II, q. 102, a. 2 ad 1.

18.   Ibid. and 100, 1.

19.   J.B. Metz, "Theologische und metaphysische Ordnung", *Zeitschrift für katholische Theologie* 83 (1961), 1-14, especially 8.

20. D. Sölle, *Phantasie und Gehorsam. Überlegungen zu einer künftigen christlichen Ethik*, 3rd ed., Stuttgart 1968.
21. N.J. Rigali, loc. cit., 242.
22. B. Stoeckle (ed.), *Wörterbuch christlicher Ethik* (Herderbücherei, 533), Freiburg 1975.
23. This type is found, for example, in the various contributions of K. Demmer (see note 10 above); natural law (autonomy) is taken quite seriously in his work.
24. Cf. the previously cited attempts of Polish moral theologians and also the work of E. McDonagh; both of these are referred to in note 12 above.
25. These and the following questions should be compared above all with similar statements in: B. Stoeckle, "Autonome Morale", *Stimmen der Zeit* 191 (1973), 723-36; *Grenzen der autonomen Moral*, Munich 1974; "Evidenz" in *Wörterbuch christlicher Ethik*, Freiburg 1975. Cf. also H. Rotter, "Die Eigenart der christlichen Ethik", *Stimmen der Zeit* 191 (1973), 406-16; "Kann das Naturrecht die Moraltheologie entbehren?" *Zeitschrift für katholische Theologie* 96 (1974), 76-96; *Grundlagen der Moral. Überlegungen zu einer moraltheologischen Hermeneutik*, Zurich-Einsiedeln-Cologne 1975.
26. Cf. DS 3004 and 3026.
27. Cf. DS 3875.
28. Compare this with section II above, "Ethical Experience".
29. B. Stoeckle, *Handeln aus dem Glauben. Moraltheologie konkret*, Freiburg-Basle-Vienna 1977.
30. B. Schüller, "Zur Diskussion über das Proprium einer christlichen Ethik", *Theologie und Philosophie* 51 (1976), 321-43; cf. also Schüller's review of J. Ratzinger (ed.), *Prinzipien christlicher Moral*, Einsiedeln 1975, in *Theologische Revue* 73 (1977), 143-5.
31. Cf. J. Ratzinger, op. cit.
32. H.U. von Balthasar, *Theologie der Geschichte*, 3rd ed., Einsiedeln 1959.
33. G. Ebeling, *Studium der Theologie, Eine enzyklopädische Orientierung*, Tübingen 1975, 67.

Norm and Responsibility

7. The Absoluteness of Behavioral Moral Norms

Christ's mission was not to establish a new moral order, new moral laws. Nor was it his primary intent to teach a moral doctrine corresponding to creation. The significance of his coming was rather to redeem sinful mankind, to transform man interiorly by grace, to make him one who believes and loves. Loving faith must and will bear fruit; it must express and verify itself in morally correct conduct, i.e., by doing what is right, thus giving witness to the truth by "doing the truth" — *testimonium veritati*. In the dynamism of faith and love, the Christian is concerned not only with living in faith and love, but also with carrying them out by a way of life proper to man as Christian. Indeed, faith, love and salvation do not depend upon the rectitude of the norms of living that are basic to one's life practice. Yet faith and love are not genuine if there is no effort to manifest through one's life practice the right mode of life, i.e., corresponding to the reality of human-Christian existence. Thus, in the dynamism of faith and love, the problem of the absoluteness of moral norms arises in this present age of uncertainty and revolution. Have we perhaps overstressed the absoluteness of our system of moral norms, and precisely for this reason failed to achieve the right life practice as an expression of our faith and love? Or are we perhaps at the point of renouncing the absoluteness of an inherited system of moral norms, and so running the risk of faith and love no longer manifesting themselves in the "right" day-to-day manner?

No small number of convinced Christians are allergic to "absolute" norms — not, indeed, to the possiblity of "right", "objective", and therefore "absolutely" binding judgment in concrete instances, and consequently the possibility of moral imperatives too, but to "universally binding" and in *this* sense absolute norms of moral action. They make their judgment on experiential grounds, so that what was yesterday an absolute, i.e., presented as always and without exception right, must today yield to other insights. They fear that the so-called absolutes, or universally valid norms characteristic of a static world-view, cannot be absolute for men of a dynamic world-view. They hold that the cultural fact of the discovery of moral norms in the past cannot be taken as a final conculsion, or rather, that man must always address himself anew to this fact, in order to examine the conclusions reached, to deepen and enlarge and adduce new experiences and evaluations. Their great concern is that abstract and therefore timeless and in *this* sense "absolute" norms do not perhaps take due account of the times; i.e., are not sufficiently realistic and responsive to the concrete mode of reality represented by (redeemed) creation; and that consequently they can obscure rather than illuminate the "objective" and in *this* sense "absolute" task of the present day. That this concern for relevant behavior on the part of the believing and loving Christian and for absolute fidelity to the order of (redeemed) creation in its concrete manifestations is genuinely "Catholic" is unquestionable.

Other convinced Catholics incline toward a view just as typically "Catholic". They fear that with the dissolution of so-called absolute ordinances and norms, in the sense of "universally valid" and "timeless" truths, truth itself will be lost. They think that if "absoluteness", understood as "immutability" and "universal validity" yields to the principle of change and historical conditioning, then faithfulness to reality, i.e., to (redeemed) creation, will no longer determine concrete action as the expression of faith and love, but will be replaced by a relativistic subjectivism. They presume that deviation from absoluteness (i.e., timelessness and immutability) might imply also a swerving from absoluteness understood as objectivity oriented to the reality of the (redeemed) created order.

Basically, both tendencies share the same interest: the believing-loving Christian must concern himself with recognizing the absolutely valid, or that which always corresponds objectively to the concrete human (Christian) reality in a moral matter. For this is the Will of God based on creation and redemption — so that what is objectively right partakes somehow in the absoluteness of God. The problem is whether and in what degree the absolute — in the sense of the objective as applied to universal or universally valid norms — is conceivable or in any sense guaranteed. When we address ourselves to this question, we do so in the conviction that global solutions of the problem are not solutions; nuanced consideration is required. Neither the opinion that love should be the sole moral absolute nor the conception of natural moral law as an all-embracing set of invariable norms is satisfactory, although there is some truth in both these points of view. It will not escape the informed reader that the problematic thus presented is of importance not only for (Catholic) circles within the Church — particularly in the present climate of "uncertainty" — but also for dialogue with those non-Catholic Christians who are experiencing and dealing with the same problematic on a broad scale, and with all men concerned with genuine morality. For God will judge Christians, Jews and pagans alike according to their works (cf. Rom. 2:9-11), the righteousness of which they can know fundamentally in their "hearts" (cf. Rom 2:15). Accordingly, the following considerations are limited to the shaping of life within the world, i.e., innerworldly actions, those relating man and his world.[1]

I. ABSOLUTE: UNIVERSALLY VALID OR OBJECTIVE?

Absoluteness in moral imperatives is directly opposed, obviously, to all arbitrary judgment and to all relativism, and thereby positively affirms the objectivity grounded in human reality itself. The real problem, we repeat, lies in determining to what degree the absolute, in the sense of the nonarbitrary but objective, is comprehensible and guaranteed in the case of universally valid norms. We are accustomed to having moral ordinances placed before us in the guise of norms purporting to be universally valid: in revelation (Holy Scripture), in the teaching of the Church, in the formulated tenets of the natural moral law, conscience finds itself confronted with moral imperatives in the form of moral norms. In what follows we shall consider what degree of the absolute character of norms is implied in each of the individual instances.

1. Norms in Holy Scripture. Moral imperatives in Holy Scripture are of the greatest interest, for God's world has absolute value, since he is The Absolute. And since he speaks, therefore, via human concepts and so in terms of universals, Christianity with good reason has been inclined to understand the moral precepts found in Holy Scripture as universal, ever valid and unchangeable norms and, in this sense, as "absolute". On the other hand, God's speaking in human mode signifies that the moral imperatives appearing in Holy Scripture should not be interpreted as direct divine "dictates". Thus we are inevitably faced not only with the question as to which moral imperatives are actually to be found in Holy Scripture, but also with the question by which hermeneutic rules they are to be understood and evaluated.[2] There is no doubt that here moral theology will have to go to school to contemporary exegesis, to avoid lapsing into unauthorized good-will reading.

Holy Scripture was never meant to be a handbook on morality: consequently it may not be so used. Inasmuch as it speaks of

God's ways with mankind, it must speak also of man's behavior
— his religio-moral behavior — toward God. Indeed, since Scripture is concerned with the conversion and salvation of the sinner,
and therefore with his personal transformation, statements regarding the religio-moral situation of man are central to the Bible.
Nevertheless, it is not the particular moral imperatives which have
this central position, but the fundamental imperative of fidelity and
obedience to God, of the following of Christ, of life according to faith
and baptism or, as with John, according to faith and love. But *these*
moral-religious imperatives are transcendental — that is, they refer
to the personal human being as a whole and not to specific moral
conduct. And even though Holy Scripture speaks also of particular
attitudes and values — goodness, mildness, mercy, justice, mod-
esty — these are still not operative norms of behavior, since it has
yet to be determined which actions are to be regarded as just, mod-
est and kind. Certainly, Scripture knows operative norms of conduct
as well — a few at least. The question is precisely with reference to
these, insofar as the absoluteness of moral norms is the point at
issue.

We shall limit ourselves to the New Testament. References
there to concrete moral behavior, norms of activity, are relatively
few; but these few are important. The critical question is: In what
sense are they absolute—in the sense of objective, nonarbitrarily
grounded imperatives or, more than that, universal norms admitting
of no exception? The answer to this question is not altogether easy.

The Christian centuries have tried earnestly to understand the
demands of the Sermon on the Mount (Matt. 5-7). No Christian
doubts their absolute validity, absolute to be understood in the sense
of objective. The question is: absolute validity, as what — as universal norms, or as models for the behavior of the believing and loving
citizens of God's kingdom who will be ready for such modes of conduct, perhaps, under certain conditions not individually specified by
the Lord? The latter interpretation seems probable from the context
and manner of expression. In recent years there has been renewed
and heated discussion of the Lord's words about the indissolubility
of marriage (Matt. 19:3-10). Regarding the scope of these words, it is
asked: Is it a question of a moral imperative or of something more?
Is the moral imperative to be understood as a norm to be followed as
universal practice or as an ideal? The discussion makes at least this
much clear: The acceptance of an absolute in the sense of an objectively valid moral affirmation in Scripture does not necessarily involve recognizing it as an absolute in the sense of a universal norm.

It should be noted first of all that while Paul ascribes to the Lord definite sayings regarding moral behavior (indissolubility of marriage: 1 Cor. 7:10 f.) and attributes others to his own personal understanding in the Holy Spirit (virginity: 1 Cor. 7, 12,25), he presupposes that most of the behavioral norms of which he speaks are valid. This is particularly to be inferred from the many ordinances in which he accepts the moral wisdom of the "good" men of his time, both Jew and Gentile; one thinks, among other things, of the tables of domestic rules and the catalogue of vices. On the one hand, this means that Paul does not present himself as a teacher of moral living, still less as a teacher of specifically Christian norms of conduct; what he does have to transmit is something quite different from a moral code. On the other hand, his having assumed a given morality can lead us to consider whether such a morality, at least in many of its regulations, is not historically and culturally conditioned. It could scarcely be supposed that the Stoic, Judaic and Diaspora-Judaic ethos which Paul represents was in all respects a timeless ethos. If it is self-evident to us today that the Pauline directives concerning woman's position in marriage, society and the Church (1 Cor. 11:2-16; 14,34-6; Eph. 5:22-4; Col. 3:18; 1 Tim. 2:11-15) are to be regarded as conditioned by his times, reflecting Jewish tradition and the position of woman in the culture in which Paul and his contemporaries lived, we must indeed ask ourselves according to what criterion we decide that those directives which Paul seeks to validate, even theologically, are historically conditioned and thus not absolute (i.e. universal), and that they hold as absolute in the objective sense rather for the age whose ideas on the position of women they reflect. Consequently, such directives cannot be normative for a period in which the social position of women is essentially different. Holy Scripture itself gives us no criteria for such a judgment, but it comes from our knowledge of the difference in the social position of women in various ages together with our own insight into moral imperatives which arises out of various social situations. This same power of discernment will permit us perhaps to make a judgment – at least in principle – as to which suits the nature of women in society better, and hence is the moral ideal, the social position of women in Paul's cultural milieu or that of women in our cultural milieu – along with corresponding moral demands.

By analogy with the instance of woman's position in marriage, society and the Church, a further question inevitably arises: whether the possibility of similar considerations regarding other behavioral norms to be found in the Pauline corpus is to be absolutely excluded —on the theoretical level at least, especially since the criteria for such reflections are not provided us by Holy Scripture itself. For the affirmation that certain explicitly mentioned modes of conduct ban one from the kingdom of God, from companionship with Christ and from the life given by the Spirit remains true if these modes are to be judged negatively, in accordance with the moral evaluation proper to that age and accepted by Paul. Paul therefore did not teach such evaluation as thesis, but admitted it as hypothesis in his doctrinal statement on the Christian mystery of salvation. Thus it remains to be established whether in Paul's cultural milieu, because of the actual conviction of the morally high-ranking segment of society, every "honorable" Christian had to share this conviction exactly, or whether this conviction was the only objectively justified one and was not based on definite options.

(In Paul we have actually a model for "Christian" discovery of moral norms. With him such discovery derives neither from Christ alone nor from the Old Testament alone. It occurs within an existing culture and as a consequence of its established moral values. It draws from Jewish tradition and from Greek popular philosophy, just as it carries along the culture in which Christianity took root. This does not exclude the fact that Paul himself also reflects upon the values he found already present, as, for example, the social position of women, and that, in particular cases, he himself independently − in the Holy Spirit—recommends practices like virginity or that he appeals to the word of the Lord.)

The foregoing considerations obviously do not permit us to conclude that the norms of behavior found in the New Testament are no longer valid today. Only, we must reflect whether the criterion of their possible absolute (i.e., universal) validity is Holy Scripture itself, whether it can be and is intended to be.[3] The moral behavioral norms in Scripture are directed to actual persons of a definite era and culture. Hence their character of absoluteness would not signify primarily universality, but objectivity; and the latter can denote either the objectively right evaluation in a particular culturally conditioned human situation or necessary conformity to the moral views of the morally elite in a given society.

2. Norms of the Ecclesial Community. Neither from Christ nor from Paul or John has the Church inherited a system of moral norms. On the other hand, the ecclesial community − how could it be otherwise? − always maintained definite moral norms and passed them on to later generations. But in this connection it may by no means be said that there was ever in the Church a definitive or in all respects universal code of precepts. Nevertheless, the Church community had "its" morality which, even if it did not derive purely from revelation, was regarded as being connected with or compatible with Christian belief. This morality — as being the morality of the Christian community — was "Christian" morality. Insofar as it had been handed down, it was a more or less codified morality, which just for this reason was lived in the one Church in different cultures and epochs. Naturally, this brief exposition is a simplification. But it enables us to understand how the Church, unlike Paul, begins not only to set forth dogmatically particular moral concepts — indissolubility of marriage (word of the Lord) and virginity (Paul's opinion, in the Holy Spirit) — but in principle the whole compass of the morality practiced by the Christian community, which Paul had not taught but rather "presupposed", as also did the Church after Paul with regard to many questions. While Paul, earlier, expressed himself *in obliquo* and hypothetically on moral questions, the Church slowly began to do this *in recto* and dogmatically. The Church teaches *in rebus fidei et morum* and indeed, as she repeatedly declared during Vatican Council II, also on moral questions about which she has had no explicit revelation. Now the question: If the Church addresses herself thematically and dogmatically to moral questions, have we then pronouncements that are true universals? Is the claim of absoluteness for the norms transmitted by the Church a claim of universal norms? Does the Church give us thereby a system of universal morally valid norms which God has not given us in Holy Scripture?

In general, then, unlike Paul, the Church "teaches" norms of moral conduct. Why, really? The answer often given runs: Because the Church has to teach the way to salvation and true morality is the way to salvation. This answer might be considered valid if taken *cum grano salis*. For ultimately there is the question whether marriage, for example, is to be understood and lived according to Congolese or Western European style; surely not an unimportant cultural and ethical question, but not in itself determinative of salvation. Still the matter admits of a different interpretation. The manner in which faith and love — which do determine salvation! — are expressed in daily life, by premarital abstinence or premarital intercourse, for example, is not a matter of totally free choice. And since man must strive to incarnate his faith and love in the "true" way of human beings, the Church assists him by her "teaching". Clearly, this answer also does not entirely satisfy. In any case, it remains true that the materiality of culturally and ethically right mastery of the concrete reality of life — education, economy, technology, sexuality, etc. — is not directly concerned with salvation, or union with God; only faith and love, together with the effort to incarnate this materiality in the "true" way in the reality of life are thus concerned.

That the material mode of this incarnation can represent only a *secundarium*, already makes it reasonable that within certain limits moral pluralism might well be possible. If, for example, faith and love have to be expressed in the maintenance of the "right" social position of woman, then the concrete expressions in the Pauline conception and in the twentieth century Western European conception must (!) be regarded as necessarily differing from each other. Yet the Christian community is obliged to see to it that moral behavior as an expression of faith and love does not come down to fulfilling one's own wishes; it must not fail to manifest the unconditional character of faith and love by unconditionality in stating moral precepts. However, it could follow from what has been said that this quality of absoluteness does not represent primarily the universality of a norm, but an antithesis to arbitrary judgment; or, positively stated, orientation toward concrete human (total) reality, and, in this sense, objectivity, truth. This objectivity-truth is achieved, on the one hand, through right understanding of the revealed word of God, insofar as it contains morally significant affirmations; on the other hand, through the right moral understanding of man's concrete reality, in which connection, obviously, the light of revelation and the moral understanding of man are not to be viewed as two completely unrelated possibilities.

With respect to norms of moral behavior, the light of the Gospel does not manifest itself in formally expressed statements alone. Rather, there is also the possibility suggested by Vatican II in the Constitution on the Church in the Modern World, when reference is made to the necessity of judging contingent realities in the world of men in light of the Gospel.[4] Edward Schillebeeckx alludes to this statement;[5] nevertheless, he is of the opinion that the Christian, on the basis of his faith, can more easily assert negatively the incompatibility of a given social situation with his faith than discover positively how the situation might be changed. Karl Rahner has spoken, in the sense of Vatican II, of a moral faith-instinct.[6] Maurizio Flick and Zoltán Alszeghy have pursued in greater detail the question of the significance of the Gospel — which itself gives no directives — for moral judgment of contingent human realities.[7] They maintain that it is possible, especially for a believer, to draw "an objective picture of revealed reality" on the basis of the content of revelation. Inasmuch as the development of dogma has often been indebted to such an "objective picture," a great deal might be gained for the proper mastering of concrete human reality via such an "objective picture." However, they are also of the opinion that actual problems — those, for example, pertaining to development and progress — can find direct solutions neither in the Gospel and faith, nor in theology, but only in a Christian ideology, which, of course, must be approached in terms of the eventual possibility of a critique by the Gospel and theology (and their "objective picture of revealed reality"). Only on this condition can a "political theology" venture an attempt to make the Gospel and faith effective for the reality of the world.[8] The "imperatives,"[9] known or determined by a "political theology," do not follow directly from faith and the Gospel, therefore, but only from an ethical interpretation ("political ethics"). And this ethics is "human" ethics; it is theological only to the extent that it has been projected by the believer as an imperative of a Christian theology which, in turn, depends in any case on an "objective picture of revealed reality."[10] It need scarcely be said that the imperatives of a Christian theology so projected are not absolutes in the sense of universalia. They represent the attempt to be as objectively relevant as possible to given realities through man's reflection in light of the Gospel, as described above; they are not to be arbitrary precepts, therefore, but the most objective possible, and in this reduced sense, absolutes.

The assistance of the Holy Spirit has been promised to the Church's endeavors. Inasmuch as the Church, to a far greater extent than Holy Scripture, has begun to address herself directly and dogmatically to moral questions, she becomes, in a much higher degree than the Scripture, concretely important because of the assistance of the Spirit of Christ. Some concepts of moral theology create the impression that the Holy Spirit slowly began to impart via the Church what he had not conveyed through Scripture — a vast collection of moral behavioral norms proclaimed for the whole world and for all time; *absoluta*, in the sense of universally valid norms. However, under this aspect, the Church is seen often in an all too spiritualized way; how very much the Spirit is merely "incarnated" in the Church is overlooked, in other words, how very human the Church is and remains despite the assistance of the Spirit. She arrives at norms of moral conduct only by way of a long process of learning to understand and to evaluate. And this comprehension and evaluation are accomplished not only by the hierarchy of the ecclesial community who, it may be, ultimately provide a decisive orientation, but by the Church as a whole, within the community of believers — where a special role often falls to the theologians.

It is not true that a moral question is submitted to the pastors of the Church, so that in solitary reflection thay can reach an authoritative decision. Before there is a question of "decision" the "teaching" Church is in all instances a "learning" Church. The Spirit assists the whole process of teaching and leading in the Church—i.e., comprehending, discovering, evaluating, mutual listening, deciding.[11] He guarantees that error, which in human comprehension-discovery-evaluation-listening-deciding can never be absolutely excluded, will not become in the end an essential component of the Church. It stands to reason, then, that the same ecclesial community or a particular cultural group within it — pluralistic, therefore — will at times begin to experience and evaluate in a new and different way, regarding specific points. In this connection it is noteworthy that in the Church's two thousand years, seemingly no definitive doctrinal decision on moral questions has been made, at least insofar as these would be related to natural law, without being at the same time revealed. On the other hand, this is not to say that the nondefinitive authoritative guidelines of the Church are meaningless, as if one might ignore them, oblivious to the fact that they also come under the assistance of the Spirit of Christ abiding with the Church. Hence a certain presumption of truth must be granted them. Yet one may not see in such instances any conclusive legislation or doctrinal definition of an ethical norm whose validity would be guaranteed by the Holy Spirit. Declarations by the Church *in rebus morum* can be understood in all cases as attempts to formulate "absolute" — i.e. nonarbitrary, but objective — imperatives, properly conformed to a concrete human reality and expressed in terms of a presumptively valid ecclesial orientation. If, on the contrary, such pronouncements had the assurance of infallibility, they could be set forth as universally valid norms, guaranteed to hold true always, everywhere and without exception. But even in such a case there would have to be a reservation; for it can be imagined and probably demonstrated, if need be, that a strict behavioral norm, stated as a universal, contains unexpressed conditions and qualifications which as such limit its universality.

The Church arrives at moral pronouncements — in the sphere of natural law morality, at least — via man's reflection on himself. But man — also a Christian and a member of the Church — is not a static being, whose nature is incapable of development. Thus, new questions will come up because of new experiences, insights and evaluations in a new light and a changed culture. Even the Christian is obliged to question in retrospect, to go back to the past in order to find out what was once believed in the Church — even authoritatively, perhaps — about the right way to embody faith and love concretely. And more than this, without losing contact with the Christian wisdom of the past, he must always be thinking out various questions that affect his life in this way or that at different times.[12] It cannot be that the Christian and ecclesial past (from which year to which year?) enjoyed the prerogative of finding the (nonrevealed) "truth" about moral behavior, while later Christians would have only the task of recording, confirming, applying the "truth" of the past—conclusive, absolute and universal in the strict sense—without advertence to really new problems never before reflected upon or resolved. Furthermore, it often happens that old problems presenting themselves in a new guise are, at bottom, new problems. Also, it is scarcely conceivable that all Church traditions or decisions concerning moral behavioral norms would be in the full sense timeless and unconditioned, i.e., absolute, completely explicit and not in some respect conditioned either by fixed ideas or value judgments or by man's limited understanding of himself.[13] For example, the Church's opposition in the past to religious freedom is understandable if religious freedom and indifferentism are equated conceptually. Moreover, it is today an historical fact that the sexual morality handed down in the Church came under the influence of certain non-Christian (Jewish and pagan) evaluations in the first Christian centuries and is conditioned by them. The Church is not a "spiritualized" reality, thinking, speaking and existing in a vacuum, unrelated to any culture, and under such conditions devising norms of moral conduct that are in the purest sense "universal." But if norms of conduct can include culturally and historically conditioned elements, only then is there a possibility that they can be expressed in a manner that will respond to concrete human reality; i.e., be objective and, in this sense, absolute. ("Can" means here that even in the moral judgment of a real situation, the Church could err.)

3. *The Natural Moral Law.* If Holy Scripture and the Church do not provide a system of universal moral norms, one expects this at least from the moral law of nature (natural moral law, natural moral order, order of creation, natural law). A well-defined concept of natural law underlies this expectation. Natural law is understood to be the summary of precepts which are based on the given and unvarying nature of man as such and which can be deduced from it. In his critical study, *The Natural Law Yesterday and Today*,[14] E. Chiavacci terms this concept "preceptive." According to this view, "immutable" nature points out to the man who "reads" and "understands" her what right behavior can and must be once and for all in the different areas of reality. A concept of this sort ends in a codifiable summation of the numerous precepts of natural law, which, because rooted in an unchangeable nature, are unvarying and universal. Thus it is maintained that all these precepts (norms) are to be applied in actual life situations — appropriately, to be sure, but unequivocally.

This notion of a static-universal system of norms is valid to the extent that it believes man is and always will be man (tautology!) and that he must always conduct himself rightly — that is, as man. But this quite accurate perception does not entail as a necessary consequence a static-universal system of moral norms. In the first place, the state of being man does not exclude that the human state may differ in different epochs and cultures, just as it is actualized in different individuals and life situations without placing man's nature in question. Against this assertion of the unchangeableness of human nature stands Aquinas' affirmation of its mutability.[15] The two positions are not in conflict if man, his component structures and even his ways of being human, together with their structures, are differentiated rather than divided. Only there must be no attempt to distinguish what precisely is changeable from what is unchangeable. For even that which essentially constitutes man, that which therefore belongs unalterably to his nature, as also his permanent structures, is basically mutable. Mutability belongs to man's immutable essence; irrevocably, man is man (tautology!). To be sure, a priori, some essential elements of man's nature can be identified: body-soul unity, personality, accountability, interpersonality; while one cannot say with equal a priori validity, respecting other components of existential man, whether they belong necessarily and unchangeably to human nature. But even these a priori and inalienable elements of man's nature subsist in it in variable modes, a fact which can be correspondingly significant for moral behavior.

Second, the question of mutability-immutability is connected with man's historicity.[16] History is possible only in virtue of the mutability of that which remains ever the same. Now man is an historical being, not only in terms of the successive variations of past, present and future, but above all, in the sense that man himself designs and brings to realization the plot-lines of his given existence and its progress into the future. He has to actualize what is sketched out for him as possibility. In the process of his self-realization he continually modifies his existence. In his spiritual and bodily aspects and his external relationships (environmental change), he becomes to an ever increasing degree a different person. Morality would have him live rightly the actual man, i.e., the man (humanity) of each actual moment, the present with the past enfolded within it and the projective future: that is, starting from each present reality he should "humanize" himself and his world. Whatever leads to our unfolding, in the fullest and best sense of the word, is good.[17]

Third, mutability and historicity are connected with the fact that man is person and nature in one. Person and nature can be placed counter to each other, so that nature expresses the intrapersonal given of man and his world, while person respresents the I, possessing and shaping itself in terms of the given nature. However, one's personhood also is given and in this sense it is nature, indeed the determining element of one's humanness, and in this sense of human nature. The man consists above all in his being a person (i.e., possessing *ratio*). Nature is not understood as human, unless it is thought of as a personal nature. Thus, it is not enough to say nature (for example, sexuality) "belongs to" the human person.[18] For then it would be possible to understand nature (sexuality) as nonpersonal;[19] hence one could speak of the meaning of sexuality, rather than of the meaning of *human* sexuality, and make the consideration of this meaning (i.e., sexuality) a moral problem for the person reflecting upon his sexuality. The term "law of nature" is not merely open to misunderstanding; it frequently is responsible for it. It would be possible and perhaps more meaningful to speak of "person" as moral norm instead of "nature".[20] But then there would be the danger that "personhood" would be viewed too onesidedly; that is, with practically no consideration of nature, provided person and nature are to be thus differentiated. In any case, nature, considered infrapersonally, cannot be the norm of moral behavior. Rather, man is essentially person and has to understand himself therefore as person — "in a human nature" — and achieve self-realization according to this self-understanding. Self-realization entails that he himself must discover the available possibilities for his action and development, and determine on the basis of his present understanding of himself which of these possibilities are right, reasonable, human (in the full and positive sense of these words), and so contributive to human progress. In this way, he arrives simultaneously at the moral judgment of a concrete situation and the affirmation of moral norms.

In reality, this is tantamount to the traditional statement that the *lex naturalis* is a *lex interna* (or *indita*), not a *lex externa* (or *scripta*). The preceptive understanding of natural law as a summary of precepts conformable to nature is not quite in keeping with this traditional concept; for, thus, a *lex interna* becomes furtively a *lex externa*, resembling general positive or positively formulated laws. The *lex interna* signifies the possibility and duty of man (humanity) to discern, as he himself evaluates himself, what in concrete "human" action here is capable of being — inasmuch as man is essentially person-reason — and what can be affirmed propositionally in the problem area of "behavioral norms." Here we are obviously dealing with moral perceptions of an absolute nature. but it is equally obvious that absolute means at least primarily correspondence of behavior to personal human reality; objectivity, therefore, and not, or at least not primarily, universal validity.

4. Conscience. As explained according to traditional manuals, the function of conscience was the application of the moral law, or its norms, to the concrete case, a formulation founded on a "preceptive" understanding of the moral law, oriented to the specificity of positive law. The traditional statement naturally has some validity; in forming the dictates of conscience, we never begin at pure zero. We always bring to our actions existing orientations and norms. Yet conscience — as judgment of concrete action — is not only, and not on the deepest level, the application of general norms. Knowledge of the essential function of conscience casts light also on the essence and meaning of behavioral norms.[21]

The function of conscience is to help man, as agent, make his action authentic (i.e., self-realizing). Hence conscience ought to assist action toward objectivity, toward truth, in conformity with the concrete human reality. It is necessary above all that action be conformable to the evaluating judgment (of conscience) with respect to the given concrete moment and its options. For this judgment itself belongs, at the moment of action, to the concrete human reality; it is, so to speak, its final form, so that the agent is enabled to realize himself only by fidelity to this judgment (mediating truth to him, yet erring occasionally). Clearly, for this very reason, the agent must strive for objectivity in forming this judgment regarding the concrete reality — i.e., that *ratio*, which makes the judgment may be *recta ratio*. (The terms *ratio, recta ratio*, derive from Scholastic tradition. Here they signify, rather than specifically discursive thinking, an evaluative observing-understanding-judging, which can also occur "intuitively".) Now the behavioral norms of the moral law should also be *recta ratio*; only insofar as they are *recta ratio*, are they behavioral norms and can they, as such, objectively have a meaning for the function of conscience as *recta ratio* in action. The difference between judgment of conscience and norm of action consists basically in the fact that man with his evaluating *ratio* forms a moral judgment of his conduct *either* at the moment of action and in reference to it *or* in advance and not with reference to the actuality of the particular event as such. In terms of the concrete situation, then, it is clear that the norm of action cannot represent an exhaustive judgment of the actual reality, and that the actor must judge in light of his conscience to what degree a norm of conduct corresponds morally to a given situation.

As only the *ratio* (*recta ratio*) of conscience judges the reality ultimately and comprehensively in terms of the concrete element in it that is to be actualized, the *ratio* (*recta ratio*) of behavioral norms exercises merely an auxiliary function. As a consequence, the decisive aspect of such norms is that they are *recta ratio*, hence their objectivity; to the extent that they are objective, they are absolute. Of course, they can be behavioral norms only insofar as they are discernible in advance; therefore they are necessarily abstract and in some way generalized. Further consideration is called for on this point.

II. THE ABSOLUTENESS OF HUMAN BEHAVIORAL NORMS

The title of this section requires clarification. Our previous reflection on behavioral norms in Holy Scripture, Church teaching and natural law, should have made it evident that the affirmations in Scripture and in the teaching of the Church on absolute norms of behavior are not as definitive as might be supposed, particularly if the absoluteness denoted is to be primarily synonymous with universality. In addition to this, Christian behavioral norms, in their material content, are not distinctively Christian norms that would hold only for Christians, but "human" norms, i.e., corresponding to the (authentic) humanness of man, which we have traditionally called norms of the natural moral law, or moral law of nature.[22] These observations suggest the need for further reflection on the absoluteness of moral norms of behavior considered as *human* (related to natural law), and hence, insofar as they can be discerned by man himself, as *recta ratio*.

1. The Human as Recta Ratio. We shall continue to employ the traditional term *recta ratio*. The human is in it, that which is humanly right. Whatever is not *recta ratio* is necessarily nonhuman, not worthy of man, antithetic to a steadily advancing "humanization". *Recta ratio* does not mean innate discernment or moral truth, "inscribed" somehow, somewhere. Hence it does not denote a norm of conduct "inscribed in our nature," at least not in the sense that one could read off a moral regulation from a natural reality. The "nature" upon which the moral law is inscribed is preeminently and formally nature as *ratio*, but only, of course, as *recta ratio*. From this viewpoint, the preferred expression would probably be that of Paul in Romans: the moral law is "engraved on the heart" (Rom. 2, 15).[23] Apart from this, realities of the natural order, *ratio* excepted, can neither provide a basis for, nor affirm, any moral laws. Considered positively, then, the task of *homo-ratio* in discovering or projecting behavioral norms consists in understanding man himself, his own total reality, together with his world, in order to assess the significance of the alternatives for action available to him and so arrive at a moral affirmation. There will be some a priori and hence self-evident affirmations: for example, that man has to act responsibly and in an interpersonal and social context. Others will presuppose experience; for instance, conduct as related to the life of another, or sexual behavior. In this regard some things will be immediately evident, e.g., that there should be respect for life (it may not be destroyed at will), that sexuality has to be viewed in relation to a particular culture, etc. Still other affirmations call for long and perhaps varied experience, until man understands the value of different possibilities for the realization of genuine humanness. How mankind and the Christian centuries as well have striven in the most diverse ways to come to an evaluative understanding of sexuality and marriage and their actualization!

2. Criteria of Evaluation. Do criteria for the evaluating *ratio* exist? A prime criterion is obviously correspondence of behavior—hence also of the behavioral norms to be discovered—to the meaning, in general, of being man and to the significance of particular givens—i.e., sexuality and marriage as *human* givens.[24] It is probable that penetration of meaning occurs far less frequently on a priori or metaphysical ground than has often been supposed. It implies varied experience on the part of man (humanity) and a long apprenticeship in unpredjudiced weighting of these manifold experiences. And it is not only the "meaning" itself of experienced realities that constitutes a criterion for the evaluating *ratio*, but also practical knowledge of the outcomes and consequences which determined modes of conduct can have—and this under all kinds of presuppositions[25]—for example, in the economic sphere, in social life, or in the area of sexuality and marriage. Of itself, experience yields no norms of conduct; assessment of its outcome is required to enable us to perceive in which direction to seek or not to seek genuine human self-realization. A basic criterion for true penetration of human reality, as well as for a just appraisal of experience, is to be found in the interpersonality of the human person.[26] The conduct of individual persons in different areas of life has to be scrutinized in terms of its interpersonal significance and implications. No one is a self-enclosed individual; each one lives as a person in relation to persons. Humanness essentially involves inter-human relations. Technological and economic progress, for instance, cannot be assessed in the concrete as "human values" unless interpersonal and social aspects are fundamentally involved in the judgment.

To arrive at a behavioral norm regarding premarital intercourse or birth control, for example, a whole complex of factors obviously has to be considered. (It should not be necessary to add that this takes place in an explicit manner only in scientific reflection.) What must be determined is the significance of the action as value or nonvalue for the individual, for interpersonal relations and for human society, in connection, of course, with the total reality of man and his society and in view of his whole culture. Furthermore, the priority and urgency of the different values implied must be weighed.[27] By this procedure, man as assessor (the evaluating human society) arrives at a judgment, tentatively or with some measure of certitude, as to which mode of behavior might further man's self-realization and self-development. As soon as this judgment has been made, it is recognized as a moral norm by the ever present conviction reflected in it that this human action is bound absolutely to *recta ratio*. The fact is simultaneously asserted that the many values to be considered according to their priority and urgency, or nonvalues, do not, strictly speaking, belong as yet to the moral sphere — that is, they are not as yet moral precepts, but are pre-moral. Only the all-embracing view and total appraisal which, as such, determine the mode of action that is good for men, lead to a moral statement. This implies that one or other aspect of an action cannot of itself, and without regard for the remaining factors, determine the morality of an action.

3. *Relativism?* Facts—social, technological, economic, etc.—change. Man's experience, i.e., those of human societies, likewise change, on the basis of changing data. Evaluations also, the mind's grasp of human realities, and self-understanding can be altered. One thinks, for example, of the efforts toward an expanded conception of marriage and sex in the milieu of the Catholic Church in the recent past. And in the process, man (that is, human society), oriented toward development and progress, also changes himself. All these manifold possible — and actual — alterations have to be brought into the moral judgment of human conduct. Such "new" aspects could call for action which, independent of such aspects, would be out of the question; or they might exclude a course of action which would be commanded under other circumstances. If the minimum family income set decades ago is linked to certain social and economic factors; if the institution of private property in our present economic, social and political situation must be viewed as differing in its concrete meaning from previous decades or the Middle Ages; if conceptual grasp and interpersonal and social experience in the realm of family and marriage necessarily co-determine behavior in this area, then on principle, corresponding changes regarding the "right" human behavior in other spheres of life cannot be ruled out. Under this aspect, behavior norms have, at least theoretically, a provisory character.

Changes in the data, differences in concepts and experiences —or even interpretations—occur not only in successive cultures, but also, in cases of actual pluralism,[28] within the same culture. This is readily understandable if heterogeneous economic, social or political situations admit, respectively, of different modes of behavior. But what if varying experiences and concepts and varying self-images of men in different societies or groups lead to different options and so to a diversity of statements on behavioral norms in relation to similar bodies of facts? One might point out, perhaps, that in many cases a given self-concept and a given viewpoint and form of a reality – e.g., marriage in, let us say, a certain African tribe – may not in themselves correspond in all respects to *recta ratio*. Then, of course, the question arises whether another form of marriage, presupposing another culture, may legitimately be imposed upon men belonging to an endemic culture – by missionaries, for instance[29] – provided the indigenous culture itself has not changed by a rather gradual process, and provided it admits of a "human" form of marriage. But might it not be assumed also that on the basis of dissimilar experiences, a heterogeneous self-concept and varying options and evaluations on the part of man (humanity) projecting himself into his future in human fashion—*secundum rectam rationem* – are entirely possible, and that these options and evaluations within the chosen system postulate varied forms of behavior? Who would expect human individuals, groups or societies to arrive at self-understanding and values exempt from all one-sidedness or merely from incompleteness? There *recta ratio* which is to guide our conduct has to allow for such conditionality, essentially connected with humanness; without it man de facto does not exist. Moreover, must it not be supposed that the behavioral norms encountered in a particular civilization or cultural area were formulated partly in consideration of just this civilization and culture, hence for them alone? And this despite the fact that definitive or generally valid norms of conduct were actually intended, simply because the possibility of other civilizations and cultures was not taken into consideration.

Is this relativism? Some time ago, when H.J. Wallraff called Christian social doctrine a "structure of indeterminate propositions"[30] and, in connection with the institution of private property, accepted only a few general statements on social ethics, the realization of which depended heavily upon economic, social and political factors, he found himself vulnerable to the charge of relativism. The title of his article was, "Vom Naturrecht zum Relativismus: am Beispiel des Eigentums".[31] Exception was taken to the subsequent statement: "Principles for a normative science would have to be drawn from social reality".[32] Here the decisive truth was overlooked, that if behavioral norms are to be operative, the entire pertinent reality (including the social factor) has to be taken into account and enter into the judgment. The a priori, hence universal, nonhistorical social ethics that stands opposed to this, that provides norms in advance for every social reality, sacrifices the indispensable objectivity and therefore validity of duly concrete solutions to an a priori universalism. The critical question, then, is not one of relativism but of objectivity, or the "truth" of the action which must be in conformity with the whole concrete reality of man (of society). Now Wallraff had spoken earlier of indeterminate propositions that must be concretized through political decisions (thus involving some compromise), but still in relation to given social reality. Our own previous consideration, however, had to do with moral behavioral norms which men (humanity) "discover" as being appropriate to their actual civilization, experience, etc. We asked: Is this relativism? And now there is the correlative question: Is it not rather the necessary connection with concrete human reality to which human behavior must be adapted if it is to be objective, true, and so, "right," *secundum rectam rationem?* The demand to be this is absolute! Rightly does Chiavacci point out[33] that the objectivity of morality is not necessarily based on an unchangeable being (in other words, on a "preceptive" understanding of natural law), but on the indispensable correspondence of act to being.

III. THE "APPLICABILITY" OF MORAL NORMS

If the absoluteness of moral norms is constituted primarily by their objective effectiveness vis-a-vis the given reality and thus not preeminently by their universality or their universal validity, the question of the applicability of moral norms to reality in the concrete inevitably arises.

1. *The So-called Exceptions to the Norm.*

A very small step in the direction of universal validity in applying moral norms brings home the realization that possibly these norms cannot be stated, as we once believed they had to be, so as to apply to all epochs or in all cultures or social groups, or in all conceivable individual cases. And so we have the problem of the exception to the moral norm, a matter discussed in past years chiefly in English-speaking circles. The title of an Irish article is symptomatic: "Toward a Theory of Exceptions."[34] The author, N.D. O'Donoghue, starts with the possibility and fact of exceptions to behavioral norms, understood, actually, in the same way as by Fletcher and Robinson, for instance, when they concede absoluteness in the sense of admitting no exceptions to only one norm — that of love.[35] An ethical system, according to O'Donoghue, is possible only because, despite change and diversity, man and his structures abide. Yet since the same man and his structures also exhibit changes and differences, exceptions must occur, but in such a way that they remain exceptions. The conclusion is then: moral norms necessarily admit of exceptions. Princeton University's renowned theologian, Paul Ramsey, the "most influential and most prominent advocate of a 'Principles Ethics'" among his Protestant colleagues, holds the contrary opinion. His title is significant, "The Case of the Curious Exception."[36] Ramsey reasons as follows. If there is an exception, it must be based objectively on the actual situation, so that when the same situation is repeated, the same exception must hold. This means, however, that the norm to be applied in general is not meant for the case at hand, or that it must give way to a "better" norm. The exceptional case obliges us, therefore, to a refining of the previous norm, since it did not take into account certain elements of the particular situation, or perhaps considered them only implicitly. Accordingly, Ramsey's solution is: fundamentally, there are no exceptions — provided the formulation of the norm becomes ever more refined and precise. This solution is the correct one. Frequently, our statements of norms are inexact, inasmuch as they do not — perhaps cannot — take into consideration all the possibilities of human reality. When, as he must, Ramsey finally confronts the question whether *all* norms can be "refined", the question will really be, at least logically, whether all the already "refined" norms are to be refined still further. In this connection, one thinks of the changeableness and historicity of man (of humanity), of his culture, his value systems, etc. Ramsey appears to incline rather to a static concept of man. Thus the "refining" entails not only an ever improved and more precise comprehension and articulation, but also a "re-formulation" for modes of reality which hitherto could not be taken into consideration.

Dennis E. Hurley, Archbishop of Durban,[37] has published another attempt to advocate the simultaneous validity of the norm and the justification of the exception. In his view, where a case of conflict occurs, duties and rights stand in opposition to each other. An overriding right can cancel the obligations of certain absolute norms of morality and so make permissible some (not all) *intrinsece mala* (killing, stealing, lying, etc.). Charles Curran[38] appeals to a "theory of compromise," in terms of which — particularly by virtue of man's situation as a consequence of original sin — what really ought not happen, may and must happen on occasion. The often invoked theory of the lesser evil (or the greater good), like the two attempts just mentioned, also seeks to maintain simultaneously the validity of the norms and the vindication of the exceptions.[39] Yet would Ramsey not rightfully reply that the justification of the exception in view of the overriding right, of the necessary compromises and of the lesser evil, must be objectively based on (human) reality itself; i.e. the norm sustaining the exception is not stated with sufficient precision, and, given this formulation, does not at all represent the true norm governing the concrete reality? The justification of the apparent exception lies in the fact that the supposed norm simply does not possess the range of validity it appears to have, judging by its inexact formulation. This does not militate against the validity of the (true) norm; rather it permits the objectively based, so-called exception to call attention more pointedly to the objective range and true validity of the norm.[40]

Further consideration leads to a like result. Hurley maintains that killing, stealing, lying, etc. are intrinsically evil; yet they might be warranted in view of important opposing obligations. According to press reports, a French bishop is supposed to have said at a conference of French bishops on *Humanae vitae* that, according to *Humanae vitae* the use of contraceptives is an *evil,* like killing; but killing in a morally justified war of defense and the use of contraceptives in certain cases of conflict would not be morally culpable (in no sense wicked). Have we not overlooked the distinction – crucial in this case – between evil and wickedness – that is, between evil in the *premoral* (physical, ontic) sense and evil in the *moral* sense (wickedness)? Objectively, there is no conflict of moral precepts, only a conflict of value judgments *(bona physica)* in the premoral sense.[41] Only the right – *secundum rectam rationem* – solution of this conflict makes the absence of conflict evident in the moral situation. Killing is a realization of an evil, but it is not always a moral evil. In this regard, there is also no moral norm applying to killing, but only such as designates unjust killing as immoral. If someone (with *Humanae vitae*) regards the use of contraceptives as a *malum*, but considers certain exceptions morally justifiable, he must understand that the *malum* of contraceptive use affirmed by him in this form lies in the premoral sphere ("it is evil") while only the objective unjustified realization of the evil belongs in the area of the moral ("it is wicked"). In general, whoever sets up negative norms, but regards exceptions as justified, by reason of overriding right, or warranted compromise, or for the sake of the lesser evil (or the greater good), shows by this that the *malum* repudiated by the norm is *not* (yet) to be understood as moral evil. Hence its realization to avoid another *malum* (or for the sake of a relatively higher *bonum*) can be justified morally on the ground mentioned previously. If, on the contrary, one prefers to give this norm moral validity, its formulation in universal terms has to be restricted, and the "exception" is no longer an exception. The norm is objective only within the limits of the restriction.

2.   Moral and Premoral Evil. The basic distinction between moral and premoral evil[42] should be carried still further in the interest of clarifying the significance of moral norms for concrete behavior. Morality, in the true (not transferred or analogous) sense is expressible only by a human action, by an action which originates in the deliberate and free decision of a human person. An action of this kind can be performed only with the intention of the agent. One may not say, therefore, that killing as a realization of a human evil may be morally good or morally bad; for killing as such, since it implies nothing about the purpose of the action, cannot, purely as such, constitute a human act. On the other hand, "killing because of avarice" and "killing in self-defense" do imply something regarding the purpose of the action; the former cannot be morally good, the latter may be.

Here we take up the question: when is human action, or when is man in his action (morally) good? Must not the answer be: when he intends and effects a human good (value), in the premoral sense —for example, life, health, joy, culture, etc. (for only this is *recta ratio*); but not when he has in view and effects a human nongood, an evil (nonvalue) in the premoral sense – for example, death, wounding, wrong, etc. What if he intends and effects good, but this necessarily involves effecting evil also? We answer: if the realization of the evil through the intended realization of good is justified as a proportionally related cause,[43] then in this case only good was intended. Man has almost always judged in this manner. A surgical operation is a health measure, its purpose is to cure, but it is at the same time the cause of an evil, namely, wounding. This, however, appears to be justified in view of the desired cure and is capable of being incorporated in the one human act — a curative measure. The surgical operation is morally right, because the person acting desires and effects only a good — in the premoral sense — namely, restoration of health. If the surgeon were to do more than was required in performing this operation, that "more" would not be justified by the treatment indicated — that is, it would be taken up as an evil — in the premoral sense — into the surgeon's intention; it would be morally bad. The conclusion in definitive terms is: 1) an action cannot be judged morally in its materiality (killing, wounding, going to the moon), without reference to the intention of the agent; without this, we are not dealing with a human action, and only of a human action may one say in a true sense whether it is morally good or bad;[44] 2) the evil (in a premoral sense) effected by a human agent must not be intended as such, and must be justified in terms of the totality of the action by appropriate reasons.

These considerations are not without significance for the question of the application of norms to the concrete case. We have already seen this in connection with the so-called exception to the norm. The problem presents itself also in the form of the traditional doctrine, morality in a comprehensive sense, as applied to a concrete action, is determined not only by the morality of the act as such, but also by the morality of the circumstances and the purpose of action, with the reservation, however, that neither the purpose nor special circumstances can recind the negative morality of an action. This point has value only as a rule of thumb (although it has also the theoretical force that something morally bad cannot become morally good in view of a good purpose). In theoretically precise reflection, one must, of course establish some additional points. For 1) a moral judgment of an action may not be made in anticipation of the agent's intention, since it would not be the judgment of a "human" act; 2) a moral judgment is legitimately formed under a simultaneous consideration of the three elements (action, circumstance, purpose), premoral in themselves; for the actualization of the three elements (taking money from another, who is very poor, to be able to give pleasure to a friend) is not a combination of three human actions that are morally judged on an individual basis, but a single human action. A surgical operation is not made up of several human actions (wounding, healing, for the purpose of restoring health), but is only one healing action, the moral quality of which is based on a synchronous view of the three — premoral — elements in conformity with the evaluating *recta ratio*. The same thing could be said about the transplant of an organ from a human living organism, about underground coal mining with its threat to health, about the moon-landing and the incalculable dangers involved, etc. But now the critical question: what value do our norms have with respect to the morality of the action as such, prior, that is, to consideration of the circumstances and intention? We answer: they cannot be moral norms unless circumstances and intention are taken into account. They can also be considered as moral norms only because we tacitly judge the action in the light of possible circumstances and intention. But since, theoretically, this is impossible, and since in practice these elements of an action are necessarily incomplete, we cannot rule out the possibility that in the practical application, an objectively based instance of conflict—the exceptional case—can show that the norm does not have, objectively, the range of validity previously supposed. The absoluteness of a norm depends more upon the objectivity of its relationship to reality than upon its universality.

"The end does not justify the means" — that is, the morally bad means. This tenet is, of course, correct. When and to the extent that it has been established that an action is morally bad, it may not be performed as a means toward attaining a good end. On the other hand, if there is a question only of evil in the premoral sense, such as death, wounding, dishonor, etc., the intention and the realization of a good can possibly justify the doing of an evil — e.g., the evil of a surgical operation in the interest of health, or a transplant. Needless to say: 1) the performing of the evil is not judged independently of the intention as morally bad; 2) in the one human action (health care, transplant) the performing of the evil is not an isolated (human) action, but only an element of one action. Therefore, a morally bad (human) action is not being used as a means to a good end. This point was often overlooked in the traditional statement of the principle of an act with a double effect. Thus, in cases in which, during the course of the action, the bad effect preceded the good, temporally or physically, opinion was always inclined toward prohibition, on the grounds that otherwise the good effect would be achieved through the realization of the bad effect (as means). Actually, many good Christians cannot understand why, in a situation where life is endangered, as, for instance, ectopic pregnancy or uterine diseases, the removal of the fetus was prohibited, while the removal of an organ from the mother, whose serious illness was anticipated because of the pregnancy, together with the fetus, was permitted; although in both cases, there was a liability involved with respect to the life of the fetus — a (premoral) value.[45] The theory failed to take into account that the evil involved is such, not on moral but on premoral grounds (like wounding, loss of honor, death, etc.), and that consequently its actualization occurs, not as a separate human act with its own morality and not, in this context, as an immoral means to a good end, but as a component of one action which is specified through the intention of the agent. Once more: moral norms are not likely to be fully expressed so long as intentions and circumstances are not taken into consideration, at least implicitly. They are objective, therefore, only when this qualification can be presupposed.

3. "Ethical" Norms and "Abstract" Norms. Under this title Edward Schillebeeckx has treated the problem of the applicability of norms to real cases in the third volume of his collected works[46] and in 1968 in *Concilium*.[47] He points out that some Catholic theologians — G. de Brie, Karl Rahner, Josef Fuchs are named — in view of the all too simple solutions of the problematic of situation ethics, have attempted to compensate by having the moral requirement of the situation from abstract norms drawn from the concept "man," as well as from strictly situation-conditioned elements. Against this solution Schillebeeckx cites the epistemological difficulty that *two* norms are posited by it. In reality, however, there would be solely the concrete reality of the particular individual's ethical norm. The abstract norm would not be an ethical norm at all, that is, a demand of reality. Rather, it would only repeat the ethical norm in the abstract and inadequately, and would have moral significance only in virtue of its existential connection with the concrete reality. This significance would lie in the fact that it is "the inadequate, indeed, but still real referent to the single operative concrete ethical norm";[48] i.e., in the direction indicated by it, the ethical norm is to be sought, without its being itself capable of providing this ethical norm satisfactorily. Apart from the question of terminology, the authors cited above legitimately suppose, precisely as does Schillebeeckx, only a single ethical norm (as required by the actual case) and admissibly understood the relationship of the "abstract" to the concrete reality as "ethical" norm epistemologically in precisely the same way as he; they have said this explicitly.

But the question of interest to us here is rather that of the significance of the abstract norm for the concrete reality as ethical norm. Schillebeeckx probably does not mean to say merely than an abstract norm cannot form the basis of an exhaustive judgment of a concrete reality. He would doubtless also wish to say that only in the confrontation with an actual situation will the moral value and the moral exigency, toward which the abstract norm merely pointed in a partial manner, be fully revealed and understood. Or he has in mind that the abstract norm can be arrived at only via the concrete reality through abstraction and conceptualization. But this would imply that the concrete reality to which it is to be applied later on, is conceivable of a different kind than the concrete reality that represented the point of departure. Thus, it can no longer serve as the ethical norm − i.e., as meeting the concrete requirements of the new reality. If he indeed meant to say this, he perceived the problem treated above and sought to solve it in his own way: the norm for concrete action is constituted by the *one* moral judgment of the whole complex (the action *in abstracto*, circumstances, intention) and not by the moral judgment of an action *in abstracto and* the added judgment of circumstances and intention.

4.   "*Intrinsece Malum*"? The question of the applicability of moral norms may arise in still another form known from tradition. If the absoluteness of the moral norm signifies objectivity more than universal validity, can behavioral moral norms be universal at all, in the sense of being applicable always, everywhere and without exception, so that the action encompassed by them could never be objectively justified? Traditionally, we are accustomed to speak of an *intrinsece malum*.

Viewed theoretically, there seems to be no possibility of behavioral norms of this kind for human action in the inner-worldly realm. The reason is that an action cannot be judged morally at all, considered purely in itself, but only together with all the circumstances and the intention. Consequently, a behavioral norm, universally valid in the full sense, would presuppose that those who arrive at it could know or foresee adequately all the possible combinations of the action concerned with circumstances and intentions, with (premoral) values and nonvalues *(bona* and *mala "physica").*[49] A priori, such knowledge is not easily attainable. An a priori affirmation would not come to be a moral judgment by way of the premoral. Add to this that the conception opposed to this does not take into consideration the significance for an objective understanding of morality attached to, first, practical experience and induction, second, civilization and cultural differences, third, man's historicity and "creative" perceptions.

Despite all this, we often make statements connoting "universal validity." But "Thou shalt not kill" is obviously too broadly stated; it would be better to say, "Thou shalt not commit murder" − that is, "Thou shalt not kill unjustly." This last formulation is universal and exact. Nevertheless, a high price has been paid for this advantage over the formulation "Thou shalt not kill." For while "killing" expresses an unequivocal fact, "murder" does not, since it leaves undetermined when killing is lawful and when it is not. Accordingly, the inference is self-evident: a precise description of an action as a statement of fact would, theoretically, scarcely admit of a universal moral judgment in the strict sense. An operative universal moral norm contains a formal element not yet defined materially, "lawful," "in an authorized manner." Hence the attempt on the part of moral theology to discover which values, realizable in this world, can justify "killing" and which cannot. If it is believed that, in moral theology, the line between "lawful" and "unlawful" has to be drawn precisely, we have once again a definitive statement of fact and, within its limits, a universal moral judgment. But here we must pause for further reflection. How could one make a judgment that would take in *all* the human possibilities — even granting that one had succeeded in understanding rightly and judging rightly those possibilities that were foreseen? Today, actually, such reflection begins thus: might there not be at the present time and in the future a society in which — as distinguished from earlier societies — by reason of its social and cultural structures, capital punishment would not be an appropriate and therefore warranted means of administering justice? Further, is there meanwhile no life situation that might justify suicide, as, for example, the only means of preserving a state secret, a possibility which presumably is open to consideration, inasmuch as it was excluded indeed in the norm as stated in the past without, however, having been reflected upon at any time? "Killing" vs. "murder" was mentioned as only one example that might shed more light on the problem of the applicability of behavior norms stated as universals.

Theoretically, no other answer seems possible: one cannot easily formulate universal norms of behavior in the strict sense of *intrinsece malum*. Practically, however, norms properly formulated as universals have their worth, and indeed on several counts. 1) Such norms, insofar as they are based on true perception, indicate a value or a nonvalue in the premoral sense. But negative values are to be avoided; in particular, as evil they may never serve as purposes for human action, and only for adequate reasons may they be actualized concurrently with relatively higher or more urgent values. 2) There can be norms stated as universals, with precise delineations of action to which we cannot conceive of any kind of exception— e.g., cruel treatment of a child which is of no benefit to the child.[50] Despite misgivings on the level of theory, we get along very well with norms of this kind. 3) Norms can be stated as universals (in the case of a specific culture or society, particularly), corresponding to human and social situations that have been actually experienced. In these instances, Aquinas' opinion concerning so-called secondary principles of the natural law, including, therefore, "operative" behavioral norms, holds true by analogy: they can be applied in ordinary cases, *"valent ut in pluribus.*"[51] And this for the reason that they are stated so as to suit conditions wont to occur in practice (and only for such); they suffice for ordinary use in practical living. 4) The extent of the inapplicability of a norm to a concrete case (for which it was actually not intended), the degree to which specific norms of our society are stated with precise relevance to present-day conditions in our society, or to those of yesterday's society (from which our present one derives) and so are not relevant to ours; or are generalized and so apply to other societies and cultures as well – such difficulties can neither be presumed as free of doubt, nor may they be completely ignored. Where the first suspicion of one or other of the conditions mentioned above exists, a point of reference is at hand for a thorough examination, to determine the factor upon which the delimiting process should be objectively based.

The absence of a distinction—made only later on—between theoretical and practical possibility characterized not only the moral-theological discussion of the past on *intrinsece malum* and the universality of behavioral norms, but also, by way of consequence, the official ecclesiastical use of these expressions. Apart from this, the terms would have a better meaning if they could be aligned with the term "absolute" in the sense given it above. Every action that is objectively—*secundum rectam rationem*—not justified in the concrete human situation (according to Schillebeeckx, the sole norm and only adequate norm of conduct) is *intrinsece malum* and therefore absolutely to be avoided.[52]

IV. NORMS AS AUTHENTIC ORIENTATION

To summarize: moral theology is concerned primarily with objectivity – its true *absolutum* – which consists in the *recta ratio* of a human-Christian actualization of the concrete reality. *Recta ratio* can be satisfactorily present only in a conscience situation. But human society requires and discovers – "creates" – norms stated as universals; the same is true of scientific moral theology. Nevertheless, universality in norms has certain limits, at least theoretically, because of the objectivity required of a true *absolutum*. What are the practical implications?

1. Formal Principles and Material Norms of Action. Undoubtedly, there are universal ethical statements in the strict sense. Nevertheless they always remain formal in a certain sense, at least insofar as they are not material norms of action, i.e., norms which indicate whether actions exactly described materially are ethically permissible or not. That our actions must be authentic self-realization or, what is the same, that we have to do the good and not the evil, is nothing other than the formal formulation of man's ethical self-understanding. This formal and hence absolutely universal formulation can be applied to different spheres of life without losing its formal character: the imperative to be just, chaste, and merciful thus materially states nothing about the materially determined actions which can express justice, chastity, and mercy. Likewise, the formal formulation of ethical self-understanding can express itself in transcendental norms, which thus do not describe the material content of actions: for example, that the Christian man has to realize himself as Christian, that he should live faith and love, baptism and the following of Christ in every action. They are universal. Categorial evaluations, on the other hand, may be influenced to a certain degree by determined experiences, by factual options in a given society, and by a specific self-understanding. Above all, this applies to the hierarchy of values — for example, in the area of marriage and family. This applies in the same way and even more to "operative" norms of action, which were treated above. In this case, to defend as a theoretical possibility the regular universality of ethical statements — perhaps on the basis of an a priori metaphysical understanding of determined actions — is to succumb to the utopia of rationalism.

2. Moral-Theological Reflection. Ethical or moral-theological reflection is always associated with moral experience. This, however, can never be a solipsistic experience. Its substance is always related to the moral consciousness of the community.[53] But this moral consciousness is shaped by manifold experiences and diverse influences. In the Christian community led by the Spirit, the human-Christian self-concept is always the matrix and potential corrective of moral understanding, even when the Christian message as such transmits behavioral norms that are scarcely "operative," definitive or universal. On the other hand, it cannot be denied that in the course of the centuries, Old Testament-Jewish concepts and the ethical opinions of non-Christian ideologies of various kinds exercised their influence. It is likewise undeniable that in the Christian communities of those centuries *errare humanum est* and that error in the moral sphere cannot therefore be excluded *a limine.*

If today, in Christian as well as non-Christian sectors, the universality of norms is being questioned on both theoretical and practical levels, with very obvious consequences, the fact still remains that men of today and also the Christian community of today are susceptible to error. There is equal a priori probability, however, that, in their reflections, they can achieve true insight. In this connection, where might the basis be found that would validate the right or necessity of questioning or rethinking, for without penetrating and common reflection in relation to this basis, will not a community run the risk of deviating from "its own" clear-sighted moral sense, which has developed within it and in virtue of its own particular reality? Theoretically speaking, three possibilities that could warrant doubt or rethinking come to mind. First, it can be shown that in the Christian past, faulty evaluations were made and false norms set. If such could be and were identified hitherto, similar identifications could in principle be made also today. Those erroneous evaluations and norms could have been objectively "false" for men of earlier times as well, although today we could probably show why the errors were scarcely avoidable or even not avoidable at all because of the state of knowledge — or awareness — at that time. Second, inasmuch as we ourselves formulate moral norms, such norms may well be imprecise or, the most likely eventuality, stated in too generalized a manner, either because there was only an implicit awareness of limits, or because limits were not adverted to at all. This helps to explain why, third, particular inherited moral statements can be related very accurately to a social situation, a culturally conditioned evaluation, a partially developed self-concept, and the like, rather than to a designated era of the past, whereas for us today those situations and evaluations are "past." In cases where we can prove this and where it is clear that a moral statement has its basis in precisely those givens that have since changed their bases, a moral reformulation is not only conceivable; it is called for.

3. The Individual and His Conscience. Undoubtedly, the question of the absoluteness of moral norms has considerable significance for the individual and the forming of his situation-conscience, in light of which (not then — directly — in light of the norms!) he acts. For since we never begin at zero to form our situation-conscience, but always include norms in our starting point, the question of absoluteness, i.e., universality, regarding the norms of the individual and his concrete behavior, becomes important. To repeat, we are not solipsists either in forming a situation conscience or in developing a moral sensibility, or in appropriating moral norms. Rather, despite the uniqueness of the individual, there is a human orientation to moral questions only in terms of a group, a community, a society, conceived as a whole. In his moral convictions and in forming his situation-conscience, the individual cannot simply detach himself from his roots in the moral convictions of the community; nor may he forget that he will find the (i.e., "his") right solution of many an individual moral problem only by relating to the moral perceptions and self-concept of his community. Specific problems usually occur in an integrated context and cannot easily find their distinctively appropriate solutions in another context. In the ecclesial community, it is to be noted further, moral traditions can also be co-determined, in that a Christian member's self-concept and ideal morality, springing from faith (even though the inferences may be partially underdeveloped), can contribute to the ratifying of a moral evaluation. On the other hand, doubts and reversed judgments occurring justifiably in a community can also, naturally, influence the mental attitude and formation of conscience taken by the individual according to his capacity and responsibility, when he decides to participate in the reflective evaluations of his community and follow the judgment of his adviser. Doubtless, much depends on a responsible discernment of spirits, perceptible through[54] and dependent upon a moral faith-instinct (K. Rahner) which, however, must not be equated with mere susceptibility to what has been traditionally handed down.

There is, of course, the theoretical possibility that the "curious exception" (Ramsey) may present itself, not only as a public phenomenon in the life of the community, but also independently in a justified individual case. For the actuality of this possibility, one should not only deal with the uniqueness of the individual and of the particular case — this would be very superficial — but with the basis which in itself is objective and demonstrable — perhaps along the lines of one of the possibilities mentioned above (under 2). Nevertheless, the individual case, granting the demonstrability of the objective basis, probably will be presented as a rule within the community in a similar and analogous manner and be carried through to a competent (not necessarily authoritative) judgment.

4.   *The "Pedagogical" Value of Norms.* The moral task of the Christian is not to fulfill "norms" but to "humanize" (Christianize) each of man's concrete realities, understood as a divine call. Norms of moral behavior should help to bring this about rightly, "objectively". The true significance of these norms consists in this "pedagogical" service — not in a universal validity that could compromise objectivity. Accordingly, the function of the norms is then "only" pedagogical.[55] They are guides to right actualization — that is, they are not intended, being abstract, to be an easy solution, nor can they even, at least normally, designate with precision their own range of validity.[56] Yet, practically speaking, they are indispensably important, because no one who is incorporated in a community is without norms. The "pedagogical" service of norms reaches its highest intensity in cases where the individual (as a member of his community) is not entirely capable of finding his way.[57] To be sure, precisely in such instances norms are liable to be understood and lived as law or tabu because they do not easily manifest their proper limits.

Once again: the moral task proper to man is not to fulfill norms so that in the final analysis life's reality would serve merely as material, so to speak, for actualizing moral values — that is, obeying norms. Inversely, the concrete reality of life itself — that is, its actualization — is the real task; hence the mandate to take up a given reality and to form it "creatively" and in a spirit of self-commitment, into something "worthy of man" (and therefore of his Creator and Redeemer).[58] The understanding of concrete reality itself could by itself enable the evaluating individual (Christian) to judge which "designs" of his shaping action are really "human" (Christian). By forming this judgment, he would simultaneously and at least implicitly recognize the norms, which he has probably carried over, just as the full meaning of the norms "carried over" reveals itself totally only in a comprehending evaluation of concrete human reality. Nevertheless, in the foreseeable future man will carry over, presumably, less numerous, less detailed and fewer behavioral norms known in advance to fulfill the work of performing responsibly the many tasks involved in shaping man's world. Rather, there will be, probably, fundamental principles, a deepened insight into human and Christian values and a heightened sense of responsibility.[59]

If moral behavioral norms have their "relative" significance for the human and Christian realization of man's world, a reflection on their absoluteness belongs to the task of a theoretical consideration of questions regarding Christian morality. Only theoretically neat attempts at solution, not apologetical efforts, can assist praxis effectively. Indeed, not only should these attempts at solution include a designation of limits, but also the indication of the limits of the designated limits. In other words, abstract discussion is not enough. There should be further reflection on how the theological analysis and its outcomes affect the daily life, not only of the "experts" but also of the "ordinary Christian". This latter provision is of very great importance, because moral judgments – concerning really contigent realities – do not require metaphysical proof, only a so-called moral certitude; with this we may be and should be content.

NOTES

1. Blasphemy is not infrequently referred to as an "intrinsically" bad act. It should be noted, however, that blasphemy, if it is really such, means expressly a contradiction addressed to God, i.e. the real essence of immorality, and therefore different from any other innerworldly acts. An analogy would be an act directed against the salvation of one's nearest and dearest.

2. Cf. J. Blank, "New Testament Morality and Modern Moral Theology", *Concilium* vol. 5, no. 3, 6-12. Cf. also A. Grabner-Haider, "Zur Geschichtlichkeit der Moral (Biblische Bemerkungen)", *Catholica* 22 (1968), 262-70; W. Kerber, "Hermeneutik in der Moraltheologie", *Theol. u Phil.* 44 (1969), 42-66, especially 52-60.

3. So also H. Rotter, "Zum Erkenntnisproblem in der Moraltheologie", in J.B. Lotz (ed.) *Neue Erkenntnisprobleme in Philosophie und Theologie*, Freiburg 1968, 226-48. The reference here is to 238ff.

4. Cf. *Gaudium et spes*, n. 46.

5. E. Schillebeeckx, "The Magisterium and the World of Politics", *Concilium* vol. 6, no. 4, 12-21, especially 16.

6. K. Rahner, "Zum Problem der Manipulation", in *Schriften zur Theologie* VIII, 303ff.

7. M. Flick and Z. Alszeghy, *Metodologia per una teologia dello sviluppo*, Brescia 1970, 47-68, 91-9.

8. Loc. cit.; cf. *Diskussion zur "politischen Theologie"*, ed. H. Peukert, Mainz-Munich 1969.

9. K. Rahner distinguishes between norms and imperatives: *The Dynamic Elements in the Church*, London 1964, 13-41.

10. In his article "'Politische Theologie' in der Diskussion", *St. d. Zt.* 184 (1969), 289-308, J.B. Metz rightly saw that political theology can lead to action only by way of political ethics (293-6). Yet it is not made clear why "political ethics", precisely as an "ethics of change" (in distinction from an "ethics of order"), is assigned specially to political theology as a "specifically Christian hermeneutics."

11. Cf. R. A. McCormick, "The Teaching Role of the Magisterium and of Theologians", in *Proceedings of Catholic Theological Society of America* 24 (1969), summarized by the author in *Theol. Studies* 30 (1969), 647f. On the action of the Spirit in the Church, cf. also K. Demmer, "Kirchliches Lehramt und Naturrecht", *Theol. u. Gl.* 59 (1969), 191-213; B. Schüller, "Bemerkungen zur authentischen Verkündigung des kirchlichen Lehramtes", *Theol. u. Phil.* 42 (1967), 534-51.

12.   For the conditioned, not ahistorical, character of the moral pronouncements of the Church, cf. A. Auer, "Die Erfahrung der Geschichtlichkeit und die Krise der Moral", *Theol. Qu.* 149 (1969), 4-22; C.E. Curran, "Natural Law and the Teaching Authority of the Church", in *Christian Morality Today*, Notre Dame, Indiana 1966, 79-91; idem, "Absolute Norms and Medical Ethics", in idem (ed.), *Absolutes in Moral Theology?*, Washington D.C. 1968, 108-53, especially 127ff; L. Sartori, "La legge naturale e il magistero cristiano", in L. Rossi (ed.), *La legge naturale*, Bologna 1970, 219-44. According to Curran, changes in the moral teaching of the Church are to be understood as development, not as contradictions of the past: "Natural Law...", 87.

13.   Cf. E. Chiavacci, "La legge naturale ieri e oggi", in F. Festorazzi et al., *Nuove prospettive di morale coniugale*, Brescia 1969, 61-91. The reference here is to p. 75.

14.   See note 13 above.

15.   Chiavacci, loc. cit., 65ff, is of the opinion that Thomas, although he cites many "auctoritates" for other formulations also, basically does not consider detailed norms as natural law; and that this theory derives from other sources. Cf. also D. Mongillo, "L'elemento primario della legge naturale in s. Tommaso", in *La legge naturale* (see note 12 above), 101-23; D. Capone, "Ritorno a s. Tommaso per una visione personalistica in teologia morale", *Riv. di teol. mor.* 1 (1969), 85ff.

On the whole problem of change with regard to moral questions, cf. J. Gründel, *Wandelbares und Unwandelbares in der Moraltheologie*, Düsseldorf 1967, especially 46-73.

16.   Cf. A. Auer (see note 12 above); I. Lobo, "Geschichtlichkeit und Erneuerung der Moral", *Concilium* 3 (1967), 363-75; A. Grabner-Haider (see note 2 above); M. Sheehan, "History: The Context of Morality", in W. Dunphy (ed.), *The New Morality, Continuity and Discontinuity*, New York 1967, 37-54.

17.   Cf. A. Auer, loc. cit. (see note 12 above), 12: "Gut ist immer nur, was der Wachstumsbewegung der menschlichen Person und der menschlichen Gemeinschaft dienlich ist. Aber das lässt sich eben nicht nur aus der Vergangenheit bestimmen; es bedarf auch der Hinwendung zur Zukunft"; J. Fuchs, "On the Theology of Human Progress", in *Human Values and Christian Morality*, Dublin 1970, 178-203, especially 185-90. From the moral psychologist's point of view, see I. Lepp, *La morale nouvelle*, Ital. ed: *La morale nuova*, Milan 1967, 78.

18.   This terminology occurs in the encyclical *Humanae vitae*, n. 10.

19.   Cf. C.E. Curran, "Absolute Norms..." (see note 12 above), 118f.

20.   B. Quelquejeu's phrasing tends in this direction, see "Brèves notes à propos de 'Nature et Morale'", *Supplément de La vie spirituelle* 81 (1967), 278-81; also L. Janssens, *Personne et Société*, Gembloux 1939, 199-243; idem, *Personalisme en Democratisering*, Brussels 1957, 93f; H. Mertens, "De persona humana ut norma moralitatis", *Coll. Mechl.* 44 (1969) 526-31.

21.   This is not the place for an analysis of the phenomenon of consci-

ence; only *one* fundamental aspect, conscience as judgment, is being considered.

22. Cf. J. Fuchs, "Gibt es eine spezifisch christliche Moral?", *St. d. Zt.* 185 (1970), 99-112; idem, "Human, Humanist and Christian Morality", *Human Values and Christian Morality*, Dublin 1970, 112-47; B. Schüller, "Zur theologischen Diskussion über die lex naturalis", *Theol. u. Phil.* 41 (1966), 481-503; idem, "Inwiewiet kann die Moraltheologie das Naturrecht entbehren", *Leb. Zeugnis*, March 1965, 41-65; A. Auer, "Nach dem Erscheinen der Enzyklika 'Humanae vitae'. Zehn Thesen über die Findung sittlicher Weisungen", *Theol. Qu.* 149 (1969), 75-85, especially 75-8; F. Böckle, "Was ist das Proprium einer christlichen Ethik?", *Z. f. ev. Ethik* 11 (1967), 148-59; K. Demmer, "Kirchliches Lehramt und Naturrecht" (see note 11 above), 200; R.A. McCormick, "Human Significance and Christian Significance", in G. H. Outka and P. Ramsey (eds.), *Norm and Context in Christian Ethics*, New York 1968, 233-61; J. McMahon, "What Does Christianity Add to Atheistic Humanism?", *Cross Currents* 18 (Spring 1968), 129-50; J.M. Gustafson, *Christ and the Moral Life*, New York 1968, especially chapter VII.

23. J. Fuchs, *Human Values...* loc. cit. (see note 22 above), 140-47. In the encyclical *Humanae vitae*, n. 12 states: "leges in ipsa viri et mulieris *natura* inscriptae".

24. R.A. McCormick insists – probably against J.G. Milhaven (see note 25 below) – upon far-reaching effects and consequences of actions whose significance is known without experience: "Human Significance...", loc. cit. (see note 22 above), 219-31; published also in *Theol. Studies* 27 (1966), 228-41.

25. So, especially, J.G. Milhaven, "Toward an Epistemology of Ethics", in *Norm and Context* (see note 22 above), 219-31; published also in *Theol. Studies* 27 (1966), 228-41.

26. W. van der Marck, in *Toward a Christian Ethic: Renewal in Moral Theology*, Shannon (Ireland) 1969, advances (perhaps rather one-sidedly) the thesis that the moral value of actions consists exclusively in their significance for the creation of positive interpersonal relations. This can be compared with the thesis of J. Fletcher and A.T. Robinson regarding love as the sole *absolutum*; also J.M. Gustafson, "Love Monism, How Does Love Reign?", in J.C. Bennett et al., *Storm over Ethics*, United Church Press 1967, 26-37.

27. Cf. B. Schuller, "Zur Problematik allgemein verbindlicher ethischer Grundsätze", *Theol. u. Phil.* 45 (1970), 1-23, especially 3f. English in *Theology Digest* 19 (Spring 1971), 23-28.

28. On the problem of morality in a pluralistic society, cf. R. Hofmann, "Das sittliche Minimum in der pluralen Gesellschaft", *Theol. Qu.* 149 (1969), 23-38; also A. Hertz, "Sitte, Sittlichkeit und Moral in der pluralistischen Gesellschaft", *Neue Ordno* 18 (1964), 187-96; W. Schöllgen, *Moral-fragwürdig? Über gesellschaftlichen Pluralismus und Moral*, Hückeswagen 1967.

29.   On the problem of "norms of morality and the christianization of nations", cf. E. Hillman, "The Development of Christian Marriage Structures", *Concilium* vol. 5, no. 6, 25-38; idem, "Polygamy Reconsidered", *Concilium* vol. 3, no. 4, 80-9.

30.   H.J. Wallraff, "Die katholische Soziallehre-ein Gefüge von offenen Sätzen", *Eigentumspolitik, Arbeit und Mitbestimmung*, Cologne 1968, 9-34.

31.   H. Schwandorf, "Zum Standort der katholischen Soziallehre heute", *Gesellschaftspolitische Kommentare* 11 (1970), 130-2, and 12, 144-6.

32.   Loc. cit., 132.

33.   Loc. cit. (see note 13 above), 81.

34.   N.D. O'Donoghue, "Towards a Theory of Exceptions", *The Irish Theol. Qu.* 35 (1951), 217-32.

35.   J.M. Gustafson, "Context versus Principles: A Misplaced Debate on Christian Ethics", in *New Theology*, no. 3, ed. M.E. Marty and D.G. Peerman, London, 1966, 86.

36.   P. Ramsey, "The Case of the Curious Exception", in *Norm and Context*...(see note 22 above), 67-135. Cf. also the excellent contribution by D. Evans, "Love, Situation and Rules", ibid., 367-414.

37.   D. Hurley, "A New Moral Principle: When Right and Duty Clash", *The Furrow* 17 (1966), 619-22.

38.   C.E. Curran, "Dialogue with Joseph Fletcher", *A New Look at Christian Morality*, Notre Dame, Ind. 1968.

39.   Thus, e.g., the commentary on *Humanae vitae* presented at the meeting of French bishops, no. 16: *Docum. Cath.* 65 (1968) 2055-66.

40.   To the cited attempts at solution, one might compare N.J. Rigali's critique, "The Unity of the Moral Order", *Chicago Studies* 8 (1969), 125-43.

41.   Cf. J. de Broglie, "Conflit de devoirs et contraception", *Doctor communis* 22 (1969), 154-75.

42.   For this distinction, cf. W. van der Marck, *Toward a Christian Ethic*...(see note 26 above); P. Knauer, "The Hermeneutic Function of the Principle of Double Effect", *Natural Law Forum* 12 (1967), 132-62; B. Schüller, "Zur Problematik..." (see note 27 above).

43.   Cf. P. Knauer, loc. cit.; the decisive question treated by Knauer is: what is a "proportionate" reason? C.J. van der Poel, "The Principles of Double Effect", in *Absolutes in Moral Theology?* (see note 12 above), 186-210. Van der Poel obviously depends on W. van der Marck, *Toward a Christian Ethic*...(see note 26 above), 65-74, and *Love and Fertility*, London 1965, 35-63. Cf. also C.E. Curran, "Absolute Norms..." (see note 12 above), 112-14.

44.   Reference is made to this especially by W. van der Marck, C. van der Poel and P. Knauer (see note 43 above).

45.   Cf. e.g., P. Knauer, loc. cit., 149: "In other words, a solution which includes both the death of the fetus and the removal of the uterus with consequent sterility is said to be better than that the fetus alone loses its life.

Who can understand this?" Similarly, C.E. Curran, "Absolute Norms...", loc. cit., 112; W. van der Marck, *Love and Fertility*, op. cit.

46. E. Schillebeeckx, *God and Man*, New York, Sheed and Ward 1969.

47. E. Schillebeeckx, "The Magisterium..." (see note 5 above), 15f.

48. Loc. cit., 16.

49. P. Knauer has a similar statement, "The Hermeneutic Function..." (see note 42 above), 138: "What is intrinsically an evil act is brought about when no commensurate reason can justify the permission or causing of the extrinsic evil, that is, any given premoral physical evil or injury." B. Schüller, "Zur Problematik..." (see note 27 above), consistent with his own approach, states (pp. 4 and 7): "These norms can only be unconditional and valid without exception when they command us to realize a good that can never compete with another more important and therefore preferable good....Whatever we can aim at in our actions in relation to our fellowman is neither an absolute good nor an absolute evil for him." An "intrinsece malum" of a concrete norm of action would nevertheless be possible when the circumstance and purpose—putting aside all other circumstances and purposes—is already fixed in the formulation of the norm; for example, "one must never treat a child with severity out of cruelty", but "out of cruelty" is not only a description of action but also a statement of ethical value (or lack of value).

50. Cf. A.T. Robinson, *Christian Morality Today*, London 1964, 16.

51. Thomas Aquinas, *S.T.*, Ia-IIae, q. 94, a. 4.

52. So also J. Coventry, "Christian Conscience," *The Heythrop Journal* 7 (1966), 152f: also C.E. Curran, "Absolute Norms..." loc. cit. (see note 12 above), 169.

53. J.M. Gustafson insists strongly, and rightly so, on this: "Moral Discernment in Christian Life," *Norm and Context* (see note 22 above), 17-36.

54. Cf. Gustafson's significant title: "Moral Discernment in Christian Life" (see note 53 above).

55. By analogy with the Pauline concept of law as a "pedagogue" leading to Christ, R. Marlé, in his "Casuistique et morales modernes de situation," in E. Castelli (ed.), *Tecnica e casuistica*, Rome 1964, 111-20, writes of a pedagogical function of moral law with respect to the actual situation.

56. With Thomas Aquinas, J. de Finance, in his *Ethica generalis*, 2nd ed., Rome 1963, 186, points out that even an aggregation of norms, being abstract, can never produce a *concretum*.

57. In opposition to many psychologists, I. Lepp, from the standpoint of a moral psychologist, maintains that "closed morality" with its norms and also the "superego" with its controlling powers are extremely important for the individual as well as for society, so long as a breakthrough to an "open morality," as he calls it, has not yet occurred: loc. cit. (see note 17 above), 91ff. In his article, "Massstäbe sittlichen Verhaltens. Zur Frage der Normfindung in der Moraltheologie," *Die Neue Ordnung* 23 (1969), 161-74, A.K. Ruff speaks (p. 164) of norms as having an irreplaceable "exoneration function."

58. Cf. the dynamic contribution of P. Antoine, "Situation présente de

la morale," *Le Supplément*, no. 92, 23 (1970), 8-27; also J.M. Gustafson and J. Laney (eds.), *On Being Responsible: Issues in Personal Ethics*, Harper Forum Books; J. Rief, "Moralverkündigung angesichts der Krise der Moral," *Theol. pr. Qu.* 117 (1969), 124-38.

59.   For positions on either extreme of this position, see P. Ramsey, "The Case of the Curious Exception," and J. Fletcher, "What's in a Rule. A Situationist's View," in *Norm and Context*, 325-49.

8. The "Sin of the World" and Normative Morality

Catholic moral theology has often been accused of an undue optimism in its treatment of natural law, and of taking insufficient account of the reality of sin in the world, even in a world which has received grace; this accusation has come especially from Protestant theologians. In this context, "sin" means not only personal sin, but also the many ways in which the effects of sin are present in the world and disfigure it. The difficulty here is focused on normative morality, meaning that abstract moral norms and concrete moral judgments are not possible without reckoning with the fact that the world is really marked by sin, and without making a corresponding adaptation to this fact. It would also mean that such norms and judgments are consequently not "human" in the fullest sense, nor do they represent what is "really" good, but only the good as this is adapted to the condition of men who must live in a world of sin. There are various possible ways of formulating this difficulty.

Recently, some Catholic theologians have adopted the ideas of their Protestant colleagues, in a variety of ways. The stimulus for such reflections is often a different concern, namely, the pastoral fear that the faithful might possibly by overburdened by absolute "ideal" norms. So the question becomes: how are moral norms to be formulated and moral judgments made, while taking account of the reality of sin in the world (a reality that is not annihilated even by the presence of grace), without neglecting the exigencies of an authentically human (and Christian) existence? Here in question is, first of all, the state of man as conditioned by sin and concupiscence, which hinder an "ideal" manner of living; also the manifold ways in which the consequences of sin are woven into the fabric of human institutions, customs and events; if moral norms were to be formulated without taking sufficient account of the latter, there could be danger of turning life into an unbearable burden. In any case, while it is necessary to take account of the fact of sin and of its many consequences, it is equally important to keep in view the necessity of overcoming the influence of sin in the world, as and when grace makes this possible.[1]

The "sin of the world"[2] is a concept derived directly from the

Gospel of John (cf. John 1:29). This is linked to the Pauline concept of sin, as entering into this world to reign in it (cf. Rom. 5:12). Its root lies in the Old Testament's concept of the solidarity of all in sin. The "sin of the world" has a relationship to "original sin". A question which is disputed, and which will here be set aside, is whether the condition of the "sin of the world" and the condition of "original sin" are in ultimate analysis the same thing(Schoonenberg's view is that our personal actual sin is an active participation in original sin and our free "realization" of original sin), or whether the "sin of the world" is better conceived as the way that original sin becomes incarnate in human history. In any case, original sin is the primordial situation of guilt in which our freedom and its history, from the very beginning, are situated and embedded (Rahner).

With respect to the relevance of the "sin of the world" to the formulation of moral norms and the making of moral judgments, the problem of "adaptation" is here understood as a question regarding the moral rectitude of action[3] rather than the theological aspect of the problem, especially as approached by Protestants, who believe that the solution is to be found chiefly in God who justifies. It should also be noted that the following observations are concerned with recent reflections developed within the field of Catholic moral theology, so that there will be no direct treatment of the various points of departure to be found within Protestant theological ethics.

In what follows I will first indicate three ways in which the "sin of the world" is relevant to the formulation of objective moral norms (sections I-III). There follows a brief supplementary reflection on the implications of the "sin of the world", in the sense of "sin-conditioned" concupiscence, regarding subjective moral knowledge (section IV). In conclusion, I will offer some systematic reflections on the relevance of the "sin of the world" to the task of formulating moral norms (section V).

I. THE "SIN OF THE WORLD" AS THE CONCUPISCENCE AND EGOISM OF MANKIND

It is not an altogether new development that the "sin of the world" should be recognized as important in connection with the making of moral norms. Such an awareness was present in the Church in the first centuries, and also in the Middle Ages, despite a considerable reliance on the natural law approach.

1. Indeed, one could hardly expect things to be otherwise, considering the theological distinction taken for granted in the first Christian centuries and the Middle Ages between the different stages or situations in salvation history. Paradise was thought of as a time in which a state of original innocence existed, whereas fallen man was seen as burdened by concupiscence due to the loss of the fullness of grace. A further distinction was made between this latter state and man's future situation of eschatological glory. There was a corresponding recognition that in a society composed of men who are burdened with concupiscence there are norms and institutions which are possible and necessary only on account of the actual situation of mankind. Thinking in terms of natural law, then, issues which at first sight are similar may be governed by different norms and institutions corresponding to the different stages in salvation history.

The chief problems (though not the only ones) which led to a discussion of those norms and institutions appropriate to mankind after the Fall were the question of private property and the matter of slavery, slavery being regarded as justified and serving to represent every form of coercion by force. This discussion still survives in terms of the theological distinction made between primary natural law, which already existed before the Fall or is independent of the Fall, and secondary natural law, which follows the Fall and is dependent upon it.[4] Regarding private property, a true communism was thought of as obviously appropriate to the state of Paradise; the view taken in the Middle Ages shows the influence of Pseudo-Clementine, among others, and it reasoned that mankind, as long as it remained free of egoism, would not have instituted an artificial division of goods not given in nature. This seems to have also been the view of Thomas Aquinas, William of Auxerre, Alexander of Hales, Bonaventure and Albert the Great.[5] Similarly, the arguments of Aquinas in defense of private property presuppose concupiscence on man's part. Regarding slavery, or coercion in general, it was thought, especially following Ambrose and Augustine, that this is a kind of punishment consequent to the Fall; that it has the purpose of compelling people to abandon the discord and disorder to which they are inclined by "sin-conditioned" concupiscence, and to make them respect order for the sake of peace in society; and that it is only since the Fall that the use of coercion has been justified.

Bonaventure above all has clearly expressed his thoughts on the variable ways in which the *ordo naturalis* is to be implemented.[6] He distinguishes between an order which is applicable to every state (*status*) of nature, to nature in the state of its origin (*suae conditionis*) and to nature in the fallen state (*naturae lapsae*). Thus, the worship of God is required by nature as such (*simpliciter*); a practical communism (*omnia esse communia*) was appropriate to nature in its original condition; slavery (*famulari* in a context of coercion) corresponds to nature as fallen and weakened; while a social order composed of such relationships as father-son and husband-wife belongs to the condition of the pilgrim (*status viae*) whether before or after the Fall, but not to the condition of eschatological glory (*gloria*). Bonaventure's additions to the patristic heritage could also be treated at greater length, so as to include, for example, the different modes of coercion and principles such as that of material cooperation in evildoing, etc.[7]

Thus, Bonaventure's theology recognizes without embarrassment that the different "orders" of nature are conditioned by the "sin of the world" and must be seen as signs of the "sin of the world"; that they do not correspond to the ideal original condition of nature, still less to the more ideal situation of eschatological glory; and that in comparison with nature "as such", they must be understood as "preternatural" modifications (*praeternaturale*). Bonaventure speaks further of the "order of nature" (natural law), which as such must take account of the realities of the different states of nature and of their various consequences.

2.　Protestant theology, especially in its Lutheran form,[8] stands in contrast to this tradition. Here, nature in its original condition is regarded as the true reality of nature and thus also as the abiding will of God. Accordingly, one must understand the order prevailing after the Fall as clashing with the primordial nature of man and with the real will of God; in brief, it must be regarded as sinful. The God of grace is likewise understood as constantly reaching out in mercy and forgiveness toward people who must, inevitably, live under the conditions which have followed the Fall.

One may find at present among Catholic theologians a greater readiness than before to stress the "sinful character" of some systems and institutions;[9] yet this emphasis is weaker than in the corresponding Protestant view, since it derives from a Catholic tradition which does not include an identification of nature with original nature, in the Protestant sense. But some present-day Catholic theologians have developed their inherited tradition by very heavily stressing an inevitable "being trapped by sin" and a consequent "uneasy conscience", though the latter is not understood as a "bad conscience" related to actively incurred guilt.

Taking account of the "sin-conditioned" character of certain norms and institutions in a fallen world (in a manner that is different from the Protestant approach) will then be right and necessary, if one wishes, and with good reason, to conceive the preservation of mankind as the object of God's grace and favor notwithstanding the "sin of the world".[10] But it then becomes clear that the real will of God is not concerned with an ideal condition that is different from the one we live in; instead it is concerned with the development of the given human situation with its component of sin, including, of course, a dynamic thrust toward continual improvement. Such continual improvement means overcoming in grace the consequences of sin in the movement toward eschatological perfection. This theme will be developed further.

II. THE "SIN OF THE WORLD" AS THE OBJECTIFICATION OF "SIN" IN HUMAN SOCIETY

The "sin of the world" sets concupiscence free, as has been said; and concupiscence in turn makes necessary certain systems and institutions which are required because of the influence of concupiscence on mankind. But there are also resulting objectifications of the concupiscence of mankind: institutionalized or noninstitutionalized situations and ways of acting, which in their turn may under certain circumstances require an "adapted" form of human response.

1. Accordingly, there follow moral norms and judgments which may at first sight shock us, since they are all too obviously conditioned by the "sin of the world." This does not mean that only formal sin leads to such objectifications, some of which may be regarded as "wrong behavior" arising from ignorance or lack of attention, while ignorance and inattentiveness may be effects of "original sin", of the "sin of the world".

In view of such objectifications of the "sin of the world", and following H. Thielecke, a theology of compromise (formerly called a principle or theory of compromise) has been advanced by Charles Curran.[11] This theology of compromise means that the objectifications of sin condition what may morally be demanded as feasible in ways that would not arise in the absence of such objectifications of sin, so that the objectifications of sin become relevant to the formulation of moral norms. These examples are offered: in a class which is prevailingly dishonest regarding examinations, complete honesty cannot objectively be demanded of an individual student. There are circumstances opposed to a correct state of affairs, so that correct behavior cannot be objectively demanded in the individual case: one thinks here of isolated instances of apparent adultery, premarital relations, homosexual relationships resembling marriage, abortion. There is also in certain sectors of business life a general understanding that what is contracted and what is done need not exactly correspond; a single individual cannot objectively depart from the general practice if he is to survive at all, and he must be able to survive.[12] In unjust situations telling falsehoods can also be justified.

It is generally recognized that such objectively grounded compromises may be called for by de facto incompatibilities between pre-moral goods or values; and such incompatibilities may result not always from "sin", but from the fact that finite goods (creatures) tend to be mutually exclusive, or from the historical complications of the given situation. (Curran cites as an example the dilemma of whether to save the mother or the child when both lives cannot be saved.[13]) Whether the examples indicated above are always to be seen as objectifications of "sin" — whether, for example, true homosexuality is always to be attributed to a "sin-conditioned" attraction — is a question that is here set aside. It should also be noted that there is a constant danger of using genuinely "sin-conditioned" situations as a facile excuse for indulging in compromise.

2.   One sees clearly then that there is a parallel between a justified compromise called for by the vicissitudes of finitude and history, and one called for by factors which are the products of sin; both, as given realities, are equally relevant to the formulation of norms. One sees equally clearly that there is a difference between the two kinds of compromise; for when a compromise involves the objectified results of sin, then some part of these results enters into what is actually done and is actively prolonged.[14] Sin-conditioned ways of acting are to be avoided as far as possible, and the avoidance of this kind of action has a motivation which is specifically different from the reason for avoiding, as far as possible, ways of action which reflect compromise but are not sin-conditioned. If a norm reflecting compromise is in fact justified, then there is no reason for an "uneasy conscience" in the proper sense of this term.[15] But a sin-conditioned compromise does create a specific motive for a genuine and conscientious regret, while such regret is not called for when a compromise is due only to the *de facto* incompatibility of goods or values arising from the finitude of the values or the complications of history.

On the other hand, it should not be overlooked that justified solutions to "difficult" solutions (found and inplemented in faith and grace) also have the effect of preventing those difficulties which already exist (sin-conditioned or not) from leading on to even greater evils. Such a solution, far from being formal cooperation in moral evil, is the only good ehich may be objectively demanded as feasible[16] or is the lesser (nonmoral) evil; in either case, it is the best possible action in the given circumstances.

The foregoing reflections, like those of Bonaventure, should not be understood as opposed to a justified optimism in the application of natural law.[17] This position clearly presupposes a vision of natural law that is not static. A dynamic conception of natural law always views human nature in the concrete, both in relation to the "sin of the world" and in relation to grace. Our moral judgments and their concrete implementation have to do with the real situation of mankind, rather than with an ideal notion of a sinless humanity.[18] Moral judgments and moral striving—by the very fact that they are human —are part of an effort to overcome the limitations of the given situation; and this holds true especially in view of him who is our redemption from sin, who is the source of our full liberation, and who points the way toward the eschatological situation of complete liberation.

It will hardly be possible in practice to make a neat distinction between compromises that are conditioned by sin and other compromises; accordingly, the task of overcoming difficult situations can proceed in principle without making such a distinction; that means evaluating the goods and evils of the given situation by way of a comparative assessment of the values involved. It is not altogether necessary that this assessment take place on the plane of explicit reflection; it will often be an immediate evaluation of the situation as a whole. This presupposes that the evils or disvalues which are brought about as part of a "difficult" solution − in spite of their being possibly conditioned by "sin" − are not moral evils, but are relevant to moral judgment as premoral evils or disvalues. Such evils or disvalues may turn out to be unavoidable in the circumstances, so that the opposite ideals are not actually part of the given "difficult" situation.[19] For this very reason, corresponding action can be both sinless and just; even when it does not correspond to an ideal which is simply not part of the situation,[20] it represents the "radical" demand of the here-and-now. More ideal norms of action must then be seen as incompletely formulated; thus they hold in the majority of situations, *ut in pluribus* (Aquinas).[21]

3. A particular class of objectifications of the sin of the world, not yet explicitly referred to, consists of the situations of injustice which exist in individual societies or on an international scale. These involve an objectively unjust distribution of economic, social, or cultural goods; in brief, any situation in which oppression is imposed. Such situations are the result of personal sin, if objective injustice is being or has been perpetrated, or when existing situations of injustice are maintained or allowed to continue in spite of a real possibility of changing them. But such situations of injustice may also arise through ignorance or inattentiveness and yet be due ultimately to a sinful attitude or to some other concretization of the "sin of the world". The way in which such situations of injustice should be detected by an alert Christian conscience, and as far as possible overcome, has already been discussed regarding the objectifications of sin in general. Unfortunately, the overcoming of injustice will often not be something that is immediately feasible, nor something to be accomplished by isolated individuals; so it will be necessary to cooperate further with unjust situations, in order to avoid a greater evil. In this case, such action is just even though it inevitably includes a partial furthering of the "sin of the world" and of its evil consequences. But this is not sin in the proper sense, nor is it some mixture of right and wrong, but the (relatively) greater good of a lesser (premoral) evil.

4. A situation is called "wrong" rather than "unjust" when behavior occurring here and now is sinful or wrong (though possibly itself in some way sin-conditioned) and compels or occasions the cooperation of others. Even the experience of bad example can be significant in this sense. Such situations have no normative significance in the sense that unjust or (morally) wrong behavior can never be justified. The moral theology of the past was also aware that such situations could, in special cases, make an otherwise unjust action right and just and therefore justify it. For instance, not returning a loan or something given as security (one recalls Aquinas' example of the sword) because of an imminent and related danger, or participation in a robbery because of similar danger, may be fully just and therefore justified. And that is — often, at least — the consequence of a situation of sin.

III.   THE "SIN OF THE WORLD" AS CONCUPISCENCE IN THE ACTING SUBJECT

Man as he actually is encounters the "sin of the world" not only in the concupiscence of humanity or in the social objectifications of sin, but also in the concupiscence that is part of himself. As was said earlier, concupiscence is understood as being operative because of the lack of that fullness of grace that was intended for man. The reality which we actually encounter is (in spite of faith and grace) that of man as marked by concupiscence, in the "situation of sin", of "sin in us" (cf. Rom. 7) and therefore in a situation of weakness. This sin-conditioned weakness specifies the reality of the acting person. In what sense is such weakness to be seen as relevant to the formulation of norms — that is, as entering into the definition of what a person objectively can do to meet the demands of values, and therefore of what he has to do? For weakness is part of the concrete person as we actually find him.

1.   The question just indicated has been, for the most part, though not exclusively, examined by authors writing in English and French (P. Chirico, N.J. Rigali, N. Crotty, G. Martelet, E. Pousset, and others).[22] The occasion for such discussion was largely the dilemma of married couples described in *Gaudium et spes*, n. 51, regarding the moral demand later formulated in *Humanae vitae*. However, this particular point will be set aside here, as far as possible.

The moral theologians who judge that human weakness may make it genuinely impossible to meet certain moral demands refer to definite demands, formulated in norms of conduct, to which they ascribe validity both in the abstract and in the concrete. But they believe that in some cases weakness arising from the concupiscence of the person is such that fulfillment of the moral demand cannot really be expected, and that therefore the demand is not binding. They believe that the "condition of the sinner" (*condition du pécheur*) demands only one thing: namely, to do what turns out to be possible, rather than attempting the impossible; this might be formulated in general norms or discovered in the individual case. The accomplishment of the concretely possible is understood explicitly as a violation of the moral (!) order; it entails the realization of a disorder (*désordre*), an evil (*mal*). Such "disorder", such "evil", is understood as "morally harmful", as something which of itself can never be justified. The choice of evil (not the evil itself) which has thus been knowingly and freely made does not count as morally wrong and in the proper sense sinful, so that one is not obliged for the time being to confess it. In this sense, and only in this sense, there is a rejection of the concept of the "intrinsically wrong and therefore always sinful" aspect of the moral norm. Thus a tension is seen between what is concretely possible and binding, and what holds "in itself" and "ideally".

In this sense the French Bishops' Conference, in paragraph 12 of the pastoral letter which it issued after *Humanae vitae*, seems to instruct the faithful that contraception is always an evil (*mal*) and a disorder (*désordre*) but, on the other hand, is not always a sin. Their reason for saying this is that the married couple in a dilemma can see themselves as being faced with a genuine conflict of values, so that the "choice between two serious duties" is often unavoidable. "As Christians we do not overlook the fact that our entire world is not yet free from contradiction and death, in spite of its participation in the resurrection of Christ." In an explanation of the encyclical shortly after its appearance,[23] Pope Paul VI quoted a work of the French dogmatic theologian, Martelet, which had been written the previous year,[24] in which the author had tried to solve the dilemma referred to in the manner already indicated. Some theologians believe[25] that the solution put forth by Martelet represents—at least in its practical application—the same opinion as the Pope's. Recently, the Italian moral theologian, D. Capone,[26] with a view to interpreting *Humanae vitae* (ten years after its appearance), again took up this contribution of Martelet's, to interpret it in the sense of the "moral truth" (*veritas moralis*) as understood by Aquinas. In this view, moral truth, as distinct from moral knowledge, does not depend on "being" or *scientia moralis*, but conforms to "right appetite" (*appetitus rectus*); this conformity is experienced in the actual decision. Only here can one establish what is really possible, as distinct from an impossible "ideal", and thus establish what is in truth demanded.

Since this theory of evil/disorder is meant to be understood as a moral theory, it insists on two points: first, that such a choice ought to be avoided if possible; and second, that one should "repent" of the sometimes unavoidable realization of evil/disorder, even if not as one repents of a sinful deed, or that at least it is to be "regretted."

The interpretation of this theory, which has been outlined, is hardly to be simply equated with the traditional subjective/objective distinction, as applied to ignorance and lack of freedom; nor, at least not for all its advocates, can this theory be identified with the currently frequent distinction between "right" and "good." For the authors in question, it is ultimately a matter of the problem of the incompatibility of different elements (goods/values) in the single given situation: on the one hand, the accepted norms which hold also in reality, and on the other hand, the demands made by the weakness of people who cannot avoid choosing — what is right behavior then?

2.   It can hardly be denied that we cannot fully determine what is here and now (not only psychologically but also morally) possible, what can be demanded as feasible, and therefore what is right, without taking into consideration man's actual weakness. "Because human freedom is constantly limited by concupiscence, the power of making moral decisions is...weakened; this fact cannot be overlooked in a utopian manner...[There is required] a recognition of what is here and now possible, in order to be able to accomplish progressively what is still impossible" (K. Demmer).[27] "It should be calmly admitted that a given demand is not yet feasible and that in the meantime it cannot be fulfilled; one should not give the impression that with a little bit of good will, everything will work out" (K. Rahner).[28] If the weakness caused by concupiscence can thus be a valid reason for an otherwise unjustifiable choice, then such weakness is obviously relevant to the formulation of norms. It is certainly a fact, and an element of the concrete reality with which we have to work: the reality of man as bound in concupiscence to his society and his world.

Should this position, represented by the French Bishops, Martelet, and other theologians, be (at least in its conclusion) a genuine instance of the normative relevance of weakness due to concupiscence,[29] it would still be only *one* example; and one must keep in mind the very important question of whether the foundation of this position is acceptable. Further, it must be kept in mind that weakness due to concupiscence in the case of objectifications of the "sin of the world" (see section II above) can have its own particular relevance.

Since the reality of man in his situation of concupiscence is the one and only actual reality, it is difficult to understand a theory based on the incompatibility of two levels: a level which is feasible for man as he is, and which is therefore not binding. Here it should be noted again that such an approach seems to operate covertly in terms of two moral orders, both binding and yet irreconcilable with each other: an order which is abstract and ideal, and an order which is concrete and possible.[30] It is better to begin with the one real moral order, which is concrete and possible, and therefore binding, bearing in mind that this always includes the thrust toward overcoming the limits of what is possible at a given moment, whether these limitations derive from the "condition of the sinner" or not. Then the "ideal" moral order, which often demands the impossible, would not be the real moral order of this world. "Hypostatizing" the ideal order only points up which values are mostly but not always binding here and now, and which values are at present not realizable but point toward a dynamic process of growth; the latter are not the object of an effort meant to realize them fully since they are really a part of the gift of eschatological glory, as Bonaventure put it, and thus not part of our historical order.

In a situation calling for action there may be more than one cause of an incompatibility of values; such incompatibility may be "sin-conditioned," or it may be due to mere finitude or historical complications. Therefore, the notion of "weakness due to concupiscence" may not be used to generate a solution to every situation in which such incompatibility arises; for that would, in the last analysis, imply an identification of the situation of creaturely and historical limitation with the situation of concupiscence and weakness. But if one at first treats all situations of incompatibility in terms of weakness and concupiscence, in order later to separate such solutions from the question of "sin-conditioned" weakness,[31] then one has presumably arrived at the insight that in all situations of incompatibility, whether sin-conditioned or not, there is really one and the same problem, as follows: How are we to determine what is right (as a norm, or as a solution to a particular situation) when an incompatibility of values occurs? It follows that, quite apart from whether the situation is conditioned by sin or not, the best available solution is morally simply right, and not just "good" or something that should be tried. In conscience this would not have to be repented of in the strict sense, but only regretted if or when the incompatibility is conditioned by sin rather than being otherwise caused.

Consequently, the statement that "difficult" or "sin-conditioned" solutions are at the same time "right" and "wrong" should not be too readily accepted as satisfactory. It presupposes that "*mal/evil*" and "*désordre/*disorder" mean *moral* evil or disorder. But such evil or disorder (in spite of its being conditioned by sin) can hardly be considered as moral evil in the strict sense, as distinct from "nonmoral" = "premoral" = "morally relevant."[32] If one wishes to call these moral evils in an analogous sense — and this has a Scriptural basis, but does not represent precise terminology — one would have to admit that while, as a reality emerging in the present they represent an evil for man, they do not, in the strict moral sense, represent the lack of a good that is absolutely necessary to man. The telling of material falsehoods, the outdated theology of a priest who is fully absorbed in pastoral work, and killing in self-defense are not things to be avoided absolutely (i.e. moral evil), even though they do represent real infringements on human well-being. Causing an "evil for man" is not morally wrong in every case. All that seems necessary is that it be justified by a comparative evaluation of all the elements of the total actual situation, without such evaluation having necessarily to take place on the plane of conscious reflection.

If, however, some theologians wish to understand the comparative goods or evils of the situation not as "premoral" (= morally relevant) but as being in some sense moral goods or evils, this presumably comes from their desire to protect (and quite rightly) individual goods or values by means of moral norms (e.g. "Take care of your life and defend it," "Protect the life of the aggressor."). The problem is that certain theologians uncritically term such norms "absolute" in the sense of exceptionless.[33] The fact that two or more norms may enter into a given situation, and at the same time be incompatible, shows that these norms are in themselves limited, without this being a matter of choice – that is, unless one wishes to absolutize one of these norms in a deontological sense, and at the same time to relativize all the other norms in a teleological fashion. Such norms of action are not absolute in the sense of "universal," unless one wishes somehow to exclude in advance the possible relevance of other and incompatible norms. The case is different for norms which are formal and thus may be genuinely universal – e.g. "Be just," or "Follow Christ"; taking another instance, the norm "Never treat a child cruelly" is formal in the sense that "cruelly" means with excessive severity and not merely "with severity"; in this sense "cruelly" defines a moral disvalue which must always be avoided. Accordingly, it is morally more exact to speak of a "compromise of values" *("compromis des valeurs")* than of a "compromise of duties" *("compromis de devoirs").*[34]

IV.   THE "SIN OF THE WORLD" AND MORAL KNOWLEDGE

Up to this point attention has been focused on the objective relevance of "the sin of the world" to defining what is morally right (sections I-III). Now another question must be introduced: to what extent may knowledge of what is right (as a norm or as a judgment of a situation) be influenced, in certain circumstances, by the sin of the world? This question will be examined only briefly, as it goes beyond the principal theme of these pages; nevertheless, it should be recognized that we can reach a knowledge of what is objectively right only by way of subjective knowledge and experience.[35]

Knowledge is itself a kind of moral achievement (K. Demmer);[36] it exists in a single subject who both knows and strives, and is dependent on a greater or lesser personal willingness to pursue what is right and good. If this willingness is reduced, an obscuring of moral knowledge and experience may follow. Such obscuration is to be distinguished from the incompleteness of moral knowledge due to creaturely or historical limitation.

Now moral knowledge is always attained within a historical and social process. This process is always negatively influenced by concupiscence arising from the "sin of the world", as well as by personal sin and sinful attitudes; the presence of grace does not fully exclude this. The individual in his moral knowing is dependent on the moral knowledge of the past, which has been obscured by the "sin of the world"; to this is also added the limitation of moral knowledge through personal participation in the "sin of the world" in the form of concupiscence, freely incurred sin, and sinful attitudes.

The manifold limitation of moral knowledge by the "sin of the world" can take effect in the incomplete or one-sided formulation of moral norms or of the good in a particular situation; this can happen also, though *not only*, where the "sin of the world" *objectively* specifies what is right (see above, sections I-III). It can also result that norms of action, which we as human beings establish, turn out to be insufficiently normative because they are formulated in an incomplete or one-sided way with regard to the individual case, which may be the case of a "sin-conditioned" reality. Not only the historical and creaturely limitation of moral knowledge is to be "regretted", but also, and indeed with special reason, the limitations on moral knowledge due to "sin". To be "repented of" in the proper sense are personal sin and sinful attitudes, which have as a consequence the obscuring of moral knowledge. Insofar as, at a given moment, we have available only our present level of moral knowledge, that level must directly regulate the decisions we take. That is the only way it can be; and in that sense it is according to natural law; and it calls for divine mercy and pardon only in the sense in which these are part of God's preservation of a world which exists under the sign of sin — and of grace. Certainly, we know that we are required to correct as far as possible the defects in moral knowledge which result from the "sin of the world", and especially from personal sin. This also is according to natural law, inasmuch as we have to overcome the incompleteness of our moral knowing; as we must also do with regard to the restrictions on moral knowledge due to creaturely or historical limitation.

V.   SYNTHETIC REFLECTIONS: THE "SIN OF THE WORLD" IN ITS RELEVANCE FOR THE ESTABLISHING OF MORAL NORMS

In the awareness which derives from faith, the Christian shares in the moral and religious consciousness of Christ. This includes the requirement of realizing in action, in an absolutely radical way, what is morally right.

1. The "radically right" should not be looked on as something that does not belong to the one and only reality and condition in which mankind exists. But the present order of reality does not include a "sinless beginning" intended for man, nor does it include the "eschatological perfection" which is promised as a gift, so these do not specify the "radically right" in the moral sense.[37] This holds true for Christians in this world, just as it was true analogically for Christ himself during his life on earth.

The reality with which we have to work, and which we have to develop, contains limitations on human possibility. These limitations can derive from the fact of creaturely or historical finitude, and would therefore also exist in a world without sin, requiring compromises there in action. They may also derive ultimately, in various ways, from the "sin of the world"; as they in fact do, on account of the concupiscence of mankind, on account of the objectifications of the "sin of the world" in society, including situations of injustice, and because of weakness due to the concupiscence of the acting subject. Insofar as creaturely and historical limitations, as well as limitations resulting from "sin", specify the concrete human reality, right human conduct, as well as right Christian conduct and analogically the actions of Christ on earth, have to be determined by way of a critical evaluation of these limitations. The reality we have to work with must not be understood as something static, fixed, but as something entrusted to us in view of a continual development, improvement, and overcoming of present limitations. This is required by an understanding of man that is dynamic rather than static; it is also required, and especially with reference to limitations deriving from "sin," by the existence of man in Christ as the Redeemer and the source of the "liberation of the whole man."

What is morally right must be discovered on the basis of man's experience in his finite existence, independently of the various kinds of restrictions to which he is subject (which in any case cannot always be precisely distinguished); this may be achieved in explicit moral reflection, or in a corresponding intuition or experience, or by the "moral instinct of faith" (K. Rahner), or by the method of "existential ethics" (K. Rahner). This is not a matter of detracting from an ideal solution because of difficulties encountered, but of seeking, finding, and living in radical uprightness that which is really right in the context of concrete human reality with its limitations. In other words, what is radically right is not to be sought in an abstract ideal, nor in a goal that seems obligatory but turns out to be unattainable, but in the best possible development of reality as it is encountered.

2. Determining what is morally right in a way that takes account of "sin," or of our present distance from "eschatological perfection," does not in any way mean alienation from oneself; alienation can only be from one's own dynamically understood reality, and not from a mode of being which we simply do not have. This is also true when our reality is "no longer" in possession of original grace, and "not yet" in its eschatological perfection; for the best course of action which is possible, with its implication of continual improvement, will mean the best attempt to find a way beyond present limitations to a self-realization which is less limited and thus better. This does not mean reaching either the primordial or final state intended for us by God; it represents the obligatory optimum, as distinct from an "ideal" which is not binding as a norm of action.

The choice which is determined in this way cannot be called "sin" or "guilt" in the proper sense of actively incurred guilt, even when it means bringing about a reality which is in some way marked by "sin"; being the best possible solution in a given situation, as such it cannot be called sinful or guilty. If, in spite of this, one still speaks of "sin" or "guilt,"[38] with an imprecise and undifferentiated use of terms, one runs an obvious risk of being misunderstood. Indeed, care should be taken to point out that "sin" and "guilt" are being used in an extended and analogous sense. We must understand in a similar way the "mercy" and "forgiveness" of God which are called for by such "sin" and "guilt," whether such forgiveness is considered as promised (the Protestant view) or as already given in the moral decision itself (the Catholic view).[39] For what is right — even when it is "only" the "best possible" attempt — as such has no need of merciful forgiveness. The term "sin" in this context has something to do with real sin, but it is being used in an anthropological rather than in an ethical sense.[40] On the contrary, real "sin...is not a metaphysical situation of finitude or limitation, nor of a mere falling short of an absolute demand of love";[41] for if that were the case, man, in all his right actions, would always and inevitably be a sinner.[42] Here, "pardon" can properly be used only in the sense of preservation of a world infected by sin so that it may be redeemed.[43] A morally right judgment would then be the "re-actualization of the event of salvation in a cultural and existential context."[44]

We must understand the expression, "an uneasy conscience" in a parallel way.[45] He who demands "repentance" of an uneasy conscience for having done what was right even though "sin-conditioned" should explain that he is using the term "repentance" in an extended and analogous sense.[46] If the term "regret" is chosen instead of "repentance," it becomes clear that basically the same terminology can be used for solutions which are not "sin-conditioned" and for those which are "sin-conditioned," not ideal, but correct; although there is still a specific motive for "regretting" a solution which is "sin-conditioned" but correct.

3. If a correct but "difficult" solution is labeled as a compromise — in a special sense when it presupposes the "sin of the world" — then it is a compromise only in comparison with an impossible moral ideal, an ideal which is not binding as a norm of action in our given situation; and therefore it is not in the strict sense a moral compromise. This so-called compromise lies "in the realm of behavior and...refers to a choice between responsibilities toward the world. In the compromise one is forced to sacrifice a particular value, which might be realized in action, in favor of another value."[47] Such values therefore do not absolutely have to be realized in individual situations. As values which are part of the well-being of the human world they are not moral values (which always have to be implemented) but premoral values[48] which have to be implemented as far as possible according to the context. Only values which determine the person as such (!) — and not merely the well-being of the person — are of themselves moral values. Therefore the compromise-solution does not allow the simultaneous realization of the morally right and the morally wrong, but only of the morally right, which, however, contains both nonmoral right (good/value) and nonmoral wrong (evil/disvalue).

With regard to norms of action formulated by human beings, which protect premoral rather than moral values, it must be asked if they really have a validity as extensive as, at first sight, they seem to have. Accordingly, the "difficult" solution, even when it is "conditioned by sin," is not a compromise with respect to exceptionless moral norms of action, but rather may represent a necessary correction of inexactly formulated norms.[49]

The expression "moral compromise" can thus be applied to such situations only in an extended analogous sense. Such a compromise means the unavoidable introduction of an evil into this world, but not sin in the proper sense. But this evil can in some circumstances be a consequence of the "sin of the world".

4. The relevance of the "sin of the world" regarding moral knowledge leads to problems which are similar to those regarding objectively right moral norms.

5. Within Catholic moral theology there is a steadily growing awareness of the relevance of the "sin of the world" to the correct formulation of moral norms. The attempt to call in question a too optimistic application of natural law should clearly proceed with great caution; in any case there is no conceivable way of arriving at moral norms which excludes reflection in terms of the relevance of "being conditioned by sin" to the definition of what is objectively right, and when he is thinking rather of its relevance to subjectively good action.

He who begins from an emphasis on the history of salvation, tends in this context to use terms such as "sin," "guilt," "divine mercy and forgiveness," "radicalism," etc., even where such formulations are, from the viewpoint of tradition, unexpected; and thus he is obliged, in order to avoid misunderstandings, to explain that he is using such terms in a special sense which is extended or analogous. He who insists above all on exact ethical formulations should not underestimate the relevance of the "sin of the world" and its importance in normative ethics; at the same time he must also indicate the limited applicability of extended conceptions in normative ethics, and will above all resist an inappropriate rejection of general ethical reasoning (natural law reasoning), or the appearance of such rejection, since this kind of reasoning will always be a necessary part of theological reflection. But this position can also mean that a good ethical solution, in "sin-conditioned" as in other "difficult" situations, requires a clear distinction between goods/values and evils/disvalues which are moral, and those which are premoral (morally relevant), as well as a further distinction between norms of action which are genuinely absolute and universal, and those which only appear at first sight to be so.

NOTES

1. On the Protestant problem, cf., for example, J.M. Gustafson, *Protestant and Roman Catholic Ethics. Prospects for Rapprochement*, Chicago and London 1978, 6-12. Cf. also H.J. Wilting, "Der Kompromiss als theologisches und ethisches Problem. Ein Beitrag zur unterschiedlichen Beurteilung des Kompromisses durch H. Thielicke und W. Trilhaas", *Moraltheol. Studien*, System. Abt., 3, Düsseldorf 1975. Cf. also K. Demmer, "Entscheidung und Kompromiss," *Gregorianum* 53 (1972), 323-51.

On the Catholic problem, cf. the literature cited throughout my presentation. First of all, cf. C.A.J. van Ouwerkerk, "Gospel Morality and Human Compromise," *Concilium* vol.7 no.5 (May 1965), 5-12.

2. On the problem of "sin of the world" and "original sin", cf., for example K. Rahner, "Erbsünde," *LThK²* IX, 1979ff; cf. idem on the theological concept of concupiscence, *Theological Investigations* I, London 1961, 347-82; cf. also P. Schoonenberg, "Der Mensch in der Sünde" in F. Feiner and M. Löhrer (eds.), *Mysterium Salutis*, 845-56.

3. Cf. A. Johnson, *Rightness and Goodness, A Study in Contemporary Ethical Theory* (International Scholars Forum, 13), The Hague 1959.

4. It is principally O. Schilling who called attention to this difference; cf. his *Naturrecht und Staat nach der Lehre der alten Kirche*, Paderborn 1914, 4ff, 10ff,227ff; idem, *Die Staats- und Soziallehre des hl. Thomas von Aquin*, Munich 1930, 7, 9ff, 25ff, 330ff. Cf. also R. Linhardt, *Die Sozialprinzipien des hl. Thomas von Aquin. Versuch einer Grundlegung der speziellen Soziallehren des Aquinaten*, Freiburg i. Br. 1932, 170ff. Cf. also P. Tischleder, *Ursprung und Träger der Staatsgewalt nach der Lehre des hl. Thomas v. Aquin und seiner Schule*, München-Gladbach 1923, especially 37-45.

On what follows, cf. J. Fuchs, *Natural Law: A Theological Approach*, Dublin 1965, 85-109.

5. Cf. R. Linhardt, op. cit., 205-10.

6. *In II Sent.* d. 44, a.3, q.1 conclusio and ad 4. (Quaracchi, II, 1008f.). Cf. also *In III Sent.* d. 37, a.1, q.3 (Quaracchi, III, 818-21).

7. Cf. J. Fuchs, *Natural Law...* loc. cit. (see note 4 above). Cf. also O. Schilling, *Die staats- und Soziallehre des hl. Thomas v. A.*, loc. cit. (see note 2 above), 10: "The extent to which sin has had an influence in changing the world can be easily shown by the example of the State; even in the state of innocence there would have been a State as well as a government and a lawful order, but the government would have shown itself to be a loving and concerned guide. Now, however, in view of the world in which people strive against one another, coercion is the indispensable means made necessary by nature, if the State is to survive. Thus there is a secondary natural law as a result of sin; it contains principles which can have importance precisely with regard to sin."

8. H. Thielicke is Lutheran Protestantism's leading theologian of ethics; cf. his *Theologische Ethik*, Tübingen 1951,especially vol. 1, passim. For reformed Protestantism, cf. E. Brunner, *Das Gebot und die Ordnungen. Entwurf einer protestantisch-theologischen Ethik*, Tübingen 1923, 2nd ed., 604-6.

9. Cf. sections 2 and 3 of this chapter.

10. J. Fuchs, "De libertate religiosa et de libertate religionis Christi":*Gregorianum* 47 (1966) 41-52, 55ff.,n.7. (The text of this note originally appeared in idem, "Christliches Rechtsverständnis", in *Vom Recht. Hannoversche Beiträge zur politischen Bildung*, vol. 3, Hanover 1963, 211-26.)

11. C.E. Curran, *Themes in Fundamental Moral Theology*, Notre

Dame, Indiana 1977, 139-44 (also in *Louvain Studies* 1977, 239-55); idem *Ongoing Revision. Studies in Moral Theology*, Notre Dame 1975, 182-90; idem, *Catholic Moral Theology in Dialogue*, Notre Dame 1972, 184-219; idem, *A New Look at Christian Morality*, Notre Dame 1968, 169-73.

12.   It is likely that in some societies this is often the case!

13.   C.E. Curran, *Themes in Fundamental Moral Theology*, loc. cit., 140.

14.   Cf. J. Gründel, "Überlegungen zum Wesen und zur Eigenart der Sünde", in G. Teichtweier and W. Dreier (eds.), *Herausforderung und Kritik der Moraltheologie*, Würzburg 1971, 131-48, especially 140ff.

15.   Curran holds this; close to him in this respect are, for example, Martelet, Pousset, Chirico, Crotty, Demmer (cf. sections 3 and 4 of this article). For the contrary opinion, cf. B. Schüller, *Die Begründung sittlicher Urteile. Typen ethischer Argumentation in der katholischen Moraltheologie*, Düsseldorf 1973, 162.

16.   Compare this formulation (in German: "zumutbar") with K. Demmer, "Hermeneutische Probleme der Fundamentalmoral", in D. Mieth and F. Compagnoni (eds.), *Ethik im Kontext des Glaubens*, Freiburg in Ue., Freiburg i. Br. 1978, 101-19; idem, "Sittlich Handeln aus Erfahrung," *Gregorianum* 50 (1978) 661-90, especially 671ff.

17.   But cf. C.E. Curran, *Themes in Fundamental Moral Theology*, loc. cit., 140.

18.   The playing-off of a concrete possible order against an ideal, concrete, but impossible order would, on the other hand, be working with two incompatible orders which at the same time make demands on us. Cf. N.J. Rigali, "The Unity of the Moral Order," *Chicago Studies* 8 (1969), 125-43.

19.   Cf. K. Rahner, in A. Röper, *Objektive und subjektive Moral. Ein Gespräch mit Karl Rahner*, Freiburg-Basle-Vienna 1971, 58: "...values, which because they are not yet actual do not yet actually obligate...do not obligate even if...one already 'theoretically' knows the demands which compromise them."

20.   N. Crotty, "Conscience and Conflict," *Theological Studies* 32 (1971), 215, holds a different view.

21.   Thomas Aquinas, *S.T.* I-II 94, 4c.

22.   Cf., for example, G. Martelet, *Amour conjugal et renouveau conciliaire*, Paris 1967; idem, "Pour mieux comprendre l'encyclique Humanae Vitae", *Nouvelle Revue Théologique* 90 (1968) 897-917, and especially 1009-63 (= idem, *L'existence humaine. Pour mieux comprendre l'encyclique Humanae Vitae*, Paris 1969); E. Pousset, *Union conjugal et liberté. Essai sur le problème traité par l'encyclique Humanae Vitae*, Paris 1970; P. Chirico, "Tension, Morality, and Birth Control", *Theol. Studies* 28 (1967), 258-85; idem, "Morality in General and Birth Control in Particular", *Chicago Studies* 9 (1970), 19-33; N.J. Rigali, "The Unity of the Moral Order", *Chicago Studies* 8 (1969), 125-43; N. Crotty, "Conscience and Conflict", *Theol. Studies* 32 (1979), 208-32. Cf. also C. Robert, "La situation de conflit: Un thème dangereux de la théologie morale d'aujourd'hui", *Revue des sci-*

ences relig. 44 (1970), 190-213; J.M. Aubert, "Hiérarchie des valeurs et histoire", *Revue des sciences relig.* 44 (1970) 5-22; K. Demmer, "Entscheidung und Kompromiss", loc. cit. (see note 1 above), 323-50; idem, "Hermeneutische Probleme der Fundamentalmoral", loc. cit. (see note 16 above), 101-19; idem, *Entscheidung und Verhängnis. Die moraltheologische Lehre von der Sünde im Lichte christologischer Anthropologie*, Paderborn 1976, 141-77; R.A. McCormick, "Notes on Moral Theology", *Theol. Studies* 32 (1971), 80-97; and 33 (1972), 68-86. and 33 (1972), 68-86.

23.   Address given on 31 July 1968.

24.   G. Martelet, *Amour conjugal et renouveau conciliaire*, Paris 1967.

25.   P. Delhaye, "Intrinsèquement déshonnête" in: idem et al., *Pour relire Humanae Vitae*, Gembloux 1970, 23-34. Nevertheless, official indications in *L'Osservatore Romano* created the impression that "Rome" was not completely happy with the formulation of the French Bishops.

26.   D. Capone, "La Humanae Vitae nel ministero sacerdotale", *Lateranum* 44 (1978), 195-227. On the question of "moral truth", cf. D. Capone, "Intorno alla verità morale" (excerpt from dissertation, Pontifical Gregorian University), Naples, 1951.

27.   K. Demmer, *Entscheidung und Verhängnis*, loc. cit. (see note 22 above), 170.

28.   K. Rahner, in A. Röper, *Objektive und subjektive Moral. Ein Gespräch mit Karl Rahner*, loc. cit. (see note 19 above), 68. The saying of St. Augustine and the Council of Trent does not contradict what was said above: "God does not command what is impossible, but instructs you by His commands to do what you are able, to ask for what you are not able to do, and he helps you so that you are able" (DS 1536). There would be a contradiction only if one were to wish to see the "true" will of God in the here-and-now impossible; that, however, would be the Lutheran thesis. One cannot also hold the contrary, that the Council understood that "true" to be the will of God; that may indeed be, but the Council did not express itself on this question.

29.   Certainly this example, which was chosen from many more, can give rise to some doubts; for in this case the ideal to be sought would be to live the married life, after some years, more or less celibately as long as the marriage lasted. Is not this a mistaken manner of thinking?

30.   Cf. N.J. Rigali's excellent contribution in this area, "The Unity of the Moral Order", loc. cit. (see note 18 above).

31.   Cf. Chirico in his two contributions of 1967 and 1970 (see note 22 above).

32.   Accordingly, "mal" (evil) and "désordre" (disorder), in the explanation of the French Bishops' Conference, should have been understood in a nonmoral sense (as morally relevant). Undoubtedly, every contraceptive act means some evil for man. With such an understanding, the bishops' argumentation would have been correct, but—as an American theologian (Chirico, 1970) pointed out—would have caused a variant reading of *Humanae vitae*.

33.   Cf. C.A.J. van Ouwerkerk, "Gospel Morality and Human Compromise", loc. cit. (see note 1 above), 10.

34.   Robert and Aubert, loc. cit., also say this (see note 22 above). Cf. also B. Schüller, *Die Begründung sittlicher Urteile*... loc. cit. (see note 16 above), 16lff.

35.   It is K. Demmer's special merit to have called attention in a cogent way to the "sin-conditioned" insufficiency of moral knowledge: cf. his "Entscheidung und Kompromiss", *Gregorianum* 53 (1972), 323-50; also his *Entscheidung uno Verhängnis* (see note 27 above), 170-77; likewise cf. his "Hermeneutische Probleme der Fundamentalmoral", loc. cit. (see note 16 above), 101-19.

36.   K. Demmer, *Entscheidung und Verhängnis*, loc. cit., 169.

37.   He who, contrary to this, joins Christian radicalism to a never possible ideal, is compelled to call attention to the fact that this radicalism "(may) not be held to be an immediately reachable norm of conduct." Cf. K. Demmer, *Entscheidung und Verhängnis*, loc. cit. (see note 22 above), 18. B. Schüller, "Zur Rede von der radikalen sittlichen Forderung", *Theol. Phil.* 46 (1971), 321-41, is of a different opinion.

38.   Cf. N. Crotty, "Conscience and Conflict", loc. cit. (see note 22 above), 214.

39.   An example of the Protestant approach is that of H. Thielicke and E. Brunner (cf. note 8 above); for an example of the Catholic approach, cf. K. Demmer, "Entscheidung und Kompromiss," loc. cit. (see note 1 above), 342 ff.

40.   Cf. C.A.J. van Ouwerkerk, "Gospel Morality and Human Compromise," loc. cit. (see note 1 above), 371.

41.   K. Rahner, *Bertrachtungen zum ignatianischen Exerzitienbuch*, Munich 1965, 39.

42.   Cf. N. Crotty "Conscience and Conflict," loc. cit. (see note 22 above), 215.

43.   See note 10 above.

44.   G. Piana, "Per un'ermeneutica della decisione etica": *Strumenti*...*Communio* 22 (1975), 13.

45.   Cf., for example, Martelet. Pousset, Demmer (see note 22 above).

46.   Cf. also B. Schüller, "Zur Rede von der radikalen sittlichen Forderung", loc. cit. (see note 37 above), 341.

47.   C.A.J. van Ouwerkerk, "Gospel Morality and Human Compromise," loc. cit. (see note 1 above), 8.

48.   Earlier I preferred to say "physical" (following the Scholastics); here I prefer "pre-moral". P. Knauer also formerly said "physical": "Das rechtverstandene Prinzip von der Doppelwirkung als Fundament jeder Gewissenentscheidung", *Th. Gl.* 67 (1967), 107-33; in the English edition, however, "pre-moral" is also used: *The Natural Law Forum* 12 (1967), 132-62. B. Schüller uses "nonmoral": cf., for example, his *Die Begründung sittlicher Urteile*... loc. cit.(see note 15 above), 39-45. L. Janssens prefers "ontic": "Ontic Evil and Moral Evil," *Louvain Studies* 4 (1972), 115-56, but also uses "pre-

moral": "Norms and Priorities in a Love Ethics", *Louvain Studies* 9 (1977), 207-38, see p. 216, n. 8. F. Scholz expands the definition when he uses "values of a physical-innerworldly type": *Wege, Umwege, und Auswege der Moraltheologie. Ein Plädoyer für begründete Ausnahmen*, Munich 1976, 24-8.

49. Cf. K. Demmer, "Entscheidung und Kompromiss," loc. cit. (see note 1 above), 328ff, 345ff, and 349ff. Cf. also J. Fuchs, "The Absoluteness of Moral Terms", *Gregorianum* 52 (1971), 415-57 (also in this volume).

9. Morality as the Shaping of the Future of Man

A somewhat longer title for the present essay, with the words "as man" added, would indicate more exactly its true intention. This addition would make it clear that what interests morality is not *any* future of man, but one which is truly human, in the best sense of the word.

In fact, various disciplines, which contribute in their own way to the totality of the sciences, are interested in one sense or another in the future of man and for this reason pursue futurology. We are speaking of those sciences which seek to arrive at some forecasts and predictions about the future of man, and which perhaps also hope to influence the direction mankind is to take, by striving to actualize these forecasts and predictions.

Clearly, futurology cannot avoid taking into account the moral comportment of man, not only as it exists now but also as it is foreseen.

For its part, morality cannot be practiced without heeding the futurological perspectives on the diverse dimensions of human reality. This is because morality as such is concerned for the multiple projections regarding man's future — whether proximate or remote — to assure not only a future that would promote human values in one or other dimension of reality — as, for example, in biology or technology — but also a future that would promote those values capable of being given a place, according to their hierarchy and urgency, within the total system of human values.

For this reason, the phrase "the future of man *as man*" is of utmost importance. Although particular advances in different sectors — biology, technology, health, science, culture — truly offer promise for man and his future, they are not yet advances of man as such, that is, contributions to his dignity as a human person. In other words, the main concern of morality is that men's undertakings do not bring about merely the advancement of some particular values insofar as they are particular, but that this advancement become that of the human person as such. Only in this way will man's progress be a human and not an inhuman one. Not all man's successes are truly human successes — that is, those worthy of man.

I. MORALITY AND HUMAN PROJECTS

1. If it is commonly asserted that morality formulates positive or negative moral norms, this in fact affirms that morality provides plans for man's life and activity which properly correspond to his being. Morality also points out human enterprises which do not befit man, since they stand in contrast to his reality and deny his true being.

With this affirmation it becomes evident that moral norms are not static laws which entered the world of man from outside the world and from outside man. Rather it is man himself (humanity) who already possesses within him at all times an (active) self-understanding, although occasionally it proves itself to be inadequate and perhaps, in certain respects, even erroneous. This self-understanding may often be neither very explicit nor reflective, but more intuitive and athematic.

Man's self-understanding is not purely individualistic; it is, instead, relational − that is, in contact with other persons (a personal Absolute is not excluded here) and with the world of human beings. The human person compretends his being neither as a static reality to be diligently conserved as such, nor as a fixed entity from which he may simply deduce behavioral norms for the future; the reason for this is that being is a static category while activity is a dynamic one.

It is rather the case that man experiences himself as a being who is not merely a "datum" but a "task". This means that man, as he finds himself in various conditions and situations − in relation to other persons, to groups, to society, to the concrete world of man, and even to the material world − can and must search for a mode or plan of acting and of realizing himself; he must do this to make of his "datum" a new and more suitable reality. This is because every actualization of the "datum" cannot fail to involve its transformation into a new reality which to some extent is different, changed, developed.

Therefore, the moral norms which we formulate are nothing other than attempts to indicate schemes for human activity and self-actualization with respect to the future. These norms, since they correspond to what man really is − even the man whose situation is defined by specific conditions − represent a true development of the human, not the contrary.

A favorite idea of Pierre Teilhard de Chardin was that sin consists precisely in not realizing − even in blocking − the true development and (in this sense) progress of mankind, insofar as this progress is human.

2. The moral norms which men formulate are not to be understood, therefore, as "limits" or "conditions" imposed from outside by a God who is man's path toward the future, as if they were street signs; man himself can eventually foresee and plan another path and another future for himself and for his world.

It is man himself (humanity), precisely due to the fact that he is personal, who plans the avenues toward his future by reflecting on his past with all its successes and failures; sometimes there are successes in a certain sector of man's activity (e.g., in industry) which are simultaneously failures with regard to the overall harmony which various human values should create, and thus perhaps with regard to the *humanum* at the core of man's person. Beyond looking to the past, man reflects on the present possibilities of "man-humanity-world", and especially on forecasts he makes and on the consequences which would follow from the various projects on the drawing-board.

Morality can approve only those projects and those choices which can be foreseen as successful not only in a particular practical domain, but also in the domain of the *humanum*, which includes all aspects of man's being. This is so because the "human being" of man is always situated in real circumstances. By keeping in mind the personal dimensions of his future, man thus formulates and indicates solutions which are "humanly" acceptable.

In doing this, man (humanity – when I say man, I always mean humanity-society) does not deprive God the Creator of his absolute supremacy; rather, man fulfills his own task of foreseeing, providing for and realizing the continual unfolding of the created nucleus which he is. Yet he must always make sure that this unfolding does not stop merely at the achievement of particular material goals but includes human progress, that is, a state of being which is worthy of man-humanity.

3. Hence it follows that the projects formulated by moral theology in the form of moral norms or of concrete solutions are personal and historical.

A. They are personal insofar as there is no being or reality outside of man – neither a *Deus ex machina*, nor a biophysical nature – which dictates to him his projects and norms; rather, it is man the person who, as such, seeks to determine which course of activity can eventually or certainly guarantee a future success for mankind which is truly human. Naturally, there are many possibilities offered by created reality (be they physical, biological, psychological, etc.), and thus man must take into account prudent plans and reasonable forecasts.

B. Such projects, formulated as moral norms or as humanly acceptable solutions, are historical, insofar as they must clearly take into account known data, experiences gained and evaluated, and reasonably possible forecasts. To the extent that the data, experiences and forecasts can change substantially, the projects-norms-solutions which have been available up to a given point do not, from the very start, exclude a necessary reformulation. For example, experience, knowledge and forecasts in the field of sexuality, marriage, or the family, if they are really novel, may perhaps require that some former schemas, norms or projects should be rethought. To a great extent it is man himself (humanity), since he is essentially historical, who actively undergoes such changes. Yet, the alteration of some element of his culture may mean that eventually new projects, norms and solutions must be formulated.

Furthermore, it follows that different cultures, with their particular knowledge of data, experience and forecasts, can at some point arrive at different judgments regarding projects which may seem to be materially the same.

This means that, per se, possible different forecasts require different judgments concerning the human admissibility, in a given culture, of determined projects-norms-solutions.

In this regard we might consider St. Paul, who could not foresee (we are speaking of futurological foresight!) the emancipation of slaves and of women, and who therefore set down norms which seemed eternal to him, but which we do not accept today, because his foresight was limited.

Finally, it follows that in extremely contingent matters pertaining to the actualization of human life, it is not normally possible, in the process of affirming projects-norms-solutions, to have evidence which is binding; rather, it is possible to attain only what we are accustomed to call "moral certainty", which man must be content with in the daily acts through which he realizes himself.

II. CRITERIA FOR JUDGING HUMAN PROJECTS

1. Man is readily inclined to search for and find criteria to enable him to make a reasonable judgment on human projects. Often he seeks these criteria outside of himself, his own reason and intuition; for example, he looks for certain "general principles" to be given to him from beyond. By acting this way, however, man is no longer that being who possesses self-understanding and who is therefore called to self-realization. He is no longer that personal being who is the image of God and who must freely take charge of himself since he participates in the general providence of God (St. Thomas). Because of this, general principles, those ultimate criteria for more concrete judgments, are made known through "man's self-understanding".

It is evidently not the individual man who comes to know these general principles; all of humanity or a particular society slowly arrives at comprehending them, and individuals participate in this knowledge to a greater or lesser degree.

Such principles ultimately permit us to judge what concrete activities and projects, formulated as norms or solutions, are humanly admissible. In other words, they allow us to evaluate the total network, composed of various data, experiences and forecasts, in the light of our understanding of man's being and dignity.

2.   Vatican II's *Gaudium et spes* tells us repeatedly that plans for the realization of the modern world should aim at a better and more human future for humanity, and thus ought to be drafted in accord with our "experience of the world" (this is the Council's wording). This means that future projects should be carried out together with other persons who have the same human experience, even with men who are not Christians.

But *Gaudium et spes* adds that Christians, in their attempts to determine such projects, also enjoy "the light of the Gospel" and not simply the experience of the world.

It was not said that the light of the Gospel itself provides solutions to the problems of the world today. Such light, however, will aid the Christian in formulating projects-norms-solutions worthy of man.

Faced with the question, "In what does the light of the Gospel consist?" we can give the global answer that it consists in the "Christ-event" itself, as the formula in general use today to express that central reality which is light for the man (humanity) who is called to seek projects-norms-solutions for his world.

More concretely, we may say: there is knowledge of the person and life of Christ; one who knows Christ, who contemplates him, will have a profound and rich experience which will make possible, or more easily possible, the drafting of projects which are more suitable remedies for the difficulties confronting mankind today. There are the accentuated themes in the Lord's discourses; in these emphasis is placed on particular values, norms and models, as is the case in the Sermon on the Mount. The values accentuated here are, for the most part, human in the best sense of the word. Yet man, insofar as he is egotistic, does not easily see them. The Lord stresses precisely these; Christians, well aware of his emphases, have a light which helps them seek solutions in their present situation.

There are fundamental orientations such as, for example, St. John's mandate to love one's brothers, or St. Paul's conviction that one who is baptized is reconciled to God and dead to sin. Thus, no project which could in some manner involve sin is acceptable to one who is baptized, who believes and is reconciled with God.

In addition to St. Paul's basic guidelines, we should also take seriously the more concrete exhortations in which he meant to indicate practical directives, precepts and advice. It is true that perhaps there are, here and there, some concrete suggestions which were determined by the age in which he lived and by the fact that his foresight too was limited.

The Gospel also contains prophetic and eschatological promises of reconciliation, peace and justice. I refer to these because J.B. Metz has taken them as the point of departure for his political theology. We have, as he claims, promises of reconciliation, peace and justice from Christ in the Gospels, which, however, will be perfectly fulfilled only at the end of time. In the meanwhile, we cannot fail to form plans for this world of ours which are, in part, already projects of reconciliation, peace and justice.

There are some anthropological implications in the Gospel which, for example, assure our definitive acceptance by God. Furthermore, this acceptance is offered to each individual man. There are also anthropological implications which assure us of the dignity of each human person. Human dignity, therefore, ought to be rigorously protected in every project of man.

I think that to arrive at solutions with regard to problems such as abortion, euthanasia, suicide, etc., the clear anthropological implications of the Gospel have their own special importance. I do not mean by this that apart from the Gospel nothing can be said about man's dignity or about that of each individual person, but the Gospel provides us with a stronger and more reassuring light.

In addition, there is the Church, as a community and as an authority, as a rich tradition (notwithstanding the errors which have occurred) and as a resolute moral force; the ethical teaching of the Church is also very rich (despite the deficiencies of every necessarily limited earthly reality). There is also the presence already in this world, of the Kingdom of God — that is, the true conversion of so many men (and not only of men who are specifically called Christian) — a conversion which is always imperfect and always to be perfected, a conversion from an egotistical closing-in on oneself to an opening in love to others: to men and God. Such a conversion opens one's eyes to the truth, and helps to prevent projects-norms-solutions which are not admissible because they are dictated by egotism.

3. There is, then, a convergence of human possibilities and of Christian light or inspiration, which enables us to conceive a future that man is capable of realizing. This can be done, on the one hand, by judging projects which have already been proposed, in such a way that, given the knowledge of data, experience and foresight, we can determine whether they are feasible human undertakings for man as such. On the other hand, we can achieve the same end by creatively proposing projects-norms-solutions which man can realize as he directs himself toward the future.

It is evident that the light of the Gospel is of extreme importance for these possible future accomplishments of man. In its radiance he can comprehend better and more deeply the meaning of life which enters into any determination of his future human activity and which is substantially different from the meaning of life advocated by other faiths or ideologies also involved in laying the foundation of future human projects. One who undertakes an industrial or commercial activity, a medical procedure, an experiment in biology or in physics, etc., ought to consider whether these activities, together with their consequences and their more or less certainly foreseen effects, are justifiable. Do they bring about progress which is merely limited to one particular sector of human reality or do they foster human activity which benefits all men as human beings? Often a man's faith or ideology will be of fundamental importance in reaching a choice or decision of great responsibility.

III. THE VALUE OF PROJECTS-NORMS

1. Forecasts and predictions are generally more or less probable, and only sometimes certain. Therefore human projects, based on such forecasts and predictions, will share in this uncertainty about success.

Many projects-norms of moral science also will not have a metaphysical certainty − not even with the help of the Gospel's light. A more profound certainty is not possible with regard to concrete decisions about human life, since such matters are quite contingent.

2. Besides this, our formulations of projects-norms are not only abstract and thus not fully reflective of the much richer reality which actual circumstances enjoy, but are also often propositions-projects which we have inadequately formulated.

Sometimes our formulation, which seeks to safeguard the *humanum* of man's future activity, is too broad; it would seem at first to be a universal. But perhaps in concrete action it becomes clear that a norm which is intended to protect one value of human action — for example, the value of fertility — is not compatible with a norm which seeks to protect another value — for example, the richness and consistency of the interpersonal life of marriage. It is our duty — at least according to some episcopal conferences on the subject — to discern which of the values protected by the respective norms-projects for conjugal life are the higher or the more urgent ones. In this way one may discern which project-norm ought to be realized in the concrete so that the life of married people may truly share in the development of the human.

It can be the case that a project-norm is an ideal, but that the conditions supposed by such a formulated ideal are not present (or are not yet present, or no longer present), so that the ideal project-norm which we have formulated is clearly not the project-norm to be realized in the given conditions; when this occurs, then an optimal project-norm ought to be realized; I am thinking, for example, of how the institution of marriage is concretely determined in certain very divirsified cultures.

It could be that either man's limitations or his existence in a world which is clearly marked (in its structures and customary modes of action) by signs of injustice do not allow him to act as if these limitations and this state of being marked by the sin of the world did not exist. This means that we are sometimes forced to act in a manner which basically does not please us; I am thinking, for example, of certain rules of conduct in the business world which at first sight might seem unjust, but are not, insofar as — within certain limits — they are accepted as common practice and presupposed by all.

The ideal project-norm is no longer, in this case and in similar situations, the true project-norm; the true one is rather that project-norm which, on the one hand, takes such a concrete situation into account, but on the other hand, seeks to lead common practices toward a more ideal project-norm.

It could be that sometimes we find ourselves faced with certain situations which require us to test the projects-norms which we have formulated: the latter no longer seem to be those which correspond to the reality which we face in today's circumstances. Thus, they seem to be norms which perhaps no longer guarantee the *humanum* in the modern world.

In that case a change of project or projects may prove to be necessary. This does not mean that we ought continually to live with the uncertain feeling that the projects-norms we possess and carry with us may be eventually surpassed or deemed invalid. Yet it could be the case that we suspect something has substantially changed. Thus we ought to reflect on what the true project might be in such a concrete situation.

3.   This question arises in a very acute manner for specialists in the sciences. The specialists in biology, chemistry, physics and many other areas are the only ones who know their respective disciplines; they are therefore the only ones capable of foresight and predictions. They are also the only ones able to judge their respective projects with regard to the *humanum* and therefore with regard to morality.

Specialists ought to be men who have developed a global vision of mankind and who thus keep alive within themselves fundamental principles for human action which is truly worthy of this designation. They ought to be men who have an idea of the dignity of mankind as a whole, and of the individual, as well as of the role of society and humanity. Only in this way will they be capable of shaping projects which are humanly valid.

In conclusion I would like to say only this: it has become clear, I hope, that there is some relation between morality and the sciences which are called futurological. Those who work in the field of futurology ought to consider and accept some of the insights which are commonly held by responsible moralists, and moralists ought to listen to the forecasts and predictions of other sciences, and should seek an explaination of them so that, as far as possible, a human judgment should not be based on "I know nothing about it", but on known facts as much as possible, and not only on these but also on the forecasts and predictions made by specialists. By doing this, morality will be able to assist in guaranteeing that man's various projects are human, humanly "acceptable" and thus properly "moral".

10. Epikeia *Applied to Natural Law?*

Epikeia as a guide in the use of human law has been well known from Aristotle's time. His doctrine exerted its greatest influence in Christian morality through knowledge of his *Nicomachean Ethics*, especially on the part of Saints Albert the Great and Thomas Aquinas. The question of *epikeia* arose from the conflict between universal law and changeable human reality, both of which exist in the concrete at the same time. Perhaps, then, the law can be in need of some adaptation — *epikeia*. Certainly Plato, considering above all the principle of law (as idea), held that every adaptation to changeable reality does violence to the law. Aristotle, however, considered *epikeia* as a virtue that creates a complete correspondence between the principle of law and changing human reality; thus *epikeia* is the virtue which properly accounts for the correspondence. It was inevitable that many theologians, both medieval and modern, began to consider the parallel question of whether *epikeia*, considered first of all with regard to positive human law, could also be effective with regard to natural moral law. It is precisely this question that I intend to treat here, since such a consideration is important for a true concept of moral norms. Many years ago, while treating *epikeia* from the aspect of positive human law, I briefly noted the following point: "In natural law (and divine-natural law), if this is considered as an internal law, there is no case of *epikeia* or excuse from the law; however, it may exist in some (inadequate) formulations of the law."[1]

There is a certain difficulty in employing the term "natural (moral) law" because it gives rise to so many erroneous interpretations; I would prefer to speak of "human morality" or of the "morality of man" as he is experienced here and now, or even of the "law of creation". I am staying with the definition "natural law" because the problem has been stated in these terms. Let us note here that the term "natural law" is not restricted to those few norms which are known very easily to all, but extends to all norms which per se are accessible to human judgment.

What has been written either about *epikeia* in general,[2] or about its specific relation to positive human law, and especially about its relation to natural moral law,[3] whether from a historical or a speculative point of view, has been presupposed in this present study and will not be repeated; these studies, however, will be utilized.

I. EPIKEIA – *THE VIRTUE OF CORRECTLY APPLYING A DEFICIENT LAW*

1. Aristotle's problem was this: the law is the work of men, made to serve society; it is an "idea", and certainly a universal one. Society, on the other hand, is itself a "human" reality, concrete and subject to change. In the conflict between these two elements, which is both possible and real, a certain "deficiency" may be observed. This deficiency is understood as necessarily belonging to the law itself, which is made by man. For the law is a human "construct" and is wholly ordered toward the service of society. Hence the virtuous citizen, realizing that a law is clearly deficient, will see what is to be done about bringing the law into conformity with the actual reality of society. Thus, as a service, which it is called to furnish, the law should correspond to the actual manner in which society exists; for otherwise, the way in which the law is employed will be useless or harmful. The true intention of the law, that of serving a concrete civilization, is therefore more essential than the written words of the law stated in a universal way. *Epikeia* does not permit anything to be taken away from the law, but states that a formally deficient law, when it is to be applied, is "corrected", or rather, that the intention behind the law is rendered effective by means of such a "correction". Aristotle, Albert, and Aquinas all held this.

Indeed, one could go beyond the words of these learned men, for, if a law which is meant to serve the community is somehow deficient, *epikeia* can also bring about an effect which surpasses what the words of the law decree. Did not the Lord, in the Sermon on the Mount, say that such a "fulfillment" of the old decrees was necessary? Along with Aristotle himself, Thomas and Albert understood and openly stated that the correction of a law which is somehow deficient, or the application of this law through the virtue of *epikeia*, is morally superior to the mere observation of the letter of the law. And more clearly than Aristotle, these great Christian doctors said that in the case of a deficient law the virtue of *epikeia* can cause the natural law, which positive law is intended to specify and render effective, to be complete and to surpass what men decreed in making the law. Natural law, however, was held to be divine in origin, or a participation in eternal law: therefore *epikeia* was understood as enhancing, transcending, and thus correcting with the virtue of divine wisdom, a law which was humanly promulgated.

However, when Aquinas spoke of *epikeia*, he always had in mind the good of society which was to be furthered by the law, and the good of individuals only insofar as the latter contributed to the good of society. Later writings, such as those of Francis Suarez, maintain that the end of *epikeia* is the good of individuals as such, and not just as members of society. *Epikeia* is therefore seen (differently from Aquinas) as not merely a subdivision of justice, but as a virtue protecting and furthering the various values of life — but a virtue that is always under the law which orders the good of society. Today, however, since society, because of its immense institutional administration, is so much "under the law," the virtue of *epikeia* serves the desired goal of individual responsibility in the face of a law which is necessarily deficient, and it thus amends, completes, and fulfills the law.[4]

2. If *epikeia* can be said to be a virtue concerned with the fulfilling of the law, and even the natural moral law — if, I say, this can be said — it must be said analogously. For when one who uses *epikeia* corrects the positive law by means of natural law, such a use of *epikeia* must be said to correct natural law through natural law. And since the correction is said to happen through natural law, natural law itself is properly declared not to be deficient.

This is certainly true if we understand natural moral law in the strict sense — an understanding which ought not to be adopted simply because it is to our liking! — namely, as a law which is not promulgated, written or "imprinted": as a law, therefore, which is understood not as being "imposed from above" on the creature of God, but which is "imprinted" on the creature to the extent that the creature, in understanding itself, posits such a law actively as well as passively. Natural law, conceived in such a manner, not only contains in itself the correction of deficient positive laws, but also necessarily dictates every possible mode of right action. In this sense we might not have to say — though it is often said — that natural law is the "sum" of those norms which are not unattainable by the human intellect; for such a "sum" de facto cannot be had.

Natural norms which have been set down, formulated, established by man, can be said to belong to natural law only in a secondary manner. The possible deficiency of such norms cannot a priori be excluded. However, norms of different types should be distinguished. One type consists of those laws which can be said to be transcendental, in that they concern the whole person as such.

Norms of this type are, for example, the adage that good must be done and evil avoided, or − and this is the same thing − that man ought to act in a rational or genuinely "human" manner; this is nothing other than saying that man should act as man, or should truly realize himself. Such transcendental formulae (or norms) are evidently analytic and therefore strictly universal. A question can arise, however, with regard to norms that are not transcendental, but categorial, in that they concern not man as a whole but particular aspects of his being. These norms can be deductions in the strict sense from transcendental norms to the various particular dimensions of human life, e.g. , that one should be "rational" and "human" in the use of the sexual faculty (be chaste), in the administration of human earthly life or in the distribution of goods of this world (be just), or that one should be duly faithful and truthful, that one should not be cruel, etc. Such norms can likewise be said to be "analytic" or "tautological" and are therefore universals in the strict sense. It follows that with regard to either transcendental norms or categorial ones directly deduced from them, *epikeia* has no application, not even analogically, because they are strictly universal.

A problem arises with norms which are categorial but not "analytic" i.e., those practical and operative norms which determine what actually pertains to chastity, justice, fidelity, truthfulness, etc. For these norms, since they are "synthetic," depend very much on the experience of worldly reality and of human life, and their ultimate concrete determination can only be derived through a due process of human evaluation. These norms are nothing other than the positions and judgments made and "formulated" by man himself, and therefore such norms per se can be deficient and consequently are general rather than strictly universal. Because neither one's understanding nor one's judgment can be very exact, it follows that one's conception and redaction of norms may be very inadequate. This happens precisely because human realities are contingent and can, therefore, change. But the deficiency of the redaction of norms will generally not be perceived at the moment of their formulation, but at a later moment when the same norms have to be applied in situations which were not perfectly foreseen and perceived, and thus not clearly appraised and described.

In such situations, one must do as one normally does by virtue of *epikeia* with regard to positive human law − i.e., the laws (to use the word of Aristotle and Aquinas) must be corrected in their application (with respect to their wording). And the reason in both cases is similar: man can often err in formulating norms and laws. Again, the word *epikeia* is evidently used analogously in both cases. This is because, in regard to a positive law, its inner meaning, belonging as it does to natural law, allows a correction of the posited law and renders such a correction possible. However, in the case of formulated norms of natural law, the true meaning of the natural law is first expressed at a certain moment, and therefore has to be formulated more exactly and adequately at a later time. This happens when one has also considered those elements within a situation which were not perfectly foreseen and appraised. It is clear that these categorial-operative norms are analytic and not synthetic, general and not universal, or at least they can hardly be shown to be strictly such. Hence, *epikeia*, understood purely analogically or apparently, can be applied to them. I say: purely analogically or apparently; properly speaking, *epikeia* is the virtue which inclines us toward understanding and expressing natural law, which is an internal law; *epikeia* always does this better, that is, more adequately and exactly, than do the norms and judgments made by men. Such a virtue can prevent these norms and judgments, once they have been made, from demanding of man anything inappropriate to a concrete situation, or from omitting to respond to his true and concrete needs. For it is more important for us to satisfy the true needs of a man in a given situation than it is to observe humanly formulated norms.

II. EPIKEIA-*DISPENSATION*, EPIKEIA-*INTERPRETATION*

1. The doctrine of *epikeia*, once it was introduced, was rather quickly linked by not a few scholars to the teaching on dispensation. *Epikeia* was not so much understood as the virtue of correctly applying a deficient law but as *epikeia*-dispensation or "relaxation of the law".

The same thing also happened rather easily with *epikeia* and its relation to natural law. This led to the possibility of reflecting, in the context of *epikeia*, on what Aquinas maintained about a dispensation from the precepts of natural law. The very use of the word "precepts" makes it clear that the question being discussed concerned particular, formally stated precepts or prohibitions of natural law — which were certainly synthetic. Thus, this discussion had to do with the secondary concept of natural law, even though natural law was said to be "internal" and thus "divinely given".

It is not surprising that this was done, because there seemed to be something in Sacred Scripture itself concerning a dispensation given by God with regard to natural law. It is well known that this question was found difficult enough by the medievals. For the possibility of a dispensation and therefore of an exception in matters of natural law had to be admitted on the one hand, but on the other, the admission of a dispensation had to be withheld, due to the concept of natural law.

Many theologians admitted such an *epikeia*-dispensation with regard to natural law. Nonetheless, there were difficult questions to be answered. Primarily, a twofold problem arose. First, is such an *epikeia*-dispensation possible with regard to all the statutes of natural law without distinction? Since the answer was negative, the question remained of distinguishing the dispensable from the nondispensable. Second, who can grant the dispensation, and if only God can, why is he alone able to do so?

Let us consider the first problem: from what statutes of natural law can a dispensation be given, and from which ones can it not? Different authors proposed different solutions, distinguishing — as did, for example, Henry of Ghent[5] — between *malum extremum* and *malum simpliciter*; the latter, even if it is "evil in itself", can in a particular case be good. Some perceived a difference between those things which are not only prohibited by natural law but also by God himself (the decalogue as the law of God was especially treated in this way). Others distinguished between those precepts which are truly necessary and those which are not so necessary, or — as St. Thomas did — between "primary" and "secondary" precepts of natural law; the latter "are derived as quasi-conclusions from the primary precepts" (e.g., the prohibition of polygamy) and are not absolutely necessary in every case.

It is evident how difficult it was for these authors to understand that the formally stated norms of natural law are set up by human beings, and that therefore there are valid reasons for making these norms with regard to certain already known or normally occurring cases, and that these reasons do not exist in certain other cases. Consequently, such norms are not applicable in these latter cases. As for the rest, there is no writer who is able to distinguish and evaluate exactly which norms are always to be applied and which are deficient. We prefer to say this: where a deficiently formulated norm occurs, the use of *epikeia*-dispensation, purely analogical or only apparently such, indeed has a place; or better: in such a case the true purpose of a natural law (understood strictly, as "imprinted"), which had been more exactly and adequately formulated, is to remove a deficient norm from the case at hand.

The second problem is this: who grants the *epikeia*-dispensation or relaxation in matters of natural law? Aquinas, with Aristotle, generously admitted, on the one hand, that the "totality of moral matters" belongs to the "secondary" precepts of natural law. Because of the great variety of ways in which men live, "when the efficacy of these precepts fails, we can licitly pass over them."[6]

Therefore, owing to the very nature of things, this holds without restriction! From the nature of things, we do not need a positive dispensation per se. Nonetheless, Aquinas, and many others after him, demand a divine dispensation (as, for example, in the case of polygamy). This, however, was not because the matter itself demanded it, but "because it is not easy to determine various matters of this sort, it is reserved for him from whose authority the law has its efficacy to permit us to pass over the law in those cases where the force of the law should not extend." In regard to the example of polygamy which he himself brought up, Aquinas says: "The law that a man may have only one wife is not humanly but divinely instituted, nor is it given in words or writing, but it is impressed on the heart, as is anything else which belongs to natural law in any way. And therefore in these matters a dispensation could be given by God alone...."

Today, we are hardly as optimistic as the learned men of other times; for we think that the divine natural law itself (neither written nor otherwise formulated) is not always sufficiently expressed in norms which are formally redacted by us men and not by God. In other words, we have difficulty in calling these norms (other than the imprinted natural law) "divine" precepts with absolute certitude. An understanding of the deficiency of these norms is attained with the same certitude with which we formulate them. Thus, it would seem that we should not speak of *epikeia*-dispensation in the proper sense with regard to natural law, but of a continuous effort to make and remake norms so that the true intention of the "nonwritten" divine natural law may be accomplished more adequately and more exactly — especially in cases which are entirely new or in those which foster doubt.

2. After Thomas and Albert had introduced and commented on the doctrine of the *Nicomachean Ethics*, other theologians held that *epikeia* was an interpretation of an existing law; such an interpretation could be either "benign" or "restrictive". This manner of speaking about *epikeia*-interpretation owes much to Francis Suarez. In this view, there is less talk about the virtue of correctly applying the law than about the prudent interpretation of the law — certainly in a benign/restrictive sense (although this is not purely a matter of whim). Nevertheless, what this understanding of *epikeia* has in common with the original understanding of the term is that in both conceptions there is recourse to the deeper though deficiently expressed purpose of the law.

When natural law (understood here as "internal" law) is the subject of discussion, *epikeia*-interpretation, strictly speaking, is not mentioned in reference to it; rather, reference is made to the human expressions of natural law which are found in certain concrete moral norms. *Epikeia*-interpretation is really needed in this area, because moral norms are too easily considered to be divine in origin rather than human expressions, and are often formulated in terms of universal laws. Hence a prudent judgment is required, so that — in the words of Aquinas which we quoted above — the different norms might exercise their proper efficacy. Many theologians through the ages have been aware that not all humanly formulated moral norms are truly universal, even though they may have been written in a universal form. They knew that the norm, "Do not kill", does not imply a universal but merely a general mandate, that the norm which prohibits incest does not hold if there is a danger that the species will not be conserved, that what has been given does not always have to be returned, or at least not immediately, etc. *Epikeia*-interpretation of this type, if it refers to particular norms of natural law and concrete norms of behavior, in fact means nothing else than discovering and trying to put into practice the true moral purpose of the natural law (in the strict sense of natural law, i.e., nonwritten) in those not infrequent cases where the norm is deficient. Again: what ought to be of primary importance is not the norm, which is formally and humanly stated, but the "true" actualization of man in any given concrete situation. I use the term "true actualization" to refer to the nonwritten natural law, which provides *recta ratio*. Concrete-operative norms which are formally stated do not a priori exclude a certain "problematic" character. Consequently, the addition of the qualifiers "benign" or "restrictive" when natural law is the topic of discussion does not make sense. We must discuss this at greater length.

III. "FOR THE MOST PART" AND "ACCORDING TO THE MIND OF THE LEGISLATOR"

1. In Aristotle's doctrine that a deficient positive law ought to be corrected, it was held that such a law is set down "according to those things which generally occur" and that it therefore only holds "*ut in pluribus*". This phrase is used as well by Aquinas,[7] and it also appears in the works of his contemporaries and in those of later authors. As far as positive human law is concerned, this phenomenon is only too evident.

In reference to natural law, however, the phrase occurs most often when various concepts of *epikeia* are discussed. It is quite obvious that it could have been used neither with regard to natural law as "imprinted", nor with regard to analytic moral principles, but only with regard to formally redacted concrete moral norms; these, however — as Aquinas says — are the "totality of morality."

Thomas thought that the natural inclination is toward those things which are *ut in pluribus*[8] and that natural rectitude in human behavior is not determined by those things which happen *per accidens* in an individual, but by those which follow from the whole species.[9] He also says that "because it is necessary that human behavior vary with different personal and temporal conditions and with other circumstances, therefore conclusions drawn beforehand from the first precepts of natural law are not always valid, but only for the most part"[10] *(ut in pluribus).* It is clear that this problem was not solved perfectly by Aquinas or by other authors. Contemporary writers perhaps realize this more readily than Aquinas did. For on the one hand, it must be said that natural law is ordered toward concrete realities, and not merely toward what generally happens; but this does not exclude considering the consequences of an act for others in determining a right moral judgment. On the other hand, the formally stated norms of natural law, since as such they are not of divine institution (as Aquinas prefers to say) but of human origin, are seen as licitly and sometimes necessarily standing in need of correction, which can help to avoid difficulties that may arise from an excessively universal redaction, or can help to render natural law itself perfectly effective. Among major authors there were some who said that the moral law is not properly concerned with what is universal, but with what is concrete.[11] Hence, the following is worthy of repetition: norms which are mistakenly formulated as "universal" must be "corrected" in their concrete application so as to preserve the true purpose of natural law; thus it seems that they must be "rendered" correct.

Furthermore, it is worthwhile to note that the adage about the value of such norms, that they merely hold *ut in pluribus*, is certainly right and useful; logically, however, it is not evident that we have always to formulate norms *ut in pluribus* and never *ut in paucioribus.*

If *epikeia*-interpretation is valid in the traditionally given cases — for example, with regard to the restitution of a sum borrowed or with regard to the command (as it was stated), "Do not kill," or even with regard to the prohibition of incest — then it is not easy to say that such an interpretation must be excluded in other cases. Contemporary opinions on correct "teleologically" determined moral judgments must be taken into consideration — precisely so that natural law may be rendered effective in the most perfect way possible. If this happens, the formally stated norms of natural law neither cease to be of great value, nor are they any longer a valid help, especially for pedagogical purposes.

2. Something else is evident from Aristotle's doctrine of *epikeia* as regards natural law: there is no place for *epikeia* unless we consider the end which the legislator intended by his law. Aquinas also observes this[12] — even though he understands the virtue of *epikeia* in terms of positive human law, which must be corrected in virtue of natural law. Such a position differs greatly from the concept of *epikeia* which, under the influence of voluntarism, insisted that the one subject to the law take into account the benevolent will which the legislator expected at the moment of the application of the law, and not the benevolent will of the legislator when the law was formulated. Today, since laws — at least civil laws — are not made by a single person as legislator but by a consensus of persons chosen for that purpose, it seems that, given the conditions of the concrete situation, less attention must be paid to the "mind of the legislator" than to the mind of the law itself.[13]

The latter interpretation is closer to an analogous conception of *epikeia* with regard to natural moral law. For if the word "legislator" with regard to natural law refers to the Creator, his mind is nothing other than the natural law itself, or "right reason" (as the medievals said) concerning the actual realization of the human reality created by him. In reference to human law, the issue was and is whether and in what cases of *epikeia* recourse should be had to the will of the legislator or superior himself; in reference to natural moral law, certain authors rightly maintained that the legislator is always present, namely, as "right reason" — which takes the place of its Creator.

This insight also pertains to the formally stated norms of natural law; recourse to the "legislator" — namely, right reason — in concrete situations is nothing other than an inquiry which has been begun and must be continually carried out into the "truth" of the natural law, especially in a case which goes beyond the redaction of those norms formulated by men.

IV. WHEN DOES EPIKEIA, ANALOGICALLY CONCEIVED, BECOME EFFECTIVE?

1. *Epikeia* cannot be considered in relation to natural moral law, except in an analogous or apparent manner, until the question of how the natural moral law itself is to be correctly proposed is treated. When the natural moral law is at stake, one ought to say in what cases such an *epikeia* is applicable. This is independent of whether *epikeia* is understood as *epikeia*-virtue, *epikeia*-dispensation or *epikeia*-interpretation; we have already stated why we prefer the first of these positions.

In the light of the various attempts proposed with regard to positive law, it was due to Francis Suarez[14] that the custom prevailed of distinguishing three cases of *epikeia*: (a) if the positive law, set out in words, is "beyond our strength" in a certain case, or impossible; (b) if the law in a particular instance is not beyond one's strength, or impossible, but is exceedingly difficult or "intolerable", i.e., "inhuman": (c) if the nonobservation is done "according to the benign intention of the legislator" (as if he were present here and now). With regard to natural law, this certainly cannot be simply said to happen in the same way but, perhaps, analogously. This is the case: (a) if the observation of an established obligation becomes ridiculous, (some writers discuss, for example, certain vows which have to be kept in sufficiently different circumstances); (b) if the fulfillment of a stated norm becomes somewhat "harmful"; (c) if it becomes altogether incongruous; (d) if it becomes impossible; (e) if the mere observance of the norms becomes altogether insufficient in a given case (cf. what was said earlier about the Sermon on the Mount). What we have said, however, requires further explanation.

2. The medieval doctors (including St. Thomas himself) and their successors correctly asserted that the "formal character of justice" (*ratio justitiae*) or the formal character of morality could never change, but that its "material" character could;[15] for an already established moral norm indicates a determinate matter or describes some action which ought not to be applied to a subsequent case. In other words, when a successive situation truly involves different matter, the issue ought to be judged by a different moral norm. This can certainly happen with respect to the various cases enumerated by us above.

We know that medieval authors applied such distinctions to difficult cases of the Old Testament such as the question, in itself extremely important, as to what factors constitute "adultery" besides those which are generally said to do so; that God had imposed adultery "in the proper sense of the word" seemed to them to be hardly admissible.[16] This medieval example is significant because, unless I am mistaken, we would hardly presume to make the absolute assertion that once and for all and in all questions we have been able exactly to decide the matter of moral norms and judgments. (Those who wish to interpret the famous "Bergmeir" case favorably must, if I am not mistaken, employ such an interpretation of the problem).

3. Recently, many authors tend to account for the possibilities listed above in another manner. It is only reluctantly that they employ the term, *epikeia*; they prefer simply to treat the nature and value of moral norms and judgments insofar as they are understood and formulated by men. They hold that we must correctly distinguish between "mixed" judgments and "purely" moral judgments.[17]

"Mixed" judgments concern certain facts (and their human perception and evaluation) and also determine the moral rationality of human activity precisely in the light of those facts. Where a judgment about facts – at least in a given case – is changed (e.g., whether in a particular socioeconomic situation a person receives a living wage for his labor; whether conjugal union might, on certain days, have negative consequences from a medical point of view, etc.), the moral judgment previously made ought perhaps to be rendered differently. The formal moral character of the prior judgment remains completely intact, however.

"Purely" moral judgments are divided, as we have seen, into "transcendental" and "categorial", "analytic" and "synthetic" ones. Transcendental and first categorial judgments are analytic and therefore strictly universal. Truly synthetic categorial judgments, namely, concrete operative norms, cannot be shown to be strictly universal, but general.

To simplify, one might say: norms of natural moral law are observed according to their value.

However, such a consideration, which is usually called "teleological", is not universally accepted at the present time for all categories of human life. Like many of their predecessors, some prefer a "deontological" judgment on some matters (e.g., on perjury, lying, life, sexuality), for such a deontological judgment is the ground of strictly universal norms; others, however, deny such a necessity.

V. CONCLUSION

When he reflected on the use of *epikeia* in applying human law, Aristotle's fundamental insight was this: concrete reality cannot perfectly conform to some universal rule; rather, the rule must be adapted to reality. Plato thought otherwise. St. Albert the Great[18] cited the following nonmoral example taken from Aristotle: when a building had to be constructed from stones of unequal size, a rigid standard could not be employed in the construction, and consequently, they made a measuring device from lead, "so that when a stone could not be reduced to the straightness of the rule, the rule was curved to the stone, so that there was not a great departure from the standard". If we are speaking of a human law which is to regulate man's life, such a "flexible" norm might not seem so easy to employ, but is the only possible norm. This is the nature of human law, this is how *epikeia* is to be used responsibly! This is the reasonable use of certain humanly redacted moral norms, which are said to be of natural law.

In fact, it can hardly be denied that there is a similar problem not only for many moral norms of natural law (of the synthetic variety), but also for human laws. Both types of norms are formulated by man in universal terms, though meant for actual living − positive law is creatively established, a moral norm is "creatively" redacted.

With regard to natural moral law, this similarity certainly does not exist, if we consider natural law in the strict sense, that is, as imprinted; it does exist, however, when we take into account the plurality of the synthetic moral norms which are humanly formulated. Then certain "humanly" and abstractly formulated norms are too easily and unqualifiedly taken for "divine" natural law itself. This identification can only be made to the extent that these norms are formulated by men who possess reason and are created and thus limited; they must adequately and unerringly consider the plural unity of man's reality as he acts concretely and then judge this phenomenon under the aspect of morality. Where a norm is known to be "deficient" *in concreto* − whether it is so in itself or in relation to a concrete situation − "the rule must be curved to the stone" and not vice versa; in other words, the norm must be corrected or at least interpreted according to the totality of the concrete reality. This means that a moral judgment must ultimately be made about what is concrete, since norms are meant to help only insofar as they have value. No one who wishes to call this practice *epikeia* should be blamed, as long as he perceives that the term is being used analogously. The problem as it has been sketched here is certainly very important. For when concrete reality is sacrificed for the sake of humanly formulated abstract norms, or when norms which seem to be only general are taken to be universal, then there is some danger that natural law in a strict sense — and therefore man himself — may be sacrificed.

NOTES

1. J. Fuchs, *Theologia moralis generalis*, Part 1, Rome 1963, 2nd ed., 140.

2. There is valuable information about the theories of Aristotle, Albert the Great, and Thomas Aquinas, concerning *epikeia*, in the following: O. Robleda, "La 'aequitas' en Aristóteles, Cicerón, Santo Tómas y Suárez", *Miscell. Comillas* 15 (1951), 241-79; M. Müller, "Der heilige Albertus Magnus und die Lehre von der Epikie", *Div. Thom.* (Freiburg), 12 (1934), 165-82; R. Egenter, "Über die Bedeutung der Epikie im sittlichen Leben", *Phil. Jahrb.* 53 (1940), 115-27; J. Riley, *The History, Nature, and Use of Epikeia in Moral Theology*, Washington, D.C. 1948; J. Fuchs, *Situation und Entscheidung. Grundfragen christlicher Situationsethik*, Frankfurt am Main 1952, 47-68; idem, "Auctoritas Dei in auctoritate civili", *Periodica de re m. c. 1.* 52 (1963), 3-18; J. Giers, "Epikie und Sittlichkeit. Gestalt und Gestaltwander einer Tugend", in R. Hauser and F. Scholz (eds.), *Der Mensch unter Gottes Anruf und Ordnung* (Festschrift Th. Müncker), Düsseldorf 1958, 51-67; E. Hamel, "La vertu de l'épikie", in idem, *La loi du Christ*, Bruges-Paris 1964, 79-106; idem, "L'usage de l'épikie", *Studia moralia* 3 (1965), 48-81.

3. Riley, "Epikeia and Natural Law", op. cit. (see note 2 above), 258-91. Also R.A. Couture, "The Use of Epikeia in Natural Law: Its Early Developments", *Eglise et Théologie* 4 (1973), 71-103; B. Häring, "Dynamism and Continuity in a Personalistic Approach to Natural Law", in G.H. Outka and P. Ramsey (eds.), *Norm and Context in Christian Ethics*, New York 1968, 199-218, especially 210-15. It should be noted that both Riley and (especially) Couture cite opinions of medieval and more modern authors, along with the more important texts, concerning this question.

4. On this point, cf. especially J. Giers, loc. cit. (see note 2 above), Chapter 1.

5. Henry of Ghent, *Quodl.* II, q. 17 (ed. Bibliothèque S.J. 1961 fol. 42 r).

6. Thomas Aquinas, *In IV Sent.* d. 33, q. 1, art. 2, sol.

7. Idem, cf. *S.T.* I-II, q. 96, a. 6c.

8. Idem, *S.C.G.* 1. 3, c. 125.

9. Idem, ibid., c. 122.

10. Idem, *In IV Sent.*, d. 33, q. 1, a. 2, sol.

11. Cf. G. Vasquez, *Comm. ac disp. in Summam S. Thomae*, Lugd. 1630ss; cf. his commentary on I-II, d. 176, c. 1, n. 3.

12.   Thomas Aquinas, *S.T.* II-II, q. 147, a.3, ad 2; I-II, q. 96, a. 6, ad 2; ibid., q. 100, a. 8, ad 2.

13.   Cf. J. Fuchs, "Auctoritas Dei in auctoritate civili", loc. cit. (see note 2 above).

14.   Cf. E. Hamel, loc. cit. (see note 2 above).

15.   Cf. Thomas Aquinas, *S.T.* I-II, q. 100, a. 8.

16.   Cf. ibid., ad 3; cf. also J.G. Milhaven, "Thomas Aquinas and Exceptions to the Moral Law", in *Toward a New Catholic Morality*, New York 1970, 141-72.

17.   Cf., for example, B. Schüller, "Zum Problem ethischer Normierung", *Orientierung* 36 (1972), 81-4.

18.   St. Albert the Great, *In lib. III Polit.: Opera Omnia*, vol. 8, Paris 1891, 300.

11. A Summary: Clarifications of Some Currently Used Terms

In many Catholic discourses and writings, in pastoral letters and Church documents, we are accustomed to hearing or reading formulae in matters involving morality which sound a little like moral positivism. Indeed, I fear that in a certain subconscious way this may accurately reflect the thinking of those who speak or write thus. In addition, some believe that we can and must make it understood to the faithful and also to men of good will that only by following the way and the norm indicated, can they—and indeed must they—build up their own lives as well as—so far as possible—those of others and that of human society. If, in rather practical matters which perhaps involve considerable commitment, a clearly defined mode of action (and it alone) is considered to be distinctively "Christian", or if such a mode of action — and it alone — is considered to be "the will of God", or if it alone is stated to be consistent with the tradition of the Church of Christ and of its magisterium, or even if such norms are said to belong to the "eternal law" of God and are therefore universal and immutable, or if, finally, such moral laws are considered as moral expressions of the being of man who as such is and remains the creature of God — if this is the way things are, then the task of man and of the Christian can only be this: to obey and submit to that with which he thinks he finds himself face to face as a superior will which is imposed on us.

All of the above formulae have a certain correct and proper sense in which they can be understood, but we often find them used and understood in the sense of a moral positivism which, for its part, implies a mistaken concept of God and of his Christ: of a God who places on man's shoulders some precepts exterior to him in order to test him. To me it seems extremely important to denounce such a concept of God and the moral law; the true conception of our life and existence, both Christian and human, the meaning which we justly or erroneously give to them, depend a great deal on our concept of God and moral law — even when we ourselves can no longer accept with sincerity such a meaning and, a fortiori, we no longer know how to engage in dialogue about it with men who have different fundamental ideas.

Our intention is to analyze some formulae which are used very frequently indeed and which are, it seems, very easily and not infrequently understood in a way that is theologically and philosophically mistaken.

I.   CHRISTIAN MORALITY

We often hear or read that this or that specific moral norm is part of the Christian moral order; insofar as a position is contrary to this norm, it is at variance with Christian existence. Is there anyone who has not read or heard this, especially in connection with certain acute moral problems which are publicly discussed, or even with reference to certain practices of many people (even Catholics) which are in open opposition to that morality which is called "Christian"?

Certainly this formula can have a legitimate meaning. Sometimes it points to the Christian character of certain attitudes, ways of behavior, and activities which are only "assertive" and not "exclusive", i.e., the possibility is not excluded that certain moral norms may also be norms of every truly human morality and that it is for this reason that they belong at the same time to the moral order preached in Christianity which has recalled to the attention of men (both inside and outside of the Church) well-defined norms of a morality which is "human" in the best sense of the word, or that Christianity has put forward certain assertation or certain truths, proposed by Jesus or found generally in the New Testament, which insist on clearly defined norms of a true human morality — e.g. the affirmation of love of neighbor and openness to neighbor, so often commended in the New Testament message.

But the way of speaking about the moral order of Christians, especially when particular modes of moral behavior are under discussion, often tends to distinguish between those moral norms for the formation of life (either of individuals or society) which are "distinctively Christian" and those which are "non-Christian"; and these are the only behavioral norms for the formulation of the human world which are mentioned. I am sure that many Christians and non-Christians think that it is a matter of distinctive norms for Christians when the Church summons the world to a certain manner of life or even urges civil legislation in matters concerning birth control, abortion, the indissolubility of marriage, sexual life, religious education in schools, etc. This belief persists in spite of the fact that the recent popes have frequently spoken on such topics, explaining that it is not a matter of questions or solutions which are exclusively or distinctively Christian, but of a genuine *humanitas* ("of all men of good will"). I fear that the great majority of Christians understands such expressions as "Christian morality" in the sense of a doctrine which is only for "us Christians", even in some cases to the extent of seeing in such "Christian" doctrines the distinction between Christians and non-Christians; I think that this may be so not only among the "simple" or "very simple" faithful, but also implicitly among the highly "educated" faithful. It is a fact that many words about the morality "of Christians", written or spoken, lend themselves rather easily to such an interpretation. If this were the true interpretation, Christians would either have to withdraw or be thrown into a special ghetto —an idea totally contrary to Vatican II's *Gaudium et spes*.

It is true that the basis of the morality of Christians is their faith, the "fundamental-transcendental" adhesion of the whole person — never fully reflected on or explicable in its depths — to the God who reveals himself and communicates himself. This adhesion to God who has revealed himself — *fides qua* — seeks to express itself in a human life worthy of the word *humanum* in terms of a morality which is made explicit in truly human moral norms. It is also true that this same faith, because of revelation—i.e. as *fides quae*— reveals to man many things regarding the ultimate reality of himself. about the meaning of his life and God's relation to this meaning. This faith which is believed can help man know better and more profoundly what truly human action is and as a consequence, it will be man's attempt to express — in a human manner — the faith which is believed.

Instead of saying that our teaching on questions such as sterilization, abortion, sexual life, social justice, etc. is true because it is Christian, it would perhaps be better to say that it can be Christian because and to the extent that it corresponds to the being-man — to whom, as has already been said, God has revealed and communicated himself. In this sense, morality and its norms are, even for Christians, *not* "distinctively" Christian but truly "human", i.e., in accord with creation and right human reason. But this human morality is at the same time "Christian" (and "distinctively" Christian) because both the faith with which one adheres to God — the Father of Jesus Christ — (*fides qua*) and the faith which one accepts because of revelation (*fides quae*) are present and are lived and thus are a specific content of the human morality lived by the Christian; and this "specific" dimension really specifies — giving a specific significance to — the same truly human morality which materially remains the same. Indeed, this faith is the highest element of the morality of the believer. Thus distinguishing, but not separating, one can speak of a "distinctively Christian" morality.

It is common practice to distinguish between morality (categorial) and religion (categorial). A religion which explicitly acknowledges a God who reveals and communicates himself in Christ will consequently be characterized by religious activity — acts of worship, prayer, contemplation, acts of faith, hope, love, acts of Christian community life, profession of one's faith, etc. — which is distinct from the religious activity (if it exists) of those who do not believe in God the Father of Jesus Christ. Furthermore, the believed and revealed relation between the Father, Jesus, the Spirit and the community of believers will often give to the actions and morality of believers an explicit and categorial motive (distinct from noncategorial intentionality) so that the intimate motive which penetrates all moral action (in its human materiality) is fundamentally a distinctively Christian religiousness. Finally, the "new man", because of his lived and believed relation to the Trinity, and listening to their inspiration, can arrive at some existential choices of conduct which are not explained solely as a realization of moral norms essential to being man. To live unmarried for other values, to deny oneself freely, to place oneself at the disposition of the poor — all of these actions can find — in their essence — a "human" justification and explanation; this is due to knowledge of human limitations and of the trying tendency to egotism, which, if it is recognized, can be overcome. But "Christian" virginity (the motive for which is belief in the kingdom of God) and every "Christian" cross (the motive for bearing which is the love shown in the crucified Christ), are Christian choices, ultimately not so much moral as religious! The same should be said with regard to many personal attitudes as well as those of the community of belief.

Sometimes it would therefore be desirable that in speaking of Christian morality one be more exact and explain — for the benefit of Christians and non-Christians alike — exactly what the undeniable Christian character of Christian morality consists of and what it does not consist of.

II. WILL OF GOD

In ecclesiastical language, just as one often finds the formula "Christian morality", so too one often hears the phrase "will of God". It would be interesting to see, in various ecclesiastical documents, how often there is an insistence on a specific kind of moral behavior with the affirmation that this is the will of God, which therefore must be accepted by both ecclesiastical and civil authority. There is, in moral theology, some suspicion about this way of speaking, which is ambivalent. Even some Christians are asking themselves: "What criterion is the basis of the observation that this or that manner of acting is the will of God?" If we admit that with regard to a norm or a precept one is really speaking of the will of God, then clearly every area of discussion is closed and every relevant problem must be excluded. But the real question to be asked is whether a norm or a moral solution is in fact the will of God.

On the other hand, a secularized world cannot understand the term "will of God", because of the fact that in this world one does not "meet" God and his formulated will. If, in spite of this, many recognize a moral order, if certain moral norms are admitted and if it is possible to individuate them, this constitutes a human cultural fact.

For Christians, naturally, to speak of the will of God has its own significance. Nevertheless it is to be feared that behind this way of speaking a considerable amount of unjustified voluntarism is often hidden. This fear is shared by many theologians who see, in this possible but imprecise way of speaking of the "will of God", a danger to man's authentic understanding of self as a creature of God. It could be that many who use this terminology do not take into account its implications.

Perhaps they think, without reflecting, of the decalogue of Sinai. But in the decalogue there are only a few commands, for the most part (in the second tablet) of a social character, and these are fundamental elements of the covenant of the people of Israel with its God. Therefore, as such — according to many exegetes — they do not hold for us, although the content of the decalogue remains valid to the extent that it is part of natural moral law. According to other exegetes, the law of the old covenant remains at the center of the new covenant, although — so they say — the content of the commandments has undergone some changes. But the appeal of Jesus and of St. Paul to the decalogue is of great importance.

Others perhaps think of certain moral formulations of the New Testament. But there are very few of these and, with regard to them, one should see what value they have — interpretatively and hermeneutically. In fact, according to many exegetes today, there is no basis for either the attempt to consider each and every precept which is found occasionally in the New Testament as a distinctively Christian norm, or the attempt to consider them as Christian revelation of moral norms. Rather, these exegetes observe that the occasional passages which speak of moral matters should be considered to be *paranesis* and not kerygma, i.e. only an admonition to do those things which are held to be morally just. It could therefore be that some of these norms — for example, the opinion of St. Paul on the behavior of women in society, and his opinion on slavery — are conditioned by certain attitudes which belong to his time and therefore are not valid for all times.

The Sermon on the Mount, often called the "Magna Carta" of Christian morality, needs not only a simple reading, but a proper exegesis and hermeneutic. It seems to me that it presents not so much a Christian moral code as a picture of the man who has been converted to the kingdom of God. The Lord proposes some exemplary models, for example nonviolence, which indicate to us what the man who has been converted to the kingdom can or ought to do when the situation demands it. In the so-called antitheses it does not seem that the Lord opposes a new morality to an old one, but rather the true morality is opposed to a purely legalistic conception of morality, and also to sinful behavior. The beatitudes, at least as transmitted to us by Matthew, indicate a human behavior which has clearly surpassed the egotism of sin and precisely because of this is "beatitude". The Sermon on the Mount represents an authentic newness and radicality for the man who is egotistical and sinful; it does not oppose a truly human morality, known by Catholic tradition as natural moral law. In this sense the Sermon on the Mount is of great value, both exhortative and heuristic.

In any case, neither in the Decalogue nor in the New Testament are moral solutions given to all the problems of an epoch in continual transformation. On the other hand, the numerous norms and moral solutions that we, in fact, have, apply according to traditional thinking to the field of the so-called natural moral law. According to St. Thomas (cf. I-II 106-108; 99,3 ad 2; 99, 4c), Jesus − except for matters of dogma and sacraments − has not added any positive moral precepts to the precepts of the natural law. Christ came to earth not to found a new moral order but to redeem and transform the sinful man who − inasmuch as he is redeemed − will continue to observe the moral order in every epoch.

Moreover, many moral theologians fear that many of those who too readily use the term "will of God" and who presume to know such a will with absolute certaintly, not infrequently have a rather voluntaristic − and hence a mistaken − concept of the natural moral law from which men − Christians in the light of the Gospel, as *Gaudium et spes* tells us − can obtain a knowledge of the will of God. Those with the rather voluntaristic conception of natural law consider and study the nature of man created by God and believe that they can read in it without much reflection the same natural law. Faced with such a conception of natural law, some today insist − not without reflection on some assertions of Aquinas − that the nature which has been given to us teaches us natural physical laws, psychological laws, etc., so that man can and ought to avail himself of these for the development of nature and himself. But how man ought to use natural reality is not directly written in nature itself: this question is a moral question. Neither the nature of sexuality, nor the reality of human life, nor the fact of the social character of man indicate what man ought to make of these. Man (humanity) himself ought to determine this — and Christians should do it in the light of the Gospel. Certainly, many years (or centuries) of long experience and reflection upon experience are needed in many questions, plus total self-understanding. According to *Gaudium et spes*, man is a being in continual historical development (an active development), and it is not easy to produce at any given moment a solution for all times and eventualities. When man, perhaps after a long and tiring search, knows how to individuate truly what way of life is not inhuman, but truly human, he will then know something of the essence of the creature with regard to the will of God the Creator and Redeemer. Therefore, when man succeeds in this work of his of determining the moral order, the norms and solutions which he finds will be at the same time autonomous and truly theonomous.

Unfortunately, man can also be wrong and be forced to correct the result of his endeavor. Because of this we should be cautious in indicating or imposing some moral norms and not insist with too much sureness upon the untouchability — in history — of certain moral behavioral/material norms just because they are supposed to be the "will of God". Ultimately, however, when we believe that we have good reasons for certain norms, they should be followed as the "will of God".

III. CHRISTIAN TRADITION – MAGISTERIUM OF THE CHURCH

In addition to the affirmation that the main question is one of the moral norms of a "Christian morality" or the "will of God", one often finds a reference to "tradition", to "Christian tradition", especially if this tradition is confirmed in documents of the "official magisterium of the Church". Moral theology today is rather cautious in referring, with too much simplicity, to tradition in moral questions. This is true above all today, since today, more than in the past, there is an awareness that the formulation of some moral norms in the Church could have been conditioned by time and culture, and even by erroneous judgments.

First of all, we must distinguish between various types of tradition; unfortunately, this is not often done. On the one hand, there is a tradition of faith, founded on revelation, which should be distinguished from, on the other hand, a doctrinal tradition, which, as such, is not founded on revelation (or even on doctrinal traditions dependent on it) but on questions which are, for example, philosophical and — in our case — questions of morality, which often are not of such a nature that their solution depends on a correct conception and defense of the content of revelation. We must take into account the fact that in both Vatican I and Vatican II, where these councils speak of infallibility (cf. *Lumen Gentium* no. 25) in matters of faith and morals, the affirmations refer to the *depositum fidei*. In this respect, Vatican II faithfully follows Vatican I (session 3, ch. 3 and 4). Certainly, formulations which are distinctively Christian belong to the *depositum fidei*; for example, that we ought to accept the reconciliation offered to us by God in Christ, and live this, since, if we are baptized, we ought to live as persons dead to sin and alive only in God. Some fundamental principles of natural law which are also revealed belong to the *depositum fidei*: for example, that God is the source and the end of our life (Vatican I, DS 3004), and those which affirm that we ought to be just, merciful, chaste, etc. But the question whether the even more concrete assertions — i.e. the Pauline lists of virtues and sins — all belong in equal measure to the immutable deposit of faith, is being explicitly raised today, especially in view of the fact that some of these Pauline affirmations are not accepted today in the Church. As examples of these we may cite what St. Paul wrote on the behavior of women in society and on slavery. But St. Paul does not give us, in his pastoral instructions, a criterion for distinguishing the different values of the actual behavioral norms that he affirmed.

If moral theology today is very cautious regarding that Christian tradition which wishes to refer to St. Paul's teachings, it is even more cautious regarding the moral doctrinal traditions which have been developing from the postapostolic period up to today. Doubtless these traditions can be called "Christian", because they have their origin in Christian communities which held that they could give expression to their faith and their willingness to follow Christ by observing these moral norms. But it does not follow from this that such traditions are traditions of faith. Often the Christians took them from non-Christian sources — as St. Paul himself did. Some of these sources and the correlative doctrinal traditions derived from them are explicitly denied by the Church. For example, consider the area of evaluating marriage and sexuality: one might think of the question of marital relations without the intention of procreation *hic et nunc* (while the Church explicitly holds other views which have their origin partially in the same sources and logically in the same moral mentality, e.g. the question of the contraceptive use of marriage). There are other traditional moral doctrines which are founded on a knowledge of facts; but this knowledge can change, so that, possibly or consequently, the doctrine of moral behavior can also change. Here one might remember what was once believed in past ages about the nature of money, the relation between religious freedom and religious indifference, sociological and psychological aspects of sexuality, etc.

Many moral theologians are asking themselves if similar traditional moral doctrines, not founded on revelation, can be definitive or valid a priori for all times, cultures, and situations, although we might not yet know what possibilities the future holds. It has been said rightly that the Church has never yet explicitly defined a moral norm of natural law which was not also revealed. Many think that the Church cannot make such a definition because of the contingency of concrete human reality and the lack of divine revelation. Consequently, they are not prepared to accept an argument taken from tradition in moral matters which is not founded on revelation, if by means of such an argument one is seeking to establish the irreversibility of a given moral teaching.

But even those theologians who think for the above reason that a definitive and irreversible decision of the magisterium is not possible if it is founded solely on doctrinal tradition and not revelation (for example, religious freedom, interest on money, due motivation in marital relations), they think nonetheless that the magisterium can and must indicate well-reasoned and well-motivated solutions to current moral questions. On the other hand, they think that the magisterium ought to do this with more cautious formulations and without referring with too much certitude to "Christian tradition", "the will of God", and "Christian" moral law. Such an official declaration of the Church would be a true and necessary help for many; in any case, it would at least have the presumption of truth.

IV. ETERNAL LAW

The Second Vatican Council, in the decree *Dignitatis humanae* (n. 3) bids us return — as the true moral norm of man — to the "objective and universal, eternal, divine law, through which God, in his wise and loving plan, orders, directs, and governs the universe and the ways of human society. God has enabled man to participate in this law so that, under God's gently provident guidance, man may always be able to know better that truth which is immutable." The *Declaration on Some Questions Concerning Sexual Ethics,* issued by the Sacred Congregation for the Doctrine of Faith on 29 December 1975, refers extensively (in n. 5) to this passage of the Council and adds: "This divine law is accessible to our knowledge."

The phrase "eternal law" has a long history. As the text cited above also says, it is regarded as a law through which the God of wisdom and love orders and governs the world which he created. But the order and the governing of the "ways of human society" are especially mentioned; man personally participates in this law, and he knows how to discover what this law says. The emphasis is obviously on the words "divine", "eternal", "objective", "universal", and "immutable truth". The formula is correct. In spite of this, it is open to misunderstanding, especially when the eternal law is considered under the aspect of the moral order of humanity. First of all, it can easily give the impression that God, in addition to being the Creator-Redeemer of all, is also an extremely wise legislator, and second, that the moral order is something eternal and immutable, because it is known by man as a participation in eternal and immutable law. Consequently, one may easily arrive at the mistaken idea of a fixedness — because of the idea of eternity — of all moral norms.

The error, as sometimes happens, has its origin in the fact that one forgets that everything is contained in the eternal law: the changeable as changeable, the unchangeable as unchangeable. There are unchangeable-universal-eternal principles or moral norms: for example, that man is called by the Creator to do good and avoid evil, that man ought to behave toward others as he would justly expect others to behave toward him, that he needs to be just, chaste, reasonable, patient, brave, prudent, etc. But there are also changeable, nonuniversal, noneternal principles; these change according to the mutability of man (together with his world), and also according to his knowledge (both of facts and of values).

This appeal to eternal law in church documents has an effect which is not totally justified, as implied in the orderly way many manualists set up their tract *De lege.* Eternal law always came in first place, then natural law, and finally, positive law. Subconsciously at least, there arose the impression that from the eternal law we men can in some manner derive something in regard to the moral order. This happened in spite of the fact that the affirmation of natural law as a participation in the eternal law should have shown that the eternal law is not directly at our disposal. Man's need and obligation to understand and seek out both the principles and the specific norms and solutions to situations for human-moral life—in the autonomy given to and imposed on us by the Creator himself—belong properly to eternal law. What has already been said about references made to the "will of God" should also be said here: to the extent that one in truth succeeds in distinguishing what is changeable and what is unchangeable and in knowing in truth principles, norms, and moral solutions, one truly participates in eternal law. If the light of the Gospel and grace have been of some help in man's autonomous work, that is all the better. Thus it should be clear: no one begins from a material participation in eternal law and proceeds to true moral knowledge; it is rather that in one's autonomous knowledge of moral truth — in which, for the most part, only a moral certitude will be gained — one acquires a certain participation in eternal law. It should also be clear that the eternity of divine law does not mean that there is no distinction between the unchangeable-universal and the changeable-nonuniversal. A fortiori it should be clear that the eternal law's accessibility to us says nothing about the extent to which our knowledge of it is adequate, inexact, or simply wrong.

V. ABSTRACT-UNIVERSAL

Eternal law was said to be objective and universal. As St. Thomas has already said, and as some today say — more readily than before — man is a changeable being. It is difficult to deny this insofar as man is a historical being. Saying this, we affirm that man is always man and that, nonetheless, he is in a continual process of change-development. We readily distinguish between the essence or unchangeable nucleus of man in his existence, on the one hand, and the variable forms of expression of this essence, on the other. Consequently, we insist that all norms are determined by the *humanum* and that therefore we cannot deny there may be some truly universal norms that hold equally for all men forever. I think that this is certain, although its application always contains some analogy because of differences in various men. But the question remains whether all norms which are determined by the *humanum* — man's nucleus—are determined by it alone, even concrete and behavioral/material norms.

What are the moral norms determined by man's essential nucleus alone? Perhaps they are norms which contain an element which, in its aspect of material content, is not yet determinate enough but is open and has to be determined: i.e. norms which contain a rather formal element. As examples we might choose the norms "be just", "be chaste", "do not kill unjustly" (= do not murder), "do not unjustly take others' possessions" (= do not steal). None of these norms indicates any element of material content that is necessary if one is to be able to say that a given action is against justice or chastity or that it is stealing or murder. Norms of this type- — i.e. which remain formal to a certain extent without indicating the element of material content that would remove or fill up the lacuna of the formal element — are, everyone agrees, in the strict sense universal norms precisely because they contain this rather formal element.

But what should we say of those norms which touch upon justice, chastity, the property or life of another, when they eliminate the formal element, substituting a concrete indication of some material content, e.g. masturbation, contraception, a specific work contract? It is true that what is abstract in any norm, being abstract as such, is founded in concrete reality. But does it follow that a norm which is abstract in itself is also necessarily a universal as regards the concrete? Would not a norm also be founded in the concrete if, insofar as it was abstract, it was not a universal but a mere generalization? A formula which says that killing a man is wrong, or which says that falsehood is wrong (or other examples from the areas of justice or sexuality) is certainly not a universal norm, but only a generalization, because the concrete realization of the object described in the abstract norm cannot be morally judged to be right or wrong a priori, i.e. independently of a simultaneous consideration and evaluation of how it fits in with other elements (circumstances, foreseen or motivating effects), without which the one human and moral act is not intended and realized.

The failure to distinguish between the abstract as universal and the abstract as generalization, and therefore the failure to distinguish between universal norms and general norms, might be traced to a nominalism which has affected moral theory — perhaps, for example, through Francis Suarez. Universal norms such as "be chaste" or "be just" refer to moral values, e.g. chastity and justice. The free relation of the person to such norms qualifies the person as such, morally. But norms of this type are not concrete behavioral/material norms because they do not indicate which personal relations to premoral values (life, sexuality, culture, health, etc.) will be realizations of moral values. Universal moral norms, being partially formal, are, insofar as they remain such, "elastic", but they, together with the right or wrong relation to premoral values, codetermine concrete judgments.

Concrete behavioral/material norms, which tend to indicate what is just behavior regarding premoral values (life, culture, but also killing, aid rendered, etc.), are therefore abstract as generalizations. The abstract judgment is formed by abstracting — without reflection — from the conditions of a concretely realized act or one which is to be concretely realized. Thus the formulae of St. Paul regarding slaves or the behavior of women in society are formulated in an unconditioned manner, although — St. Paul could not have known this — they are conditioned. In the application of such norms we must see whether, for certain conditions, the norm ought to have been formulated differently. This must be done because such norms, which are already materially determined in their formulation, might refer to certain conditions without any consideration being given to other possible conditions. Therefore their value — the universal formulation notwithstanding — is perhaps not really universal but, because of the generalization which has taken place, more limited than the formula indicates. The abstract character of such norms, then, is not derived from a still elastic formal element of the norm, but from the nonconsideration of all the possible conditions which can accompany the realization of a correlative action. No one is capable of foreseeing and morally judging — a priori — all the elements which together determine a human act, and are described as a behavioral/material norm.

The norms in question could have become true universals if an elastic-formal element had been joined to them, for example, "possibly", "normally", "if there is a sufficient reason", etc. They could also have become universal if they had been formulated exclusively for certain specific conditions, to the exclusion of the presence of other conditions, for example: it is always morally unjust to treat a child cruelly solely for the pleasure one might derive from this! (I grant, however, that this example is not perfectly ad rem, because "being cruel" — and not only "being harsh" for a sufficient reason — might already be a moral disvalue). Yet every just judgment on a concrete activity in a situation *hic et nunc* is a true universal in the sense that a recurrence of the same activity in the same situation would be judged in the same way. But without such ulterior determinations, concrete behavioral/material norms, for their part, cannot have more value than that of a generalization. The concrete human act always contains some elements which are not taken into account by the abstract norms in question; on the other hand, true judgment on an action ought, in order to be objective, to take into account the complete reality realized in the action; therefore the presence of an element which would require a different norm regarding the object-act judged by a "general" abstract norm cannot be excluded a priori. This would not mean taking exceptions, but knowing and recognizing the true extension and the intrinsic − unexpressed − limits of behavioral/material norms which in fact concern only one element − the object − of a true human and moral act, and which disregard the other elements. Moral judgments, however, as has been said, ought to take into account the totality of the action, considering and evaluating all elements which are present.

VI. AGERE SEQUITUR ESSE

This assertion means something regarding the manner in which we know moral norms, the will of God; it has to do, then, with the essential elements of a Christian ethics. Therefore it is discussed nearly as much as it is known! In the first place, this axiom establishes an absolute correlation between man's being and his acting. Second, it does not in itself say anything about the changeability or unchangeability of man, or about the consequences of this for moral judgments. Third, being is the foundation of an obligation only insofar as it is that being given to us to be developed by us toward the fullness of being man; this affirmation includes another, i.e., that a particular obligation cannot be deduced from the abstract concept "man" and, that this concept notably codetermines concrete obligations. The correlation of action and therefore also of moral norms with the meaning of being human and with the meaning of particular human data − e.g., sexuality and marriage − is a criterion of utmost importance for moral truth.

A difference of opinion on the part of various authors arises in the interpretation of the saying "action follows being" in the discussion on the understanding of the "given" and the "task", and on what the normative correlatives of these should be. There are some authors who, using this axiom, think that some particular human realities − e.g., sexuality − with their natural (infrapersonal) finality insofar as these really exist in man ought therefore to be normative for the fullness of being human. In opposition to such a theory, I think that one should not affirm the normative power of particular elements of man unless this is done in the totality of the various aspects which determine man's being and acting. Otherwise, the formula "action follows being" is not being taken seriously enough − because the truest "given" and "task" of man are not the elements or particular aspects of human existence, but the *person* (*ratio!*) himself, who is real in a human nature with all its particular elements and a concrete historical condition. This human nature can be "arbitrary" not only because of an insufficient consideration of the "essential human nucleus", but also because of an insufficient consideration — on the part of the *persona-ratio* — of the totality of the various particular aspects of our action in a specific field of being and action. This last consideration is required precisely by the fullness of being man, which is real only in the totality of the concrete reality of a man. Only the "overall vision" can guarantee the truth of action.

It can be rightly said that everything receives its norms from the *humanum*, since otherwise one would not be dealing with human norms. But it can also be formulated this way: everything receives its norms from the concrete fullness of man, i.e. from the real person in an historically realized human nature. This would mean that neither the *humanum* alone, in its abstractness, nor the determinate (particular) elements alone permit the establishment of a judgment or moral norm. It is rather the two together, or even better, the one unique human reality with various aspects, that permits a moral judgment. The concrete cannot be deduced from the universal! One eventual possibility may already be foreseen from this, namely, that a different realization of the same humanity, as well as of certain sectors of life in different sociological, economic, cultural and individual contexts, cannot exclude a priori somewhat different practical solutions. This is because action should correspond to concrete being as a given and a task; it must encompass the whole significance of the totality of the unique human reality, insofar as the — at least attempted — personal realization or nonrealization is the acceptance or refusal of self. But it seems impossible to foresee the various diversities per se which might be possible and to express them once and for all in a norm.

It is clear that the judging of the totality of human reality does not mean a just arrangement of all occuring elements or even a simple addition of them. Rather, what is needed is a "human" — "rational" evaluation of the various values contained in the various elements. This holds true especially for the relation between acts (as means) and effects (either foreseen or motivating). Man's evaluative reasoning is in a certain sense passive-receptive (everything is already present in eternal law and in some way in creation). But this same evaluative reasoning is, at the same time and a fortiori active-creative, since it, itself, is the subject of rational evaluation. "That which is to be done" is a "given", but it is shown only to autonomously and actively evaluative reasoning. In this sense it can also be said that actively-creatively seeking (on man's part) is a continual search for man's own future. In fact, man often reflects on the various possibilities of his future action, and comes to think finally that he has found his own task — the future, the will of God.

Even the first Christians — perhaps without too much reflection, although with a fine sense for the kingdom of God and the following of Christ — surmised what their duty was by rational evaluation. Man today must do the same, and he should do it under the conditions of today and of specific cultures. Does not St. Paul tell us that even the pagans were able to find and partly succeeded in finding by themselves what action corresponds to man's being (Rom. 1 and 2)? It is obvious that a Christian theist understands reflection on authentic human self-realization as an image of the will and call of God and his Christ — this will and call are not merely formal ("behavior worthy of man — the creature of God"), but they have content, and are particular and concrete.

It seems to be important that certain moral formulae — such as those discussed above — find in time a more cautious and exact use in the teaching and exhortation of the Church, and a fortiori in public proclamations regarding problems of acute public interest, especially in a pluralistic society such as ours. Two things are required, and neither of them is easy: (1) a reflection on the formulae employed and on their meaning, and (2) a search for a translation which renders the meaning of these formulae accessible even to those persons whose task is not precisely the study of ethics and morality.

12. The Question Addressed to Conscience

For a long time now people in the West, including Catholics, have been departing from the past by immediately directing to their conscience those questions which require a moral solution. In earlier times people decided such matters in terms of a fixed set of norms through the observance of which they could properly realize themselves and their world, and thus behave in a correct moral way. Contemporary man, on the other hand, understands himself to a greater extent and in a more profound way as a person; he is given and is responsible for an "I" unique to him, which possesses a dynamism proper to itself and which is to actualize itself through the exercise of personal conscience. In realizing his potential, man likewise lends shape to his interpersonal relations, to human society and to the material world.

I. CONSCIENCE: PERSON AS FREEDOM AND AS SOURCE OF PERSONAL DECISIONS

The human person is characterized by a self-consciousness which allows him to view himself as a person growing to greater maturity through encounters with other persons (who likewise enjoy self-consciousness), with a society composed of such persons, and with the nonhuman world which surrounds society and stands at its disposal. In his innermost being man's experience is that, in the attempt to form relationships with the above-mentioned "givens" of his experience (understood as essential extensions of his own self), he not only tries to determine this interaction but at the same time, and above all, he realizes his own self in his totality as a free, self-determining and interpersonal being. As a person who has been endowed with freedom he knows himself as having been offered and having accepted freedom, and thus not as a primordial and self-sufficient absolute.[1] As a result, the man who has already come to maturity has at all times actualized that freedom of his which is directed toward self-determination (himself in his totality as person). To be sure, he has either truly realized himself by accepting the self given to him, or he has alienated himself by insisting on his absolute self-sufficiency. Each mature person, precisely as such, *is* freedom not as a mere possibility, but as an already freely accomplished self-realization or self-alienation; there is no middle option, but only the possibility either of standing by this free self-determination or of changing it.

The self-actualization of the person as gifted freedom therefore means self-realization or self-alienation in relation to a freedom which attests to an originative and self-sufficient Absolute. It is better to refer to this Absolute, which reveals itself as related to the free human person, in personal rather than in apersonal terminology; we call it God. It is true that individual decisions are only meaningful and good if the whole of reality is meaningful. An atheistic philosopher, Ugo Spirito, claimed that he guided his life not by norms and moral reflection, but by the findings of science. An atheistic friend of a theologian in New York objected violently when an unscrupulous barman cheated a drunken soldier of some change which was due him.[2] Certainly, no one will heedlessly continue to drive down a narrow street if he suddenly sees someone drunk lying on the road in front of him. In all these examples a genuine duty is perceived, even if in a perhaps unreflective manner. Such duty is only understandable on the presupposition that there is an Absolute in which all meaning itself is grounded, and not only the meaningfulness of a particular action or of human duty understood as an isolated phenomenon.

Indeed, the personal self-as-freedom can only be determined through a series of concrete decisions in this world which embody expressions of one's self. One thing should thus be clear: the transcendental self-disposition which the human person has of himself as a totality is the decisive means by which he exercises human freedom; we are often deeply conscious of this fact, at least implicitly. The total freedom spoken of here is thus not that freedom which acts insofar as it makes particular decisions which can in diverse ways but only peripherally determine human behavior. All too often it is the case that it is not a person's most profound self-made decisions but other manifold aspects of his being, whether interior or exterior, that to a great extent determine or codetermine his various thoughts and actions. Thus, that freedom which allows man to be a personal self is truly his only when it causes him to decide about himself as a whole, and not when it allows him to make individual decisions and enables him to select a particular option.

We are speaking of freedom and conscience; one is unthinkable without the other. It is important to know where, in what depths, conscience and freedom, as well as personal self-determination, are located in man. Conscience, freedom, and self-determination can only be that depth of the human person in which he is, according to St. Thomas,[3] totally present to himself, therefore at a point which cannot be "extended". In this depth, the following are present in a unified yet distinguishable manner: (1) an understanding of the nature, meaning and destiny of man; (2) an experience of the imperative character both of the inner demand to realize the self and also of the type of behavior by which such self-realization can be correctly known and experienced; (3) a comprehension of the importance which self-realization and self-alienation have for the genuine and final destiny of man; (4) a spiritually attractive impulse to achieve all of these goods. This mystery of conscience, which is experienced in its ultimate profundity and plenitude, accompanies everyone at all times; it is a total experience which, however, can never be fully grasped through intellectual reflection. It is, in fact, possible, even in all good faith, to misinterpret or deny the existence of conscience theoretically; in doing so, guilt may or may not be involved.[4] One who is able explicitly to believe in God and in the importance of the Christ-event will bear within himself a more deep-seated and a more clearly delineated experience of conscience. He will also be able to come to insightful knowledge and make significant assertions through his reflection on his original experience and likewise through reflection, even if it be only partial, on his spontaneous experience of morality, of moral demands, and of the anguish arising from an uneasy conscience. This anguish might cause one to undergo a dramatic experience. There could be anguish involved also in seeking to form one's conscience properly, above all in the face of very grave decisions. This is always the case, especially because through one's conscience one experiences oneself as a human person endowed with freedom and face to face with the primordial, self-sufficient and absolute freedom of God, in whose freedom man's entire being finds its meaning.

II.   THE ANSWER TO THE QUESTIONS OF MAN WHO IS CHALLENGED TO A PARTICULAR DECISION BY CONSCIENCE

It may be that I was not expected to take a penetrating gaze into the very essence of moral conscience.[5] The questions normally treated tend to be these: in the face of real problems, how can I question my conscience and how should I understand its authority? How does conscience act so as to bind me to norms and laws which are formulated in an obligatory way? Where do I find, to use a theological phrase, "the will of God", "God's voice" and the inspiration of the Spirit, the gift of the Father and Son? Is the answer to these questions to be found in the innermost experience of conscience or in a formulated norm? This question is important. For, on the one hand, we can at any given moment actualize our self as personal freedom only through actions resulting from free particular decisions; on the other hand, neither our freedom nor the reality of man and the world originates with us. The person, as "entrusted freedom" in a world which is likewise completely "entrusted" to him, must continually seek to experience this freedom within him as conscience. It is only through objective decisions and behavior, and not through whimsical acts, that human freedom can legitimately realize itself. Such proper exercise of freedom also clarifies the previous acts by which a person has realized or alienated himself, either at the periphery or at the center of his being. However, having said this, we intend to remain with the everyday question addressed to our consciences: "What must I do?" This question includes queries about how one is to shape interpersonal relations, human society, and the material world; thus, the question of conscience is not only a "private" concern.

In asking "What ought I to do?" one poses a question about the "moral knowledge" contained in conscience and about the content which will be given as an answer. Each person must find this answer for himself; once it is found, however, precisely because it is given by conscience, this answer reveals itself as an absolute demand which concerns the total person endowed with freedom — his entire destiny and salvation. For this reason, the search for and the discovery of the right answer through conscience takes place in a way different from the theoretical search for and discovery of moral knowledge and moral opinions. Thus, the search for the answer of conscience is always accompanied by the chiefly unreflective awareness that it is a matter of searching for and of finding both moral knowledge and judgment. The honesty of the search, as well as the implementation of the judgment, involves the person as such, his destiny and salvation. The man who is searching for and forming the answer of conscience is therefore engaged and impinged upon quite differently from the ethician who is speculating in an abstract manner. It is not general principles which the individual seeks but the compelling, totally concrete and unique self-realization of, and not self-alienation from, his person in the here and now.

In contemporary theology there are primarily two models being used to describe the role of conscience in finding "knowledge in conscience". For centuries the predominant model was that in which one's conscience plays the role of simply applying to individual actual instances previously determined principles or behavioral norms. Without doubt this model is marked by legalistic and static characteristics. It scarcely notes the fact that predetermined norms are due to a particular intellectual perspective which may no longer exist in the present, or that the concrete situation may exhibit certain elements and may require a certain behavior in the future, neither of which were foreseen in a universally formulated norm which can only prove valid when certain conditions are presupposed.[6] For, an "application of the norm" in using one's conscience really means discovering an original norm which meets the situation and which is objectively correct, even when this is done by means of a serious yet critical testing of already existing norms. What is always involved is a hermeneutic of the "here-and-now-morally-correct".

This last remark helps us understand why modern man is inclined to juxtapose the earlier model of describing the role of conscience to another. According to this latter model, the one who forms and probes his conscience should not primarily dwell on a search for predetermined norms, at least insofar as these − as is usually the case − are due to human experience, searching and discovery, and thus are limited and conditional. The person's efforts should rather be directed primarily toward an objective, original and immediate moral understanding of his "I" as it finds itself in his concrete world. The "I", of course, is not exempt from considering the appropriate aid and the touchstone character of predetermined moral norms, counsels, etc., and the "I" should not disregard the light of faith or fail to trust in the constant assistance of the Holy Spirit who does not, however, guarantee the solution. Yet, the "I" must hermeneutically "read" its actual situation with a view to genuine self-fulfillment and thus creatively draw up a plan of action for the proximate or remote future. Such a model possesses not so much a legalistic and static character as a personal (but not necessarily private) and dynamic one.

In developing one's conscience toward a position and a judgment, one gains a glimpse of the innermost essence of conscience: experienced insight into, inclination toward, and demand for genuine self-realization through a multiplicity of particular decisions. It should not be overlooked that such an experience of conscience is a personal activity; conscience is not an "it". The experience of conscience is accompanied by an active search for the certainty of fundamental values and moral insights. The further attempt to arrive at a personal judgment in particular situations takes place with the aid of many criteria derived from knowledge and experience, from norms which have been handed down or personally acquired, from orientations given with the light of faith and also from man's abiding (and at least implicit) self-understanding, even though this may be inadequate. In this way the personal "I", as a "*point* without extension", becomes at the same time a light sufficiently clear to arrive at a concrete decision, one which automatically signifies another decision to abstain from any further formation of conscience since this is now superfluous. At this point, we experience our position, that "word" of conscience which ultimately enlightens and binds us, takes hold of us and compels us from the very depths of our being. Here we find the answer to our question.

In spite of the binding character of the experience of conscience, the concrete material assertion which is made will by no means enjoy the certainty of metaphysical evidence, but, in accordance with the contingent character of human reality, will reach only moral certainty which does not prevent reasonable doubt from arising and cannot a priori exclude the possibility of false value judgments. But this is true not only of a judgment made by human conscience here and now, but also of our attempts to formulate abstract moral norms.

Thus we must also reckon with the not infrequent occurrence that, after consulting his conscience, a person does not arrive at the right answer in the sense of the correct draft which will lead to the formation of a genuine human-Christian future; this fact can be recognized, according to circumstances, either by others or by oneself, at least subsequently. The question is how such an "erroneous conscience", which is formed and experienced in good faith, can claim absolute validity and obedience. This question has been discussed through the centuries and has received many answers. For example: through faithful adherence to a conscience which has consented to something objectively unjustified, the person: (a) is guilty in spite of good faith (Bernard of Clairvaux), (b) remains innocent (Averroes, St. Thomas), (c) is guiltless but perhaps not morally good (St. Thomas), (d) acts correctly in a moral-personal sense and is thus morally good (the majority of Catholic moral theologians today). The last answer ought to be clarified; I would certainly prefer the formulation "only personal but objective" instead of the hitherto widely used restriction "only subjective". For, one ought not to overlook the fact that a judgment of conscience, made in good faith, is an additional determination, and, indeed, the final form of the "here and now situated person". The person, however, in his totality (together with his final form) has to realize himself through freedom. One who decides and acts in this way thus does so — from the personal point of view — impartially, "in an objectively correct manner". This formulation leads to a further one concerning the normative power of conscience, which has to be questioned in relation to the normative power of abstract norms.

III.   A QUESTION: DOES MAN'S CONSCIENCE WHICH HAS TO BE CONSULTED HAVE ONLY A SUBJECTIVE NORMATIVE POWER IN COMPARISON TO ABSTRACT NORMS?

Although the position taken and the judgment rendered by conscience are pronounced and experienced totally in solitude, face to face with the Absolute, and thus in a sacred place, one is still not without help when it comes to formulating this position. Every man always carries within himself norms of some type, acquired either from prudent persons or from the people of God or from some other source. It has to be so: if we did not have such aids, we would be all too easily overburdened in the formation of our conscience. Norms attempt to assert something about an objective moral plan for the correct and concrete self-realization of the person in this world. Therefore norms are genuinely helpful in the formation of conscience. On the other hand, they can only be an aid to the extent that through conscience both of the following can be adequately judged: the reality of our given situation and what it requires, and also the range of validity which humanly formulated norms prove to have with regard to the situation to be brought about. Put succinctly: norms are aids for conscience, but they are such only insofar as conscience can make judgments about them. If a person correctly understands the entire concrete situation in which he finds himself, he can more adequately judge the true significance which the norm has for that given situation. The more he comprehends the norm, the more will its ability to aid in the formation of conscience increase.

Because of this auxiliary function of norms in the formation of judgments of conscience, conflict situations, at least apparent ones, can arise.

First, it can indeed happen that one's personal theoretical opinion on a matter differs from a predetermined norm; both, however, intend to help make possible an existential formation of conscience, although both can be erroneous. Now, on the one hand, a theoretical opinion is only an aid and not an already formed position of conscience itself; perhaps a responsible self-examination must, in opposition to authorities of various kinds, come to the conclusion that the presumption as a whole does not correspond to one's theoretical opinion. But the reverse can also be the case, namely, that one must competently and responsibly come to the stance that the pre-given norm, which in its objective wording applies to the present situation, either does not take into consideration decisive elements of this situation or does not meet today's understanding of reality. This stance can be based on new factual knowledge or on a new intellectual perspective which has emerged (here, one may think of questions of social justice or of other human rights in the last hundred years); in some instances, even the Church has officially allowed new dimensions to be made clear. It would certainly not be easy, however, to determine where, for example, with regard to Church teaching, norms are to be found which, even after one has attempted a valid interpretation and hermeneutic, are definitively guaranteed either by God or the Church; surely there are relatively few norms (and indeed very few concrete ones) of this type.

Moreover, one is usually not alone in one's doubts about the validity or extent of validity of a norm; thus a common search begins and, occasionally, a common opinion. Are those, then, who are themselves less competent the sorry losers? I do not think so; for even they will be able, within the community, reliably to determine who is to be regarded as truly competent and responsible in the doubts he has expressed or in his stand against current norms; and who is to be regarded as a mere "innovator". A highly regarded Canadian theologian[7] wrote some years ago in an American work on conscience that if competent and responsible theologians timidly conceal their best insights, they can find themselves in the position of not being advocates of the "poor", i.e. of those who are not competent. This is a valid aspect of a very delicate problem!

A second possible conflict in the formation of conscience results from the search for an exact understanding of norms with their various differences, rather than from the situation just mentioned in which personal theoretical opinion stands in opposition to predetermined norms. Certainly, norms exist which are absolute in the sense that they are universally valid, since they invariably hold true and always express something essential for the proper realization of man and his world. These norms, however, are more or less formal and indicate nothing about the material and concrete way in which they ought to be put into practice here and now. Examples of such formulae are: do good, follow Christ, be just and chaste, protect life as much as possible! Precisely because they are strongly formal in character and do not as yet deal with concrete situations, they are always valid, but they are also less useful for the concrete formation of one's conscience. We must search further, until our conscience can make a judgment. According to Aquinas,[8] more helpful are decidedly concrete norms with some content, which describe a particular matter and qualify it from a moral point of view. Examples of such norms are: the forbidding of suicide, of telling untruths, etc.

It can surely be the case, however, that such norms, which are formulated abstractly after the manner of a universal, depend on definite factual knowledge, horizons of understanding and social conditions which are not explicitly included in the formulation and which furthermore do not hold today in general or in given instances. The Pauline or Thomistic view on the position of slaves and of women in society can no longer be fully accepted by us; we generally tend to take the opposite view of suicide to that stated above when it is the suicide of one who is carrying a state secret and who is in danger of having that secret taken forcibly from him; here we regard the taking of one's own life as a justified exception in spite of the generally accepted opinion of the past which regarded suicide as forbidden and unjustified in every case. It is more difficult in the concrete order to determine what invariably pertains to social justice and to chastity than to say that man must be just and chaste. Therefore the corresponding concrete determinations of these values can hardly be valid "universally" in the strict sense; they are, more often, generalizations, which hold "for the most part" (Thomas's phrase is *ut in pluribus*).[9] One of the sometimes extremely complicated tasks in the formation of conscience is to discover, so as to enable a genuine stance of conscience to emerge, those changing yet essential circumstances in otherwise identical behavior. If this is not done, the generalization might be allowed to become a universal without good reason. The norm alone does not suffice!

From the foregoing reflections on the importance of both personal theoretical opinion and of the different types of norms employed in developing a position and in making a judgment of conscience, we can gain a critical perspective on the widespread notion that conscience is merely the "subjective application" of "objective norms" to individual cases. In maintaining this standpoint, one allows norms the significant advantage of being "objective", while at the same time denying conscience this privilege, since it is seen to be "only" subjective. Obviously, there is fear that, if the importance of conscience's stance is strongly emphasized, this will lead to a subjectivism which unjustly ignores objectivity. One could retort by asking whether a person is content to regard the necessary application of norms in the constant process of forming conscience as "only" subjective or whether he must demand that such an application be also objective. Furthermore, are not the discovery and formulation of norms tasks which must be accomplished chiefly by individuals but also by all mankind, and, besides, are carried out "only" by the probing subject, in order to arrive at abstract objective statements? And is not every attempt to form one's conscience likewise the act of a subject aimed at the attainment of an objective position of conscience? Why should the search for norms by the subject be called "objective" and the discovery of a conscientious position "subjective"? Both the abstract and the concrete determination of what is morally right are directed toward objectivity and are brought to completion by human subjects who consider all the aids given them in proportion to their true importance. Both these activities entail a "creative" element in the true sense of the world.

The attempt made here to analyze the question modern man puts to his conscience and its answer, which led us to define conscience as an experience of coming to a position in which insight is guaranteed, accepted and absolutely compelling, is clearly intended to achieve two purposes: it has set out, first, to procure for the answer of conscience some recognition of its due value and importance, especially when compared with abstract norms; second, to remove the "question put to conscience", a very popular phrase today, from the danger of an arbitrary subjectivism — that is, from misuse.

Everyone must at all times, more or less explicitly, and in all earnestness, pose the question of conscience for himself. There is no sector of life in which the answer of conscience is not relevant and must not be heeded. I call explicit attention to this, since decisions made in conscience are of vital importance in the field of social sciences and of political praxis.[10] Employing the key insights of this chapter as a point of departure, I would like briefly to allude to four concerns:

1. Work done in public for society is in the last analysis always work done by personal subjects, even when they work together or in the name of society or of various organizations. One who works in the public area or is engaged in social activity decides and acts as a morally responsible person. All his decisions and actions must therefore result from an inquiry put to conscience and from the answer which is given, even when this happens spontaneously and without explicit reflection. His activity is thus always carried out with absolute and personal freedom, be it thematic or athematic.

2.   In such activity, the question posed to conscience is not primarily one of norms for the sake of a norm-justified decision and behavior, but above all, for the sake of decision and behavior justified by reality, which correspond to the nature and dignity of man and of society in their situation as it now is, insofar as this "now" leads to a future. Norms which have already been thought out can indeed also be of great help for the work to be done in society and in the state, and these norms must be taken into consideration in accordance with the normative influence they exert in the process of arriving at the answer of conscience.

3.   No one can avoid the fact that norms alone do not always offer themselves as a simple solution, and that even those norms which seemingly illumine the given data in a definitive manner can lead, if adhered to in a one-sided manner and out of a servile mentality, to false solutions. Not all questions concerning the public order or the work done in the area of genetics, to take two examples, can create a solution from sufficiently concrete predetermined norms. A norm which suffices as a solution would presuppose, if it were to be applied, an adequate and comprehensive knowledge of data at hand. In many cases, the one who himself has experience in a given area and is called on to decide and to act, will be faced with many questions. What is needed in order to enable him to arrive at an objectively justified answer of conscience is, beyond a knowledge of his particular field, on the one hand a genuine readiness to act as a human being in the fullest sense of this word (as everyone can possess this sense in the light of his personal guidelines, e.g., the light of the Gospel), and, on the other hand an adequate acquaintance with human goods and values, their hierarchy and urgency. He must also be familiar with basic moral principles and have had corresponding past experiences which involved determining which values are to be preferred over others. Making such basic elements available for human decisions and actions must be regarded as the most urgent type of assistance which ethics or morality can lend to contemporary man. In passing, it might be said that interdisciplinary cooperation, wherever it is possible, can prove to be immensely helpful; this collaboration, however, does not free anyone from the necessity of putting questions to conscience.

4. These reflections expressly call attention to the fact that even in collective activity the individual may not appeal to a decision from above or to that of the majority without consulting his own conscience. The moral question may indeed have been explicitly considered in the decisions already made by superiors or in the working sessions of a committee. Nevertheless, the moral decision, in the strict sense of the word, is entirely up to the individual concerned. The answer of a person's conscience may and indeed ought to be influenced, according to circumstances, by others on a committee or by a higher authority. On the other hand, one should keep in mind the important distinction between a decision for the moral good of society and a decision to carry out that moral good publicly. But the question as to what moral values should be protected in the public sphere is also to be determined by considering the various degrees and particular urgency of values in themselves, as well as the necessary possibility that through them the common order and common good can be maintained, especially in a pluralistic society; this, too, requires that a question be put to conscience.

NOTES

1. On this point, cf. H.U. von Balthasar, "Neun Sätze zur christlichen Ethik", in J. Ratzinger 1975 (ed.), *Prinzipien christlicher Moral*, Einsiedeln 1975, 2nd ed., 67-93. The reference here is to pp. 86ff.
2. Cf. J.M. Gustafson, *Can Ethics be Christian?* Chicago-London 1975, 1ff.
3. Thomas Aquinas, *S.C.G.* IV, 11; *S.T.* I, 8, 1. This insight is a continually recurring fundamental theme in the theological anthropological theory of K. Rahner.
4. Cf. also the assertions of St. Paul in Rom. 1:18-23.
5. The foregoing reflections were originally part of an interdisciplinary symposium.
6. To anticipate an objection, it should be noted that, according to contemporary exegesis, concrete behavioral norms come only rarely (if at all) from divine revelation. This also holds true for norms given to us by the Church. Nor do competent theologians, ethicians or groups in society give us norms. Concrete norms are the result of human experience, insight and reflection in which the Christian engages "in the light of the Gospel" (but the light of the Gospel itself does not give us norms). Cf. *Gaudium et spes*, n. 46.
7. Cf. the exposition of F.E. Crowe in W.C. Bier (ed.), *Conscience. Its Freedom and Limitations*, New York 1971, 312-32.
8. Thomas Aquinas, *S.T.* II-II prologue; *In Eth. Nich.* II, 1. 8, n. 333ff.
9. It is indeed possible to describe and qualify a state of affairs with an exact material content, but only by excluding other possible circumstances:

e.g., harsh treatment of a child merely for the sake of cruelty is without exception always immoral (cruelty is immoral!), but this leaves open the question concerning what grounds could justify harsh treatment of a child (harshness is not cruelty!). The moral solution to an individual case here and now can be considered as a universal (i.e., it is "universalizable") insofar as a completely identical case, should it happen, would have to be judged in the same way. But the condition of complete identity is usually not formulated; an act which is essentially the same under different circumstances may possibly have to be judged differently.

10.   The reader should know that during the interdisciplinary symposium, mentioned above, at which the present paper was delivered, there were also conferences and discussions on special topics such as the human sciences and social and political problems.

ACKNOWLEDGMENTS

Chapter 1, "Moral Theology as *Sacra Doctrina*." Paper, "Lehrfach Moraltheologie als 'sacra doctrina'", delivered in Rome in 1977; first published in *Studia Moralia* 15 (1977) 191-206.

Chapter 2, "Moral Theology and Christian Existence." Article, "Theologia Moralis et Vita Theologalis", *Seminarium* 20, NS 8 (1968), 647-59.

Chapter 3, "Vocation and Hope: Conciliar Orientations for a Christian Morality." Article, "Vocazione e Speranza: indicazioni conciliari per una morale christiana", *Seminarium* 23, NS 11 (1971), 491-510.

Chapter 4, "Is There a Distinctively Christian Morality?" Lecture, "Gibt es eine spezifisch christliche Moral?" delivered to university students in Zurich in 1968, and published in *Stimmen der Zeit*, Vol. 185 (1970/2), 99-112.

Chapter 5, "Is There a Normative Non-Christian Morality?" Article, "Esiste una morale non-cristiana?", *Rassegna di Teologia* 14 (1973), 361-73.

Chapter 6, "Autonomous Morality and Morality of Faith." Paper, "Autonome Moral und Glaubensethik", delivered to a meeting of German-speaking Catholic moral theologians in Freiburg, Switzerland, in 1977, and published in *Ethik im Kontext des Glaubens Probleme-Grundsätze-Methoden*, ed. D. Mieth and F. Compagnoni, Freiburg (Switzerland) and Freiburg-im-Breisgau, 1978, 46-74.

Chapter 7, "The Absoluteness of Behavorial Moral Norms." Article, *Gregorianum* 52 (1971), 415-57.

Chapter 8, "The 'Sin of the World' and Normative Morality." Article, *Gregorianum* 61 (1980/1), 51-76.

Chapter 9, "Morality as the Shaping of the Future of Man." Lecture, "Morale come progettazione del futuro dell'uomo", given as part of a series of lectures on futurology, Rome, 1975-76, and published in *Pensare il Futuro: questioni sistematiche di futurologia*, ed. P.C. Beltrão, Rome, 1977, 137-48.

Chapter 10, "*Epikeia* Applied to Natural Law?" Article, "'Epikeia' circa legem moralem naturalem?", *Periodica de re morali, canonica, liturgica* 69 (1980/1).

Chapter 11, "A Summary: Clarifications of Some Currently Used Terms." The first four sections of this chapter are a summary of a paper delivered in Rome in 1973 to a meeting of representatives of Bishops' Conferences; the fifth and sixth sections are a summary of an article, "Sittliche Normen-Universalien und Generalisierungen", *Theologische Zeitschrift* 25 (1974), 18-33.

Chapter 12, "The Question Addressed to Conscience." Paper, "Die Frage an das Gewissen",delivered during a workshop on conscience in Nuremberg in 1978, and published in *Das Gewissen, Vorgegebene Norm verantwortlichen Handelns oder Produkt gesellschaftlichet Zwänge?* ed. J. Fuchs, Düsseldorf, 1979, 56-66.

During the preparation of this book, two of its chapters were published in books of collected essays. Chapter 7, "The Absoluteness of Behavioral Moral Norms,"appeared in *Readings in Moral Theology No. 1: Moral Norms and Catholic Tradition*, edited by C.E. Curran and R.A. McCormick, S.J., New York, 1979, 94-137, as "The Absoluteness of Moral Terms." Chapter 4, "Is There a Distinctively Christian Morality?" appeared in *Readings in Moral Theology, No. 2: The Distinctiveness of Christian Ethics*, New York, 1980, 3-19, as "Is There a Specifically Christian Morality?". In this book the English translations and the contents have been slightly changed.